The

Autobiography

of

Maud Gonne

— · — · — · —

The

Autobiography

of

Maud Gonne

A Servant of the Queen

Edited by
A. Norman Jeffares
and
Anna MacBride White

The University of Chicago Press

The University of Chicago Press, Chicago 60637

This edition was originally published by Colin Smythe Limited,
Gerrards Cross, Buckinghamshire, in 1994, as *A Servant of the
Queen: Reminiscences* by Maud Gonne MacBride.

University of Chicago Press Edition 1995

Printed in the United States of America
01 00 99 98 97 96 95   6 5 4 3 2 1

ISBN 0-226-30251-2 (cloth)
ISBN 0-226-30252-0 (paper)

Library of Congress Cataloging-in-Publication Data

MacBride, Maud Gonne, 1866–1953.
    The autobiography of Maud Gonne : a servant of the queen / edited
by A. Norman Jeffares and Anna MacBride White. — Colin Smythe ed.
        p.   cm.
    Includes index.
    Rev. ed. of: A servant of the queen. Colin Smythe ed.
    1. MacBride, Maud Gonne, 1866–1953.   2. Women revolutionaries—
Ireland—Biography.   3. Women politicians—Ireland—Biography.
4. Feminists—Ireland—Biography.   I. Jeffares, A. Norman
(Alexander Norman), 1920–   .   II. White, Anna MacBride.
III. MacBride, Maud Gonne, 1886–1953.   Servant of the queen.
IV. Title.
DA958.M25A3   1995
941.508'092—dc20
    [B]   94-39713
                                                                            CIP

CONTENTS

ILLUSTRATIONS

INTRODUCTION

Gifted, adventurous, energetic and forceful, Maud Gonne wrote an autobiography that reflects her unorthodox nature. She began the book in the thirties, writing in bed as she always did. Her income had been declining since the First World War. She had always been most generous in her support of charities and individuals, selling her jewels in the process. Since among her many activities she had earlier been an effective journalist and had continued writing letters and articles for newspapers and journals to the end of her life, she thought that she might make some money out of writing these memoirs, a hope in which she was probably encouraged by Seumas Mac-Manus, who was writing his autobiography at the time (it was published in 1938) and Dorothy Macardle, whose *The Irish Republic* had been published by Gollancz in 1937. Gollancz also considered Maud's text and decided that he would publish the book. The memoirs would allow her to tell some of the adventures in her life and to explain what had motivated her to work for Ireland's freedom.

She may, perhaps, have thought of the idea when considering how Yeats had written about his life. He had finished the first volume of his *Autobiographies*, which he entitled *Reveries over Childhood and Youth* (1915), on Christmas Day 1914, and, as he told his sister Lily four days later, he regarded it as 'some sort of apologia for the Yeats family'. He followed it up with *Four Years 1887-1891* (1921) and *The Trembling of the Veil* (1922), the three volumes being collected as *Autobiographies* (1926), and supplemented by *Dramatis Personae* 1896-1902 (1935), *Estrangement, Extracts from a Diary kept in 1909* (1926), *The Death of Synge, Extracts from a Diary kept in 1909* (1928) and *The Bounty of Sweden* (1925) in the 1955 edition of *Autobiographies*. Maud was delighted with the first chapter of his *Reveries* in 1915. When she began reading it she commented that 'it must be very hard to select out of the mass of one's child memories, the essential things which have really influenced one's life.' She herself had tried in a desultory way, she told him, to note down childhood memories and had found that they crowded back in an extraordinary way—'much more vividly than memories of later life.' If she had jotted down any notes at that time, they no longer exist and may have been destroyed with her other papers and letters when the Free State soldiers raided her house and made a bonfire of them in the street during the Civil War.

Though Yeats was careful to describe his first book of memoirs as 'less an objective history than a reverie' he did have a desire to impose pattern upon that reverie, often using a phrase 'getting it all in order' which suits the process; he also recorded finding it 'curious how one's life falls into definite sections.' With the deliberate aim of making known the unusual qualities of his ancestors—something to which he had been spurred by George Moore's comments upon both sides of his family, the first response to which he made in the '[Introductory Lines]' and '[Closing Rhymes]' of *Responsibilities* (1916)—he was selective, concentrating upon what seemed to him critical moments or periods in his life, imposing a premeditated pattern upon each of the autobiographical volumes.

Maud could afford to be less inhibited than Yeats. Socially as well as financially secure in her youth and middle age, she did not have to justify a lack of family funds (Yeats's father had defended his financial fecklessness with the dictum that a gentleman is not concerned with getting on). Besides, she was into her seventies and many of the people about whom she wrote were now dead. Yeats had had to take care not to write of the living—for instance, his father's friend, Edward Dowden had conveniently died in 1913 thus allowing Yeats to attack his attitude to the Irish Literary movement in *Reveries*; but he had to wait a long time before taking his revenge upon George Moore, who did not die until 1933, in the lively prose of *Dramatis Personae*, long meditated but not published until 1935. Maud, however, did find that she could not write as freely as she would like; she had to be careful not to include some matters and not to name some people, coming under pressure from both her publisher and her family not to do so. Gollancz feared libel actions and took legal advice about some aspects of the book.

she had aimed for—and indeed helped to bring about in Ireland—was not what she had hoped for. Her dream and that of others was lost in the Civil War; thereafter she concentrated on the welfare of prisoners. Yeats perhaps had envisaged this:

> But even at the starting-post, all sleek and new
> I saw the wildness in her and I thought
> A vision of terror that it must live through
> Had shattered her soul.

Fife Ness   A. Norman Jeffares
Dublin, 1994   Anna MacBride White

to an end. But Maud did not indulge in self-analysis. She did not want to discuss herself. It is possible that the strain of leading her secret life with Millevoye in France compelled her into such discretion, as well as her membership of the IRB, and her awareness of being spied upon. In his old age Yeats wrote of her in 'A Bronze Head', a poem stimulated by seeing a bust of her in the Municipal Gallery of Modern Art in Dublin:

> You that have not lived in thought but deed
> Can have the purity of a natural force.

How far she deliberately avoided intellectual activity in favour of action is uncertain; she could be sharply intelligent and effectively forceful in argument, but she frequently said that she found acting on her first impulse rather than on careful analysis was more effective. She valued the ability to keep silent (and knew how indiscreet Yeats was) and must, for instance, have deeply resented Dr Ryan's inability to maintain confidentiality, especially in the matter of the betrayed French intelligence agent and the filching of the money for the proposed bombing of British troopships. Her political influence in France was deeply damaged by these incidents. There is no doubt, however, about her incisive intelligence; while she was at times content with a superficial approach, she was quick-witted, purposeful, indeed at times exigent in her desire to get things done; and that desire prevented her from deep analysis or complex theorising.

Though she continued to enjoy the irony of many events in her life, when she tried to write a sequel to *A Servant of the Queen*— firstly in a straight sequence of about seven chapters and then, when that proved too painful (as she told her family), by describing episodes in her life—giving it the title *The Tower of Age*, she found that she simply could not do it. There were all the old problems of what she had had to leave out in *A Servant of The Queen* and then life after the tragedy of her marriage was, perhaps, too grim and painful to contemplate in old age, too hurtful to others, outweighing for once the crucial element of willpower to overcome such feelings. She would have had to mute too many of her passionately held views about people: while she was never inhibited in stating her public views, what having no valid visa. She was well aware of her beauty and the effect it had on men.

There is a youthful exuberance about her early encounters with the plain-clothes police in Dublin, the G men, to whom she easily managed to give the slip on many occasions. Action released her sense of joy as the chapter 'Victoria's Jubilee' indicates (something also emerging in Yeats's account of her part in the Jubilee riots) and as her description of the proscribed Beresford Place meeting in 'England's Difficulty' clearly shows. There was perhaps a superfluity of self-confidence, though backed up by certitude in such matters as challenging Camille Dreyfus to a shooting match, as she recounts in 'Spies'. Always there was courage: in battling for the evicted in Donegal and Mayo, in making her first political speech in England and in her public protests in Dublin.

Despite the moments of excitement, of dramatic tension, what emerges most lastingly from the book is Maud's incessant concern for the unfortunate, for the evicted, for poor children, and, above all, for prisoners, and especially the unfortunate Treason Felony prisoners.

Millevoye had suggested to her the role of Ireland's Joan of Arc; she had taken up the suggestion with conviction and brio being described in headlines in the newspapers as such, the part and the work combining to give her added influence. This was useful: it assisted her to achieve her ends as when, for instance, she realised that those in distress in Donegal and Mayo saw her as the Woman of the Sidhe. She lived up to this part too, just as in 1902 she incarnated Yeats's Cathleen ni Houlihan in that highly emotive nationalist play about which he pondered in old age:

> Did that play of mine
> Send out certain men the English shot?

A Servant of the Queen is a romantic book: it heightens sensibility when it describes the meeting with Millevoye, when it uses an image Yeats also employed, of the stone of the heart, or the heart turned to stone, to convey Maud's coldly detached feeling of finality when she realised that her affair with Millevoye had come documents—especially as most of her papers of that period were by then lost or burnt. Some of the chapters were not placed in chronological order, something that has been amended in this edition.

The book reads well, its stories carried along by her ability to write prose with the accents of speech. She may have been helped to achieve this flowing, at times racy style because she was not relying on written records, but was, rather, retelling stories that had settled into their shape over the years. Chronology, then, was not important but the events of the narrative move easily backwards and forwards in the manner of flexible conversation. Details which must have seemed irrelevant to her are not allowed to hold up the flow. For instance, she does not tell us much about her French governess, nor about 'Bowie' (Mary Anne Meredith), her old nurse. Nor do we learn much about the times her father spent with herself and Kathleen when he was on leave and took his daughters travelling in Europe. Instead, we have the dramatic advice he gave her: never to be afraid of anything, not even death; and to realise what willpower can achieve.

What we do get, however, is a series of exciting episodes. It was obvious to some of the older Irish nationalists, particularly John O'Leary, that she was in search of excitement (she distressed Yeats's father on their first meeting by her praise of war) and her enjoyment of action, of dramatic tension, which, with her courage, was what directed her into and made her so effective in the line of work she undertook, much of her strength being in the efficacy of her public demonstrations. She was always anti-establishment, firstly in reacting against the norms of her upper middle class conservative relatives, then later in espousing the causes of evicted tenants and prisoners, the victims of what to her was the Establishment par excellence—the British Empire. Before her emergence politically these qualities first appear clearly in such episodes as her carrying secret documents to St Petersburg for the French Boulangists and obviously getting immense pleasure out of persuading a Russian diplomat (who ironically, was carrying counter proposals from the Germans) to get her through the frontier controls despite her

Maud had wanted *One of those little Stones* as a title but after some discussion with Gollancz agreed to *A Servant of the Queen* instead. This title also suggests Queen Maeve of Connaught with whom Maud sometimes associated herself (as Yeats did) having taken Maeve as her name in Inghinidhe na hEireann, the Daughters of Ireland, the woman's association which she founded and of which she was President.

A Servant of the Queen presents a crowded canvas but it is none the less selective once it moves into Maud's political life, which began after her meeting with a French politician, Lucien Millevoye, in Royat, a French spa where both were recovering their health. She had inherited weak lungs; her mother and both her grandmothers died of consumption and her sister Kathleen also died of it in 1919. At twenty, declaring her independence from her relatives, she attempted an acting career which ended in the illness which brought her to Royat. It was while rehearsing as leading lady in *Aidrienne Lecouvreur*, a play by Scribe and Lejouré, about the tragic actress of that name, that she fell seriously ill. The twenty-seven chapters of the book cover her life up to her marriage in 1903, in her thirty-seventh year, to John MacBride. They are selective in a way that differs from Yeats's approach, for Maud was careless about detail. She wrote with vigour; she had good narrative skills, telling a story well and supplying significant dialogue at high moments of drama. Various events in her life impressed themselves upon her memory indelibly, and she was very aware of the importance of the history of the times she lived through, but sequence and historical dates seem to have mattered little to her. Few of her contemporaries in the period she covered were alive and at that time there were few reference books covering the period. When Seumas Mac-Manus was writing his autobiography they did discuss the Battle of the Rotunda and who was present there, their memories differing slightly according to her. Iseult, who helped her with typing and editing, though she was highly intellectual, did not have an historical perspective, so the chapters deal with different aspects of Maud's life simply as she remembered them. As a result they range over the fifteen years of her political life which the book covers without the benefit of being checked against and many of Maud's and Iseult's good friends would have found it difficult to accept it. Perhaps some guessed, but the more innocent did not. While Iseult herself had dearly wished to be acknowledged as her mother's rightful daughter, Maud's son, Seán was especially anxious that none of the family skeletons should be aired in public, being very conscious of the worldly position—though he himself later worked towards the easing of the illegitimacy situation by supporting the shortened birth certificate which left out parents' names. Gollancz, too, was wary; his concern naturally was the possibility of libel. So Maud, whatever her personal views were, continued the fictions she had had to practise throughout her life.

In this edition, however, we have decided to clarify this situation and give the names of others omitted in the final revised text of the first edition. None of her notes or early drafts are available except for a few attempts at a very poor chronology, but two names which were both left out were those of Dr Mark Ryan, head of the IRB in London, who was still alive at the time of publication at one stage during the Dr Leydes betrayal [see the Chapter titled 'Betrayal'] he was described as Mr X and of the man who did the betraying, an ex-MP named by Yeats in his *Autobiographies*, Frank Hugh O'Donnell. Also in the chapters 'Countering a Plot' and 'In America' the agent provocateur was a British agent by the name of Merrick Shaw Copeland Jones.

The Queen of the title of the book was Cathleen ni Houlihan, as the opening section 'I saw the Queen' explains. In it Maud related how, tired but glowing with satisfaction, she was returning to Dublin from Mayo where she had applied her willpower to a famine situation and imbued the local people with the strength to force an amelioration of their conditions. She looked out of the window of the train which was passing through bogland dark in the fading light and saw

a tall beautiful woman with dark hair blown in the wind and I knew it was Cathleen ni Houlihan. She was crossing the bog towards the hills, springing from stone to stone over the treacherous surface, and the little white stones shone, making a path behind her, then faded into the darkness. I heard a voice say 'You are one of the little stones on which the feet of the Queen have rested on her way to Freedom.'

Her family, particularly her son Seán (who left the IRA in 1937, and, finally being called to the Bar, took up legal practice) did not wish her to discuss her private life, particularly her affair with Lucien Millevoye, nor to go into the details of her divorce case against Seán's father, John MacBride. So Millevoye appears not as her lover and the father of her son Georges Sylvére, who died in infancy, and her daughter Iseult, but as her political ally in the struggle against the British Empire. Iseult is referred to as 'the charming child I adopted' or 'my lovely niece', and Eileen, Maud's illegitimate half-sister, is called 'Daphne'. John MacBride's behaviour to her and to Iseult, then a child, was brought up in the divorce proceedings.

Maud, however, though writing only of a much earlier period, found difficulty in many different regards. There was always the question of libel, of family sensibilities and the social attitudes of the time, all of which came under discussion. Autobiographies in those days—more than half a century ago—were much more bland than they are in the current fashion for startling revelations, and only the good and not the controversial was liable to be touched on, as, for instance in *Seventy Years Young* by the Countess Fingall, published in 1938, and *Past Times and Pastimes* by the Earl of Dunraven, published in 1922, whose authors' lives at one time or another ran parallel to Maud's own. So to reveal the name of her half-sister, her own love affair with Lucien Millevoye, the birth of her son Georges and her daughter Iseult by him, given the social rectitude of the time, would have been injudicious. To mention other names would have affected descendants of other families. For instance, Eileen Wilson, had married Maud's brother-in-law, Joseph MacBride, in 1904 and lived in Ireland with her five children. Georges had died at nineteen months so there was little need to say anything much about him. But at the time of Iseult's birth it would not have been acceptable to have acknowledged her parentage for very obvious reasons, as Millevoye's political career would have been at stake, Maud's social and political credibility, especially in Ireland, would have been severely damaged and, last but not least, Iseult's own social acceptability would be very badly affected. Even in the 1930s, and for long after, illegitimacy was a stigma,

CHRONOLOGY TO THE EVENTS
REFERRED TO IN
A SERVANT OF THE QUEEN

1865   Premises of Fenian paper *Irish People* raided in Dublin; many arrested, including John O'Leary.

1866   MG born at Tongham, near Aldershot, Hampshire on 21 December.

1867   Fenian rising in Ireland.

1868   Gonne family moved to Ireland (April). Kathleen Gonne born on 8 September.

1871   Fenians released into exile, including John O'Leary, O'Donovan Rossa, and John Devoy (January). Edith Gonne died in London on 21 June.

1875   Charles Stewart Parnell elected to Parliament (April).

1878   New Departure, a proposal for co-operation between parliamentarians, agrarians and republicans.

1879   Irish National Land League founded in Dublin by Davitt, Parnell and others.

1880   Gladstone's second Liberal administration. Founding of Ladies' Land League in October.

1881   First issue of Parnell's paper, *United Ireland*, edited by William O'Brien (August). Parnell held prisoner in Kilmainham Jail, Land League outlawed (October).

1882   Parnell and other leaders released under the Kilmainham Treaty. Phoenix Park Murders claimed by Invincibles.

1883   Start of Fenian dynamiting campaign. Thomas Clarke and others imprisoned for dynamiting conspiracy.

1885   Thomas Gonne takes up appointment in Dublin as Asst. Adjutant General (January). Culmination of Fenian dynamiting campaign.

1886 John Morley appointed Chief Secretary for Ireland. Gladstone's first Home Rule Bill defeated and Conservatives returned to power. *United Ireland* publishes 'A Plan of Campaign' by Timothy Harrington. Clanricard estate becomes model for Plan of Campaign. Thomas Gonne dies in Dublin on 30 November.

1887 Victoria's Golden Jubilee (June). MG meets Millevoye, travels to Constantinople and becomes 21 on 21 December. 'Bloody Sunday' Socialist meeting in Trafalgar Square on 13 November.

1888 Pope Leo XIII condemns Plan of Campaign (June). Commission to inquire into allegations made against Parnell by the *Times* in 1887 (September).

1889 MG and WBY meet (30 January). Richard Pigott shoots himself on being found out as forger of Parnell letters. District Inspector murdered when attempting to arrest Father James McFadden of Gweedore (February). Ellen O'Leary dies (October). Parnell cited in O'Shea divorce Case (December). Boulangist movement collapsed.

1890 MG's son by Millevoye born (January). WBY initiated into Golden Dawn. MG active in Barrow-in-Furness by-election where Liberal and Home Rule candidate Duncan won (June). 'New Tipperary' opened by Plan of Campaign leaders. WBY asked to resign from Madame Blavatsky's Theosophical Society. In O'Shea divorce suit Parnell found guilty of adultery. Irish Parliamentary party splits, majority opposing Parnell (December).

1891 WBY proposes to MG (July). Her son dies on 31 August. Boulanger commits suicide (September). Parnell dies (October). MG ill in St Raphael (?). Death of Rose Kavanagh. WBY's poem 'A Dream of Death' published (December).

1892 Stead writes of MG in *The Review of Reviews*. Amnesty Associations formed. MG's first article published. She lectures in France. Liberal Government elected with Gladstone as PM (August). John Morley again appointed

Chief Secretary. Irish Literary Societies formed in London and Dublin, and libraries scheme commenced. Famine in Russia. John Redmond's article on Treason Felony prisoners in *The Fortnightly*. Margaret Wilson (Mrs Robbins) goes as governess to Russia.

1893   John Redmond's pamphlet on Treason Felony prisoners. Gladstone's 2nd Home Rule Bill rejected by Lords. MG publishes her account of Treason Felony prisoners in Portland prison.

1894   Dreyfus arrested. WBY in Paris, sees MG (February). Gladstone retires from politics. Iseult Gonne, MG's daughter by Millevoye born (August).

1895   Conservative government in power with George Balfour replacing Morley as Chief Secretary (July).

1896   Alice Milligan and Anna Johnson commence publication of *Shan Van Vocht* in Belfast. James Connolly comes to Ireland, founds Irish Socialist Republican Party. WBY meets Edward Martyn, Lady Gregory, George Moore. The Ivory Case (see Chapter XIII, Countering a Plot) when Czar Nicholas visited Paris (October). In Paris Yeats meets John Millington Synge (December) and helps MG to form Paris Young Ireland Society.

1897   MG starts *l'Irlande Libre*. Charles MacCarthy Teeling episode. Queen Victoria's Diamond Jubilee. WBY's first long stay with Lady Gregory at Coole. The '98 Centenary preparations commence, MG goes to USA. Potato blight causes famine in winter of 1897-98.

1898   '98 celebrations under way. Famine in the west and Kerry. United Ireland League founded by William O'Brien. Local Government Act. MG's mystical marriage with WBY.

1899   WBY visits Paris, proposes to MG. First production of Irish Literary Theatre, *The Countess Cathleen*. MG in Mayo, evictions. *Shan Van Vocht* ceases publication and *United Irishman* commences (March). Francis Tully and Evicted Tenants Restoration Scheme. Boer War begins (October). Formation of Irish Brigade, Irish Transvaal Committee, anti-enlistment campaign, visit of Joseph Chamberlain, Colonial Secretary, to Dublin.

1900 MGs 2nd tour in USA. Dr Leyds episode. Irish Parliamentary Party unites. 2nd season of Irish Literary Theatre (February). Queen Victoria's visit. Suppression of *United Irishman*. MG's libel action against Colles. WBY's trouble with the Order of the Golden Dawn and quarrel with MacGregor Mathers (April-May). Patriotic Children's Treat (June). Nationalists' delegation to Paris (July). Founding of Inghinidhe na hEireann and *Cumann na nGaedheal* (October). Major MacBride in Paris (November).

1901 MG's 3rd tour in USA with MacBride; he proposes to her there. *Inghinidhe na hEireann* theatrical productions. 3rd Irish Literary Theatre Season (October).

1902 MG's lectures in Paris. MG's nurse 'Bowie' dies. Eileen Wilson (Daphne Robbins) comes to live in Paris with MG. Inghinidhe na hEireann and the Fay brothers perform WBY's *Kathleen ni Houlihan* and Russell's *Deirdre* (April). Irish National Theatre Society formed. MG rents house in Coulson Avenue, Rathgar, Dublin. She decides to marry John MacBride, visits deFreyne estate.

1903 MG received into Catholic Church and marries John MacBride (February). King Edward VII visits Dublin; Battle of Rotunda. MG and Douglas Hyde withdraw from National Theatre Society.

1904 MG's son Seán born (January). First productions in the Abbey Theatre. MG decides to seek marriage separation (December).

1905 Legal separation proceedings commence. Cumann na nGaedheal Samhain convention does not re-elect MG as vice-president. MG starts painting.

1906 Marriage separation verdict only valid in France.

1907 Dungannon Clubs, *Cumann na nGaedhael* and National Council form *Sinn Féin*.

1908 MG's appeal for divorce, as against legal separation, fails, which means she has to live in France to retain custody of her son, Seán. WBY and MG begin second mystical marriage (June).

1909 Lady Gregory seriously ill. Synge dies. Madame Avril ill. MG in Dublin, later with family in Bernex and Colleville.

1910 MG helps during Paris floods. Commences work for feeding Dublin school children. Ella Young's *Celtic Wonder Tales* published with MG's illustrations. Accession of George V.

1911 School meals campaign. MG in Italy (April).

1912 MG in Brussels and Dublin in relation to organisation of school meals.

1913 Home Rule Bill does not pass Lords. Ulster Volunteers organized. MG in Dublin at time of strike and lock out. Formation of Citizen Army and Irish Volunteers.

1914 MG and family in Pyrenees for summer. Ulster Volunteer Force gun running. Convention re Amending Bill to Home Rule for exclusion of Ulster. Irish Volunteers' Howth gun running. Home Rule Bill passed as Government of Ireland Act (1914) but suspended because of outbreak of First World War. Beginning of Irish Volunteer split. MG and Iseult nursing the wounded in Pyrenees. WBY begins his memoirs.

1915 MG nurses in Paris Plage and Paris. Military Council of IRB formed (December) by future signatories of Proclamation of the Irish Republic.

1916 MG nursing in Paris. Family spend Easter in Normandy where they hear of the Easter Rising. Execution of leaders. WBY visits MG and proposes, she refuses. She commences attempt to get back to Ireland. Ulster Unionists agree to immediate implementation of Home Rule provided Ulster is temporarily excluded. Sinn Féin opts for a republic.

1917   Sinn Féin wins first by-election (February). WBY accompanies MG and family to London, where they are not allowed to proceed to Dublin. WBY marries Georgie Hyde Lees. MG escapes to Ireland in disguise.

1918   MG buys house at 73 St. Stephen's Green. Millevoye dies. German Plot arrests in Ireland (May), MG in Holloway Prison, released (end of October). Sinn Féin wins general Election. World War ends. MG escapes to Ireland in disguise.

1919   MG working for Sinn Féin Government. Her sister Kathleen dies in Switzerland. Guerilla warfare in Ireland, Seán MacBride joins IRA. Sinn Féin Dáil declared illegal.

1920   Extra forces, Black and Tans, arrive in Ireland. Iseult marries Francis Stuart. Sectarian riots in Belfast. MG begins relief work as war of independence escalates.

1921   White Cross formed (February). Truce (July). Anglo-Irish Treaty Signed (December).

1922   Provisional Government takes over (January). Anti-Treaty forces seize Four Courts (April). General Election. MG in Paris (16 June) for Provisional Government when it attacks Four Courts. Civil War. Griffith dies suddenly. Cosgrave's Free State Government. (November-May 1923). 77 prisoners shot as reprisals. MG forms Women's Prisoners Defence League. MG and Mrs Despard move to Roebuck House, Clonskeagh, Co. Dublin. They start small industries to give employment. WBY's father dies; he moves to Dublin. He becomes an Irish Free State Senator.

1923   Civil War ends. Irish Free State enters League of Nations. MG and Mrs Despard continue protests against Government's repressive measures. Seán on the run and active in IRA. WBY wins Nobel Prize for Literature.

1926   Seán MacBride marries while on the run. De Valera forms political party. MG still active for relief of prisoners.

1927 Kevin O'Higgins shot, Seán arrested for his murder, finally released.

1929 WBY dangerously ill in Rapallo.

1932 De Valera wins general election. WBY spends winter and spring at Coole. Lady Gregory dies.

1934 MG active in support of prisoners and presses for solution of the border problem caused by the Treaty.

1936 WBY seriously ill. IRA declared illegal. MG stands for local elections for new republican party which loses badly, but she continues working for prisoners.

1937 De Valera's new constitution approved by referendum but MG along with other women objected to its paternalistic attitudes.

1939 WBY dies (28 January) in South of France. Second World War declared.

1946 Seán's party, Clann na Poblachta, founded.

1948 De Valera loses general election, Seán a member of new Inter-Party Government. Republic of Ireland leaves the Commonwealth. Official re-interment of WBY in Sligo.

1953 MG dies.

A NOTE ON THE TEXT

W HEN FIRST published in 1938 and reissued in 1974 the order of the chapters in *A Servant of the Queen* was not correct, nor as originally intended. We have altered the sequence of chapters (with the exception of the last chapter) from Chapters XIV to XXVI, to keep to an approximate chronological order. The order is approximate, as some of the events she recorded occurred either immediately before or after Maud Gonne's marriage. She was, for instance, baptized into the Catholic Church in February 1903, just before her marriage. The Battle of the Rotunda occurred a few months after her marriage and it marks the end of her major political demonstrations of that era in her life. *Fine*, a group founded by Ella Young is mentioned (p. 334), its activities continued well into the twentieth century and are probably referred to in a letter written by Maud Gonne to Yeats on 10 November 1915 (see *The Gonne-Yeats Letters 1893-1938. Always Your Friend*, ed. Anna MacBride White and A. Norman Jeffares (1992), Letter 312, p. 361). The new order of Chapters in the second half of the book follows, with the original numbers in brackets given after the titles, XIV. Spies (XV); XV Occult Experience (XVIII); XVI Victoria's Jubilee (XX); XVII In America (XIV); XVIII Famine (XVII); XIX The '98 Centenary (XXI); XX England's Difficulty (XXIII): XXI End of the Alliance (XXII); XXII Betrayal (XXIV); XXIII Days of Gloom (XVI); XXIV The New Century (XXV); XXV The Battle of the Rotunda (XXVI); XXVI The Inevitability of the Church (XIX); XXVII Dusk (XXVII).

We have silently corrected various misprints. We have identified 'the gentleman from your party', and 'an Irish Member of Parliament' whose actions are described in Chapter XXII, Betrayal as Frank Hugh O'Donnell. 'Mr X', in the same chapter, is Dr Mark Ryan, 'One of John O'Leary's Chief Lieutenants', also mentioned in this chapter, is T. W. Rolleston. Brief notes are given on them in the 'Notes on Persons and Organisations'.

I SAW THE QUEEN

I WAS RETURNING FROM Mayo triumphant. I had stopped a famine and saved many lives by making the people share my own belief that courage and will are unconquerable and, where allied to the mysterious forces of the land, can accomplish anything. Had I not seen death and despair recede! That afternoon, at the Wishing Well in Ballina, where the girls of the town had led me while waiting for the train, I had seen the fish which they said none of our generation had seen; it had darted across the clear water which bubbles up unceasingly at the foot of a green mound where legend says a queen lies buried. I had wished the wish of all our hearts—a Free Republic, but had refused to tell for it is unlucky to tell wishes. I had been seen off at the station by a cheering crowd and a band; the Town Council had presented me an address and a spinning wheel painted green and gold.

Tired but glowing I looked out of the window of the train at the dark bog land where now only the tiny lakes gleamed in the fading light. Then I saw a tall, beautiful woman with dark hair blown on the wind and I knew it was Cathleen ni Houlihan. She was crossing the bog towards the hills, springing from stone to stone over the treacherous surface, and the little white stones shone, marking a path behind her, then faded into the darkness. I heard a voice say: "You are one of the little stones on which the feet of the Queen have rested on her way to Freedom." The sadness of night took hold of me and I cried; it seemed so lonely just to be one of those little stones left behind on the path.

Being old now and not triumphant I know the blessedness of having been "one of those little stones" on the path to Freedom.

FOREWORD

Every logical mind will assent to the proposition that omelettes cannot continue to be manufactured without a continual breaking of eggs. No more can the British Empire stand or go without famine in Ireland, opium in China, torture in India, pauperism in England, disturbance and disorder in Europe and robbery everywhere.

"You cannot have a British Empire and repudiate the conditions *sine qua non*. There stands your British Empire and here is what it costs; everyone can determine at his leisure whether it is worth the price."

(From John Mitchell's *Apology for British Rule*.)

By the time that I, the daughter of an Irish father and an English mother, with Scotch and French blood in my veins, had arrived at the age of reason and was a free agent I had determined that it was not worth the price.

How I arrived at this determination and how it affected my life is the story I have tried to tell.

In telling it I may seem to ignore events and people deserving to be mentioned. In a fight one sees only the corner of the field in which one stands. That is my excuse to those other soldiers in the fight for freedom whom I have not mentioned and who have made as great efforts and perhaps greater sacrifices.

CHAPTER I

WORDS REMEMBERED

Tommy said: "you must never be afraid of anything, even of death." And because his voice was so strange and far-away although he held me in his arms and because I was very frightened though I did not know why or what death meant, being only four, these words sank into my mind never to be forgotten.

Tommy was my father. He stood with me in his arms beside Mama's coffin. Nurse, carrying my younger sister, Kathleen, stood beside him.

All the day and night before the gloomy London house had been full of hushed bustle and strange sounds and strange people; I was very curious, and escaping early from the nursery that morning in my nightgown, I had gone to find Mama. My small fumbling fingers succeeded in turning the handle of the door of her room; I was afraid nurse would catch me before I got it open. The room was dark and lit by candles although it was daylight. Tommy was kneeling by the bed. As I opened the door he turned his head. He was crying. Harshly he said: "Go away," and nurse, coming down the stairs, captured me.

It was only when the men were there waiting to carry down the coffin that Tommy came and fetched us to say good-bye to Mama. Mama was tall like a lily and very beautiful. She wore white and blue like the sky and all her jewels were pearls and turquoises.

Like those the gods love she died before romance faded, five years after her wedding day. She died in that gloomy

London house on her way to Italy where Tommy was taking her in search of health. The night when she knew she must die, she asked to be buried in a little green country church-yard in Surrey near the house where I had been born, not very far from Aldershot where Tommy's regiment had been stationed and where they lived on return from their honeymoon. At her grave, a marble cross, uninscribed for fifteen years, stood beside the one bearing her name, as a memorial to that unfaded romance. Tommy had had it put there so she would feel less lonely and himself less hopeless. I only knew this when his will was read fifteen years after in Dublin.

That night, before she died, she told Tommy how unhappy she had been at the boarding school to which she had been sent by aunts when her mother died and she made Tommy promise he would never send Kathleen or me to school or let us fall into the clutches of the aunts.

Floraville, our home in Donnybrook, was too big without Mama and I think Tommy found it too intolerably lonely without her, so I watched him on a ladder take down Mama's picture and my picture also by Wall, a Dublin artist of great merit, and the golden Fra Angelico angels Mama loved and had had copied when they were on their honeymoon in Florence, and pack them in packing cases. He hammered his finger in nailing the case; it bled and I ran to get nurse to make it well but Tommy would not let her put on a bandage. He always, in all our many moves, insisted on hanging and packing these pictures himself. He got very expert at it.

It was in the garden of Floraville, while Mama was still with us, that I first saw the white wonder of snow which one so seldom sees in Ireland, except in the mountains. I stood at the big nursery window, howling because nurse said it was too cold to go out, and Tommy came and told her to muffle me in my red Connemara cloak and took me out to run in it. His big foot-prints and my little ones made such funny patterns. I found a broken branch of holly on the path all covered with glistening snow and rushed back into the house with it to Mama.

"Oh Lambkin, what a darling to have brought it for me."

"It isn't for you," I said, clutching it; "Tommy says it will melt at the fire; I want to see."

She looked disappointed. I had not brought it for her, I had not thought of her as I danced in the snow, and because of that I always see her eyes with a sad look in them. When death stands between me and someone I love, a cruel little memory of something done or left undone suddenly arises to make sorrow more bitter; trifles, unnoticed at the time, loom up and seem of more importance than sins not confessed.

The reproach in the eyes of Dagda, the Great Dane dog who was my girlhood companion, made me cry at nights in my cabin all the way to America, where I was going on an important mission. The letter telling me of the dog's death was given me as I was going aboard at Cobh. I had hardly noticed the sorrow and reproach in the eyes of the old dog when I had brought a young strong dog into the house and told him, because he was old and wise, he must train the young dog in the ways he should go. He had put his great paws on my shoulders and looked at me and the sorrow of his eyes suddenly haunted me, now that I would never be able to ask his faithful forgiveness. He had been such a wonderful understanding companion and had guarded me in many tight places, and I had failed him when he was old and weak. Is this sentimentality? I don't think so. It is so hard to know what is important and what is not in the quickly moving incidents of life. Death suddenly alters all values. Things which were important become as nothing; things that we considered trifles suddenly loom immense. Which are the true values, the values of life or the values of death?

We went to live in a little wooden hut in Kildare with a verandah running round it and a sun porch where Tommy grew flowers and taught me to sow seeds and make cuttings. Soldiers in red coats constantly came and went. A grey donkey lived in the paddock; Kathleen and I strapped in panniers used to ride it. The donkey and I were close friends. I often fell asleep with my head nestled in the warm sweet-smelling fur of his neck when he lay down on the grass in the sun; he was so careful never to roll on me or step on me when he got up. If I was in trouble after a noisy row with nurse, the donkey would come and put his head through the window and bray loudly and help me to make more noise. Animals and I always understood each other; I was never afraid of them and they never hurt me. There was a kennel of fox-hounds reputed to be dangerous to any but their keepers near my uncle's house. I succeeded one day in getting into the yard. No one was there and the key was in the door of the kennel. When the kennel man returned he was horrified to find me happily playing in the kennel with the hounds. If you have no fear, conscious or subconscious, I believe things will hardly ever harm you.

"You must never be afraid of anything, not even of death."

Because those words were said under terrible emotional strain to a child whose mind was made receptive by awe and curiosity they became indelibly fixed and influenced my whole life. I deliberately conquered fear, and I used to be afraid of many things, especially of the dark. As a child I saw strange shapes moving in the dim gleam of the night-light, creeping under the bed, and a veiled woman with dark sad eyes often bent over me at night. Nurse hated it when I used to tell her and talked of nightmares and of fever. There was a rather gloomy shrubbery near Uncle Charles's home at Ascot; we children used to avoid it at dark. After dinner in the evening, I forced myself to go out alone into it. At first I ran all the time and was breathless when I reached the house, but I took that fearsome walk every night till I could do it slowly and without a tremor and later I have walked quite fearlessly at night through the forest of Fontainebleau, which few men would have done at that time, for it had ill-repute. It is true that Dagda, the Great Dane, walked at my side and I had a revolver in my pocket. So in the war, when I was an old woman in Dublin and bullets were flying and crowds swayed like corn ears in the wind, it never occurred to me to take cover; and because I literally felt no fear, nothing ever happened to me, though some who took cover were wounded. Outside General Mulcahy's house in Portobello, the Women's Prisoners' Defence League had organised a great protest meeting against the murder of prisoners of war for which Mulcahy was held responsible. The Free State soldiers were drawn up inside the railings; some shots had been fired over our heads; a woman's hat had been pierced by a bullet. I heard an order given and the front line of soldiers knelt down with rifles ready,—some of the young soldiers were white and trembling. I got up on the parapet of the railing and smiled contempt at the officer. He had curious rather beautiful pale grey eyes and a thin brown face. We gazed at each other a full minute. The order to fire was not given. Later I was told I was brave and had saved many lives. But that is not true; you are not brave when fear is dead. I was much braver when I ran breathlessly through my uncle's quiet shrubbery. It is the young who ARE afraid, and yet take risks, who are brave. They have not the protection which the total absence of fear gives, —a strange aloof power. I can never see why old people should be afraid, but they mostly are more fearsome than the young.

Some other words of Tommy's I record here because they also influenced my life. They were spoken laughingly as we sat in a little albergo in Rome and talked of hypnotism and of the curious shows Pickman, a conjuror hypnotist, was giving. These words only became significant to me a few years later in an emotional crisis in my own life when Tommy was dead. Tommy said: "Will is a strange incalculable force. It is so powerful that if, as a boy, I had willed to be the Pope of Rome, I would have been the Pope."

I don't think Tommy ever concentrated his own will on anything for long. He loved life in all its many forms,—art, sport, drama, travel,—and had many interests and occupations and was always turning aside to help people he knew. His death left a blank in many lives, in many different circles.

We were leaving the Curragh.

Packing-cases again. Mama's picture and the golden angels were taken down. I think a doctor had told Tommy I needed sea air. People often said I was very like Mama and Mama had died, and nurse was worried whenever I coughed and pursued me with cod-liver oil and orange juice.

The sitting-room in the ugly little house opposite the Baily lighthouse at Howth was too small for the golden angels to surround Mama's picture. They were hung over the beds where Kathleen and I slept, in the room above.

Howth was different then from what it is to-day. There was no tram, and very few houses. The ugly little house we rented had been built by the enterprising man who drove the one outside car in the district to and from the station at Sutton. He and his large family lived in a little cabin near by and his mother lived in another, even smaller and smokier, cabin farther up in the heather.

Tommy used to come for week-ends and Kathleen and I used to be strapped securely on to one side of the car, with our feet in a big sack of hay for the horse and a rug to keep us all compact, tucked in at each side of the cushions if the day was cold or windy; our landlord sat on the other side till we arrived at Sutton where Tommy, coming off the train, would take his place and he the driver's seat in the middle, while Tommy's bags and exciting parcels of cakes and toys filled the well of the car and the drive home seemed very long till we could get opening them.

No place has ever seemed to me quite so lovely as Howth was then. Sometimes the sea was as blue as Mama's turquoises, more strikingly blue even than the Mediterranean because so often grey mists made it invisible and mysterious. The little rock pools at the bottom of the high cliffs were very clear and full of wonder-life; sea-anemones which open look like gorgeous flowers with blue and orange spots and, if touched, close up into ugly brown lumps, tiny crabs, pink star-fish, endless varieties of sea-snails, white, green, striped and bright buttercup-yellow. Nurse must have been a wonderful climber, for she often took us down to bathe in those ready-made bathing pools where Kathleen and I boastfully declared that we were swimming, with our feet and hands firmly touching the bottom. The waves used to come splashing into them and made us feel very brave. It must have been a fairly perilous enterprise for her to convey safely two young children up and down those zig-zag narrow cliff paths among the wheeling crying sea-gulls. We were never allowed to go near the cliffs alone, but on the other side of the house far up the heather-covered hill to Granny's cabin, we were free to wander and play as we pleased. The heather grew so high and strong there that we could make cubby houses and be entirely hidden and entirely warm and sheltered from the strong wind that blows over the Head of Howth. After I was grown up I have often slept all night in that friendly heather. It is as springy as the finest spring mattress and, if one chooses the place well, so cosy and sheltered and quiet. From deep down in it one looks up at the stars in a wonderful security and falls asleep to wake up only with the call of the sea birds looking for their breakfasts.

Nurse was a sociable soul. Very soon she knew all the people who lived in the little cabins along the road to the Post Office and away in the heather, and while, over a friendly cup of tea, she chatted, Kathleen and I played with the barefooted children and shared their slices of hot griddle cake baked at the turf fire, or their potatoes out of big iron pots hung in the chimneys. No potatoes and no bread ever tasted as good. All the hospitality was on their side for nurse would never let us bring them to share our meals, carefully set out by Annie the housemaid in the little sitting-room, and woe to Annie if our silver christening mugs and spoons were not brilliantly polished. Those elaborately set-out meals and the steel hoops of her own crinoline were nurse's way of keeping up respectability.

Our feelings towards the ragged children were mixed; they were better climbers than we were and better riders of donkeys, but we could boast of our exploits in swimming pools. If we had better clothes, they had more learning, for every day they trudged off to the far-away school-house, while we played all day with the kids and donkeys in the heather. On the whole honours were fairly equal and we all kept our self-respect and enjoyed exciting games together and all united in admiration for a big boy called Bobby. Bobby used to get sea-gull eggs and tell us wonderful stories of dangerous caves in the cliffs where men had hidden,—some said rebels, some said smugglers,—none of us had ever been allowed to visit those caves. Bobby occasionally drove the car to Howth village for provisions. Nurse was a knowledgeable woman and gained great reputation for having saved a sick baby's life. She had a store of nursery remedies and came to be consulted whenever there was a sick child or a minor accident in Howth. She was very proud of this reputation; it gained her forgiveness for her crinoline and English accent, of which also she was proud, but which, if it had not been for her reputation as a doctor and her unfailing good nature, might have marred her popularity; all the cabins were hung with coloured pictures of Wolfe Tone, Emmet and Michael Dwyer and of Allen Larkin and O'Brien and the early Land-League heroes side by side with chromos of the Sacred Heart and of the Blessed Virgin. If nurse knew who these men were, she never said anything; but when she was not there, the old people used to say they were great men, the Lord have mercy on them, but would not say more because after all we too, as well as nurse, belonged to the other side,—the English garrison; nevertheless they made us welcome to their glowing turf fires. Many presents nurse used to get of eggs and butter-milk and mushrooms and periwinkles in return for her lime-water or powders or ointments, for the people were very proud and insisted on making some return. Only their hospi-tality to Kathleen and me was allowed to go unrequited. It was given so naturally, so ungrudgingly that I doubt if they ever noticed it was unreturned.

One Sunday Tommy looked worried and thoughtful. He had taken Kathleen and me over the heather to church at Howth and after we had lunched with Lord Howth, at Howth Castle, and while Kathleen and I, dressed in black velvet and pink silk stockings and big straw hats with ostrich feathers which nurse spent hours in recurling, were having a glorious time in the afternoon eating giant strawberries in the garden, some lady playing croquet on the velvet lawn had told Tommy that his daughters were being allowed to run wild like little savages and,—which was quite true,—were quite shockingly ignorant. The result of the worry and thought was a letter to the aunts in London and the subsequent arrival in Howth of an English governess, a clergyman's daughter, who had undertaken the impossible task of teaching us reading, writing and arith-metic, music and painting and all that little ladies should know.

She was a kindly stupid woman who did her best, but, as she had herself only a smattering of the wide knowledge she was supposed to impart, we learned very little from her. It was the end of our liberty. That winter, with nurse and governess, we were sent to visit Aunt Augusta in London.

CHAPTER II

EDUCATION

AUNT AUGUSTA WAS Mama's aunt. She lived alone in a very big house with very big rooms in Hyde Park Gardens. She was waited on by eight servants, not counting the stable boy who waited on the coachman but never appeared. She was secretly afraid of them.

She had a cross little black and tan dog called Tiny whom, I think, she loved. Tiny's manners had not been properly looked after in his youth; when he made a mess, which he often did, it was a serious household affair; the bell had to be rung,—that became my job,—the footman answered it and was told of the event in apologetic terms by Aunt Augusta; he then reported to his superior, the butler, who in his turn reported the matter to the upper housemaid, who then delegated authority to deal actively with the nuisance to the under-housemaid who finally appeared with dustpan and sponge and a pail of water. If the event recurred too often in the same day, Aunt Augusta's courage failed her and, blushing, she would ask our obliging governess to do the necessary with the fire shovel and hearth brush, because she said she didn't like to disturb the servants too often at their work. She was less afraid of the governess. Every morning, the tall footman, in striped yellow and black livery, used to take Tiny for a walk on a lead; in the afternoon, Tiny used to drive with Aunt Augusta in her yellow chariot in Hyde Park, or to the Army and Navy Stores, or Covent Garden market, where she used to say cheaper fruit could be bought than in the greengrocers' shops. The footman used to sit beside the coachman on the box and be ready to hold Tiny while Aunt Augusta did her shopping; Kathleen and I, dressed in our velvet frocks and ostrich-feathered hats, were expected to accompany Aunt Augusta and Tiny in the yellow chariot, an honour we soon failed to appreciate.

In the shops Aunt Augusta used to spend much time haggling over the price of apples and pears and oranges, and when the paper bags had duly been passed from Aunt Augusta to the footman and from the footman to the butler and finally appeared, a measly collection on a magnificent silver dessert-stand in the centre of the dining-table for dinner, their prices used to form the principal subject of Aunt Augusta's discourse. For company's sake, she had honoured our governess by inviting her to share her evening meal; Kathleen and I were brought down, dressed in starched muslin dresses and blue sashes, only for dessert. The butler used to stand behind Aunt Augusta's chair, the footman behind our governess at each end of the long table while they ate; places at each side were prepared for Kathleen and me and we were duly supplied with half an apple or half an orange and a biscuit, on pink dessert plates with hand-painted pictures of Windsor Castle and other royal residences. Aunt Augusta never failed to tell us that fruit was a very expensive luxury and must be indulged in sparingly; I think she had intimidated our poor governess into refusing it altogether.

Dessert finished, Aunt Augusta used to say grace and bow to our governess; the butler opened the dining-room door and they both walked upstairs to the drawing-room, the door of which was opened by the footman, and Kathleen and I and Tiny used to follow. Aunt Augusta requested our governess to play on the grand piano, which she did very feebly; the butler reappeared and opened a card table and Aunt Augusta settled down to play patience. At nine nurse came to take us up to bed.

At eight forty-five, every morning, Aunt Augusta used to read family prayers. The butler arranged two imposing-looking family prayer-books at the head of the table at Aunt Augusta's place, and three chairs at the opposite end for our governess and Kathleen and me, and eight chairs by the side-board for the servants. The first morning there was some confusion as no chair had been placed for nurse, who was duly waiting with the other servants in the hall for the summons to enter. The scullery maid humbly relinquished her chair, but even so, it needed much reshuffling because the servants sat according to rank and nurse's place would have been with the upper servants, next to cook, and, as a guest, before Aunt Augusta's lady's maid. I learnt later of these distinctions; that first morning I was conscious only of a great deal of shuffling after I had been told by our governess to kneel down and close my eyes, which I naturally opened again to find out what was stopping Aunt Augusta's part of the performance from beginning.

It seemed to me a long performance, but at nine o'clock the silver urn was lighted and Aunt Augusta was pouring out tea. Generally there was no hitch, and at five minutes to nine the butler brought in the silver urn. Only once, years after, when for a few days I was again staying with Aunt Augusta, an incident occured which is worth recording. It was before the occasion of one of Queen Victoria's numerous jubilees; prayers were over; the servants had risen from their knees, but did not file out as usual. Aunt Augusta raised her hand and asked the butler to request them to remain. She had a large sheet of paper in front of her and a pen and ink. She gave several embarrassed coughs, for she was not used to public speaking; at last she said: "I know you all are anxious to give something to show your love and gratitude to our queen."

The butler and Aunt Augusta looked at me and waited. I am not generally lacking in moral courage, but on that occasion I was so taken by surprise that, instead of saying anything, I merely gazed out of the window. Aunt Augusta thought it wiser to say nothing, and the butler hastily put half a sovereign on the plate at the end of the table and Aunt busied herself writing it down. Cook followed the butler with the same amount, and, one by one, each of the other servants, according to their wages, down to the scullery maid with her half a crown, contributed. All had evidently been prepared and knew that on this spontaneous demonstration of loyalty to old Vic. their places depended. I understood then how Jubilee funds attained their noble proportions, for, in every reputable English household, as well as in most of the shops and factories, the same pressure was brought to bear.

My one attempt at verse was severely checked by both nurse and governess when, on the day settled for us to leave Aunt Augusta's, I was discovered dancing in front of the great mirror on the landing leading to the drawing-room and singing at the top of my voice:

"Hooray, hooray, hooray!
To-day we are going away."

The assurance that I had made it up myself won no praise, even from Nurse, usually so admiring of our efforts in the field of art, whether recitations of nursery rhymes, paintings of ready-traced cards or piano exercises.

We were driven in the yellow chariot that afternoon to Richmond where Uncle Frank, Aunt Augusta's brother, lived. He had inherited from his elder brother (Mama's father who died very young) a marvellous collection of pictures and art treasures and had built two long picture-galleries onto his house to hang them. He had also a winter garden with tropical palms and bamboos the whole height of one side of the house. He had married a very beautiful Portuguese lady, Aunt Emily, whom he treated abominably. She seems to have been the only one of the aunts Mama had loved and she was my godmother. She was old and faded when I knew her, and in her long black silk dress and mantilla moved about among all these riches and splendours like a neglected ghost. Uncle Frank would not allow her even a carriage to drive in the beautiful Richmond Park; when she occasionally visited London, she had to go in a hired fly. Her excursions to London were generally to buy magnificent dolls for us children and she never forgot her godchild's birthday; but these extravagant presents had to be kept secret from Uncle Frank and the money to pay for them had to be craftily saved from the house-keeping accounts which Uncle Frank always examined every week himself. Aunt Emily had insisted on Tommy letting us stay with her and he was to come and fetch us from Richmond; she wanted to see her darling Edith's children.

Women of that generation don't seem to have had a dog's life, or to have counted for anything.

How Uncle Frank, who was Mama's guardian, managed to possess himself of all grandfather's art treasures, leaving Mama, his only child, but one solitary unsigned picture, a beautiful Venus and Cupid which hangs to-day on my wall, I do not know. As I have said, women counted for little and girls for less in that generation and I fancy Mama was too happy to escape from the aunts, and Tommy too happy helping her, and both too happy in being together, to spoil their happiness by sordid investigations. As grandfather Cook died long before I was born, it would be useless for me to try to unravel the mystery,—I have little use for the dust of past generations. Anyhow I can't picture Tommy or Mama building long galleries onto their home, to which on certain days the public were ceremoniously admitted. They were useful to Uncle Frank, no doubt, as supplying a plausible reason for the title conferred on him by grateful England after he had paid certain Royal gambling debts.

Aunt Emily had beautiful hands and played the harp. She was not altogether satisfied with my health, nor with our musical education nor with our deportment nor with our way of pronouncing French. Though too kind to say much to us or our governess on the subject, she had a long conversation with Tommy, from which we were excluded. A doctor was called in to see me; then with Tommy and Nurse, Kathleen and I started for the South of France. I never saw Aunt Emily or Uncle Frank again. Aunt Emily died, a pale sad ghost; Uncle Frank married again an enterprising American, imbued with distinct ideas on women's rights, who took over the keeping of accounts; and Uncle Frank faded away and Lady Cook's widow's weeds floated over pages of society journals,—a just retribution!

Tommy rented a tiny villa for us on the road between Cannes and the ancient little citadel of Grasse, the great perfume centre of France. The villa was called Villa Fleurie and was a nest of flowers. Mimosa trees and pepper trees hung their long feathery foliage over it. It stood in fields of orange and lemon trees, carpeted with Parma violets for the flower market. A tiny fountain in the garden, where tiny emerald frogs croaked unbelievably loud love songs, was a source of joy to Kathleen and me. A French governess took charge of our education.

Mademoiselle was a strong Republican and the most efficient French woman I have ever met, and that is saying a great deal, for all French women seem to me so efficient. She succeeded in making us love our lessons and find them as exciting as play; she taught us history, some would say with a republican bias, but it was human history and she taught us to love human beings and to love beauty and to see it everywhere. She was building a little villa for herself to which one day she was going to retire with her dog, Toutou and her cat, Catichat, which meantime she had brought to live with us. Occasionally she would take us with her to inspect the progress of the workmen who were building it, and to plan her garden. Like our garden, it had big fragrant mimosa trees; in the tiny unfinished kitchen of her house, mademoiselle would cook most delicious dishes and teach us how simple it is to cook if one uses intelligence; and afterwards we used to picnic under the mimosas. She was happy herself and had a way of making everyone else happy.

I visited her later when I was grown up and she and Catichat and Toutou were old. She was just the same; she sat in her tiny drawing-room and showed me all her new books and was very interested to hear I was working for Ireland's freedom; then she put on her big straw sun-hat and showed me her garden with its mimosa trees, its roses and its minute rows of salad and vegetables. She tended it all herself and said it provided for almost all her needs. "Independence, *ma Chérie*, is the most precious of all things and everyone can be independent." Catichat, her tail in the air, and Toutou walked sedately after her.

I owe to her most of the little education I possess. What was of more importance, she had given us the desire to learn; she made us love literature and took the trouble to discuss it with us. Tommy had to leave to go to India. It was a heart-break, but he left us in good hands.

For six years we lived abroad; in the summer, among the snows of Switzerland; in the winter, in Italy or the South of France. Whenever he could, Tommy was with us and then we travelled. We visited cathedrals, museums, picture galleries, theatres. We spent much time in little old bric-à-brac shops where, amid endless junk, Tommy often discovered some real treasure, some piece of wonderful embroidery or wood carving which he would buy. He had sure taste and some knowledge and was a born collector. The expense of our education must have, I think, taken up most of his spare cash, for he often turned away from things that he would have liked to buy, if they were too costly.

More and more he treated me as a companion and sometimes, to our great amusement, when he and I were on some excursion alone together, people would take us for a honeymoon couple. At fourteen I was five feet ten and, having a great desire to be grown up, I made Nurse lengthen my skirts and dress the masses of my gold-brown hair in great coils at the back of my head. Tommy looked amazingly young; he was only fifty when he died.

I was sixteen and Tommy left us in Rome with an old friend of Mama's while he returned to Ireland to take up an appointment of Assistant Adjutant General in Dublin. He had kept his promise to Mama; he had never sent us to school and he had saved us from the clutches of the aunts. He intended that we should stay abroad another year. But one night, visiting the Colosseum by moonlight, a young Italian had proposed to me,—it was the first proposal I had received. A young Austrian had proposed the year before, but had made the mistake of addressing the proposal to Tommy and I heard of it only a month later after the young man had suddenly gone away. I determined no such mistake should occur again and though I would have preferred the proposal to have come from an American artist who was painting my portrait, the Colosseum by moonlight seemed such a suitable place for a proposal, that I accepted the Italian. Mama's friend was much perturbed when I told her and we both wrote to Tommy to announce the engagement,—I fancy, in very different terms. The result was a telegram summoning us back to Ireland at once. The American artist brought me a wonderful armful of flowers to the station and the Italian a large bag of chocolates which the heat had rendered sticky. I regretted the American had not been in the Colosseum, but it could not be helped; it was his fault, not mine. I afterwards learned he had a wife in America, which evidently rendered him ineligible, so he was not really to blame. The Italian and I promised to write to each other and kept our promise for quite a long time. Tommy got disturbed seeing the arrival of numerous letters with an Italian post mark on them and did the shockingly conventional thing of confiscating them and of opening all my letters; so my fiancé took to writing to me with milk on the pages of fashionable papers and circulars which Tommy unsuspectingly handed to me; letter-writing always bored me and Tommy's education seemed to me more important than the letters. Tommy was far more interesting than the writer of them; so, one morning after breakfast, when Tommy handed over to me several open letters and a few unopened circulars and sat down in the armchair by the fire with a cigar to read his own correspondence, I sat down on the fender stool, leaning my back against his knees. After a few minutes, I said I wanted to show him something and, opening a wrapper containing a circular advertising Italian hotels, I held it close to the fire and an impassioned love letter gradually emerged in brown letters. "Look, Tommy, at what you have just given me, you have given me a lot like this. Don't you realise how absurd this inspection of correspondence is? If I show you this little trick, it is because I know of several others equally good; so let us be reasonable. In three or four years I shall be of age, and if I want to marry this young man you can't prevent me. But if he goes on writing me letters like this and expects me to answer them, I certainly shall not want to marry him. So, for the sake of *l'amour éternel*, I will write and explain he had better not write for three years and you must stop helping to make him interesting by opening my letters."

There was an awkward pause; then Tommy burst out laughing and he never opened any more of my letters; as soon as he had finished reading his own correspondence, he told me he had seen in Atkinson's window a buttercup-coloured poplin shot with white which made it shimmer like gold in moonlight and he thought it would make me a wonderful evening dress and proposed we should go and look at it together. That was Tommy's way; if ever we had the slightest difference of opinion on any subject, it always ended by his giving me a present, to show there was no ill-will and because Tommy enjoyed nothing so much as giving presents.

We arrived in Dublin the day after the departure of one Lord Lieutenant and the State entry of his successor.

Tommy had many friends who were curious to see his daughters and our advent created almost as much interest in garrison circles as the arrival of the Lord Lieutenant. People were calling on us all day and invitations to teas, dinners and balls were piling up on the mantelpiece of the drawing-room under Mama's picture. Tommy said he would help me to answer them and that I must start keeping an engagement book. I was to be presented at the first Viceregal court by Lady Dunraven. Kathleen was not to come out till two years later. My presentation dress, embroidered with iridescent beads, looked like a fountain, and on the white satin train, three yards on the ground (regulation length), I had insisted on having water lilies to look like a lake, and Tommy had fetched Mama's pearls from the bank where they had been stored for years. I was told that a dancing-mistress was holding special classes to instruct débutantes how to curtsey and how to manage their trains, their bouquets and their fans before and after the ceremonious curtsey; but I declined to attend this as I felt I could manage quite well by myself and I rather resented all the fuss made about it. This didn't prevent me practising in private before the long mirror in my room, for it was no easy matter to manœuvre gracefully with so many impediments and mine were considerably complicated by the water lilies.

At a tea party given in our honour by a colonel's wife, I was told by some lady that the Lord Lieutenant kissed all the débutantes. "An old Irish custom," she said. I created much consternation when I said I had no intention of allowing myself to be kissed.

"Oh, but you must. The Lord Lieutenant represents the King."

"But it's not done at the English Court."

"No, because there is the Queen, and of course she doesn't kiss the girls. But in Ireland the Lord Lieutenant, representing English Royalty, keeps up the old customs."

"The sooner he gives it up, the better, then; anyhow he will not kiss me. No man will ever kiss me but the man I choose."

The ladies looked at each other, as though I had said something rather scandalous and I heard someone say excusingly: "She was brought up in France," which remark encouraged me tactlessly to insist on the feudal origin of the *droit du seigneur* and on the necessity for abolishing such relics of barbarism. The teaching of Mademoiselle didn't seem to be appreciated in Dublin; however the occasion did not arise as the Prince and Princess of Wales came over to hold the court and the Prince, not being King, had no right to kiss the débutantes in public. The Viceroy only stood smilingly in the background.

Places had been reserved for us in the window of the Kildare Street Club to watch the Viceregal procession and the State entry of Lord and Lady Spencer. The streets were lined with military and Royal Irish Constabulary, while Dublin Metropolitan policemen kept order behind the lines. There was much talk among the ladies seated in the window about the shocking state of the country and the chances of disloyal demonstrations. From their vantage point on the railings of

Trinity College Park the College boys were throwing paper bags of flour on the helmets and blue uniforms of the policemen. I gathered they did not approve of the D.M.P.; they said the Royal Irish Constabulary were a far better lot. An old colonel standing behind us disapproved of these foolish pranks and said the D.M.P. were a decent body of men, trying to carry out difficult duty; he liked them better than the R.I.C. who, he said, were neither flesh nor fowl, but a police force trying to ape the military.

Then came the sound of bands, the clatter of horses, and Lord Spencer, with his fiery beard and his "Faerie Queen", drove by in a coach drawn by four magnificent horses. I thought the "Faerie Queen" looked rather old and portly for the title, but so no doubt did her prototype Queen Elizabeth. The ladies and the College boys cheered vociferously; some of the crowd raised their hats, others had their hats knocked off. The befloured D.M.P. men, trying to look good-humoured, shouldered people about. As a show I thought it not worth the hour we had spent waiting for it and was glad when Tommy, his military duties over, came to fetch us to tea with the Humes in Dawson Street, where I heard much talk of a reported attempt to shoot Lord Waterford.

CHAPTER III

DÉBUTANTE

I WAS DULY PRESENTED at Court and manœuvred my shimmering dress and water-lily train and huge bouquet of lilies of the valley and ostrich-feather fan quite successfully; and in the shimmering dress, without the train, I danced at the great Court ball in St. Patrick's Hall on the following night with the Duke of Clarence, who danced very badly and trod excruciatingly on my satin-slippered toes, the shining paste buckle of which cut into the flesh. Respect due to Royalty prevented me from crying out.

Clarence had the vacant look of an idiot and his mouth hung perpetually open. After the dance we stood at the end of the great hall and, by way of making conversation, Clarence said:

"I was told that Dublin was celebrated for pretty girls. I have not seen one since my arrival."

He was suddenly and most unceremoniously pushed aside by his royal father who had overheard his remark:

"Get out, you young fool, saying such a thing to a beautiful woman!"

And the Prince of Wales led me on to the Royal dais.

Shortly after this I received a diamond pendant from Aunt Mary, who had seen my picture in some of the Society papers, and an invitation to go with her to Homburg in August.

Aunt Mary was a remarkable personality; she was Tommy's aunt and a striking contrast to Mama's aunts. She had been a noted beauty and had buried two husbands of whom she

often spoke affectionately and regretfully; the last was the
Comte de la Sizeranne and she was still living in Paris in an
exquisite little flat hung with red damask in the Place Vendôme.
In the course of our travels Tommy had taken me to see her.
She always wore black velvet and had snow-white hair dressed
à la Marie Antoinette; I thought she wore a wig, as its curls
were so perfectly arranged, but when her French maid got ill
at Homburg and I tried to replace her I found it was all
growing on her own head. She was seventy and told me she
had been to the dentist for the first time in her life that year
to get a tooth stopped. Her hair had turned white at forty
and she had never dyed it. "Women are so foolish to try to
pretend they are young; every age has its beauty, if you
accept it," said Aunt Mary and certainly she was beautiful and
looked as if she had stepped out of a picture. But if she did not
try to ape youth she took extraordinary care of old age and
spent much time preventing unbecoming wrinkles. Her chief
hobby, I soon found, was launching professional beauties. It
was quite a dilettante hobby, for she had ample means of her
own and I don't think was influenced by pecuniary motives.
She did not mind how ugly her men friends were, but women
must be beautiful. She loved to discover and present to the
world a beautiful girl and obtain for her the royal prerogative
of beauty. I was fifteen when I met her and she decided at
once that I fulfilled the requirements for her hobby and
begged Tommy to leave me with her, which he had refused
to do; she succeeded in keeping me for only that one afternoon
to drive with her in the Bois de Boulogne. We went first of
all to Guerlin the perfumer's, where she was well known, for
we were at once taken from the shop into a little private parlour
where many shades of powder and face creams were produced.
She made the attendant try some of these on me and then
ordered her to wash them all off: "The child's complexion can't
be improved," and ended by presenting me only with a

bottle of perfume. "You should always use the same perfume and one that suits you." She then took me to a modiste and bought me a beautiful black lace hat. Finally we started for the Bois at the fashionable hour and Aunt Mary's whole attention was concentrated on noting whether people duly appreciated her latest artistic production.

Her establishment consisted of a man cook and general factotum, a French maid and a young English secretary whom she addressed as Figlio, while he called her Madre, though neither spoke Italian and his secretarial duties were purely fictional,—I suppose to explain to a conventional world his constant presence. He was well off, with a charming flat of his own in London ; he was a good musician and a queer, nervy type; he literally didn't seem able to live without Aunt Mary. They sometimes quarrelled, for I think he used to bore her, but he would always be on the doorstep next day begging for forgiveness. Some years later, when Aunt Mary had changed her tiny red damask apartment in Paris for a tiny red plush house in Chelsea and, on her way to Homburg, was staying in Paris to buy some clothes, I called on her one morning at the Hotel Continental and found her half amused, half enraged. She had quarrelled with Figlio in London and had forbidden him to accompany her to Paris; but he had followed by the next train, and when she still refused to see him, had come up to her locked door at night and made such a noise, knocking and crying in the corridor, that he had been expelled by the Manager and she had received a letter with her morning coffee, pointing out the impropriety of such scenes. "And I am seventy-five!" said Aunt Mary. At that moment the waiter brought in a gigantic basket of red roses, which must have cost a small fortune, with a card: "To Madre from her adoring Figlio."

In Homburg Aunt Mary had rooms in a fashionable hotel; she did not get up till twelve, so I had my mornings to myself.

After that we were continually on parade. She overhauled my dresses and said which I was to wear; she always managed to secure a table at the Casino or a box at the theatre where we would be most noticed. At the dances she would never let me dance except with men who were either celebrated or very good dancers, so that people would stop to watch us, and always she insisted on leaving early and arriving late. She was furious one night at the opera at Frankfort because she said I had made less of a sensation than an English girl she had chaperoned a few years before.

She certainly succeeded in getting me spoken of as "the belle of the season"; enterprising photographers requested me to sit for my photograph; my pictures appeared in society papers; strangers even began asking me to sign autograph albums. Aunt Mary was delighted but it was beginning to get on my nerves, though I was vain enough in some ways.

The Prince of Wales arrived and also some very pretty ladies. "You are better looking than any of them. He will certainly remember you and will ask us to supper," said Aunt Mary.

That afternoon, on the promenade the Prince of Wales came and spoke to us. That evening Tommy arrived, a week before we expected him. My room opened onto Aunt Mary's sitting-room; the door was ajar while I was dressing for dinner. I heard Aunt Mary's voice raised in loud remonstrance with Tommy:

"But no, you shall not take her away, it is ridiculous. You are spoiling her chances. The Prince of Wales talked to her to-day on the promenade; he admires her. Lady S. is wild with jealousy; he will ask us to supper."

"That is exactly why I am taking her away. An invitation from royalty is a command. If I refuse to let her go, my military career would suffer and I don't choose she should be talked about. I am taking her away before any invitation."

"Tom, you are ridiculous."

I thought it time to interrupt the tête-à-tête and came in. Tommy said: "You wanted to hear the *Ring* at Bayreuth; I have got tickets, we shall have to make an early start to-morrow morning."

"How lovely! I wanted to hear Wagner so much in his own opera house but thought all the tickets were booked for the whole series," I exclaimed.

"I got two tickets that had been thrown up at the last minute and came quickly to fetch you."

"Aunt Mary," I said, "is it very bad to desert you? But I want so much to go. You have only a few glasses more of water to drink so you won't have time to be lonely."

Aunt Mary looked cross but said nothing and Tommy and I started next morning and again were mistaken for a honeymoon couple.

On our return to Dublin I found at first the new life very full and entertaining. I was not seventeen and, everybody said, too young to be at the head of Tommy's house without a chaperone; so I was terribly anxious to show I was efficient. Tommy, much amused at my efforts, helped me to keep my engagement book and my visiting book. It was not all play. It was one of my duties to call on the officers' wives of every new regiment stationed in Dublin and to entertain them at least once at some social function where they would make contact with the rest; after that they could sink or swim according to their abilities. This part of the work I soon found deadly boring; the veneer of uniforms and mess training which made the men fairly presentable, though not entertaining, was lacking in their women folk; some were vulgarly pretentious; others, decent, drab little creatures struggling with children and household difficulties. With very few had I a single idea in common. Of course there were exceptions. The wife of an artillery officer, Captain Claude Cane, was one

of these. She came from Malta, she was almost as young
as myself and very pretty. She had such heavy plaits of hair
wound round and round her small head that I thought the
weight must be uncomfortable; so, because she had the same
frank unEnglish way of speaking naturally of things, I put
the question to her about her hair and, on that first visit,
persuaded her to let me take out the hair pins and undo the
plaits. Her hair was of the same gold-brown colour as my
own and quite as thick, but it touched the ground while I
could only just sit on the ends of mine. I called her Eve and
found her name was Eva. I was thrilled and the usual ten
minutes visit extended to an hour, so that Eva's husband, Claude
found us both happily discussing hairdressing problems and
laughing at the dullness of garrison life amid hand-mirrors
and combs and brushes. He was an unusual type also, tall
and dark, with strange philosophical ideas which interested me.
He is now the Grand Master of Freemasonry in Ireland and,
therefore, we are in opposite camps. But then, we became friends,
and I invited them to dinner; I wanted Tommy to know them.

By way of proving how grown up I was, I took much pains
in making friends with all the generals. They really interested
me far more than most of the young officers, whose conversation on sport and racing I found tedious. They had all
travelled and some of them had read a lot and could tell
me things of which I liked to hear,—and I was a good listener.
My afternoon teas, which I got these elderly generals into
the habit of dropping in, became an institution. I discovered
that, incidentally, this was quite useful to Tommy who had
many differences of opinion with some of them on the employment of troops in Ireland. It was hard to quarrel with Tommy
and be on friendly terms with his daughter.

At first I used to go to the kitchen every morning after
breakfast and discuss housekeeping with the cook, but very
soon I discovered nurse was more efficient in this than I was,

so I left this duty to her and replaced it by visits to the stables with sugar for the horses. Kathleen and I had each our own riding and driving horses and of course Tommy had his chargers and hunters. My love and understanding of animals made each horse an individual to me; I knew their characters and could do what I liked with them. Most mornings, Kathleen and I rode in the Phoenix Park; it was marvellous galloping across the fifteen acres. Sometimes Tommy came with us; more often we rode alone because he was busy at office work or, on field-days, had to attend in uniform in his official capacity. These field-days were a great amusement to us. The horses loved the military bands and used to dance to them, especially an old charger of Tommy's, almost too old to work. He was called Yellow Jack and I sometimes rode him because of his dancing and of his adorable character. I loved him better than my own horse. On the field-days Kathleen and I took malicious joy in watching fat infantry colonels tumbling off their horses. This often happened. We used to make bets as to the ones who would come croppers.

Tommy loved hunting, but he hated me to hunt. He said that he never enjoyed a hunt if I was there, as he was always afraid of an accident. The idea of conquering fear would always make me take risks. He said I had a loose seat and, for all my understanding of animals, didn't ride as well as Kathleen. I think this was true, though I was very hurt when he said it. One day, he was out hunting in Kildare. He had lent my horse to a friend of his who was staying with us; I think he did this to make sure I would not go. I was very cross, but said nothing. Yellow Jack, the old charger, was at grass in a farm in Kildare; after breakfast I took the train and arrived at the farm. The old horse was in the field and came at once to the gate as I arrived, to welcome me. I explained matters to him; he also resented being excluded from the hunt on account of age. I saddled him myself and we

started. The hunt was well away. He knew the country, I
didn't, so I let him go as he pleased. He knew, and I did too,
that his old legs couldn't jump; but he was very clever; he
found gaps in hedges and scrambled over ditches in an amazing
fashion. We caught up with the hunt near the end. The poor
little fox was run down in a valley. The horses were galloping
down a long stretch of grass. Suddenly Tommy caught sight of
a familiar chestnut with groggy legs tearing down a precipitous
short cut which brought him into the first line of horses. He
won me the brush.

To hide the terror he had felt, Tommy pretended to be
very angry with me and I slowly started alone to take Yellow
Jack back to the farm; the old horse was very tired and I
walked a great part of the way by his side but we were both
happy and so proud of our achievement that we did not feel
as sad and ashamed, as we should have, of that pitiful little
red blood-stained brush which the huntsmen had hung onto
the bridle behind Yellow Jack's ears. I spent the rest of the
evening bandaging his swollen aching legs with salt and water.
The bandages I made by tearing up my chemise, as I could
find nothing else available for the purpose at the farm. I was
standing in the loose-box, watching the old horse munching
his corn and vaguely wondering how I should get back to
Dublin, for I had missed all the trains, when Tommy on an
outside car drove up and solved the difficulty. He was not
pretending to be angry any more and came and patted Yellow
Jack's neck and congratulated him.

It was Jack's and my last hunt. The old horse died two years
later when I was far away in London amid troubles in which
hunting and horses had no part.

Tommy and I got back to Dublin too late to go to a big
dinner at the house of a rich Dubliner in Merrion Square. I
don't think either of us regretted it very much. I hated the
long ceremonious feasts which the townspeople delighted in

giving. They slavishly and lavishly entertained the British Military, I could never understand why, for the younger officers hardly concealed their contempt for the natives. Tommy checked me when I too openly joined in laughing at our hosts and I heard him sharply rebuke a young captain who deliberately pretended to mistake the master of the house for the butler: "If you accept a man's hospitality, at least behave like a gentleman," I heard him say. Tommy himself was always friendly and, alas, he and I became great favourites and received endless invitations which Tommy said his official position obliged him to accept. "So as you hate being bored alone, you must take me to keep you company," I ruefully objected. "You can't always have headaches," said Tommy sternly. So wearily, I had to sit through seven-course dinners and, in the drawing-room with the ladies, receive absurd compliments for wearing poplin dresses. "So sweet of her, isn't it. She has had it embroidered with shamrocks to win our hearts." I wore a silver grey poplin and Tommy and I together had designed scroles of shamrocks which had been embroidered in silver on it because they seemed to suit the material so well. "You are really Irish. Isn't it wonderful, etc."

Next day I was going to the country to stay with the wife of a big landowner for a hunt ball. She was an American with a very beautiful voice, and Holman, a Russian 'cello player, was to be of the party. Tommy was not going and was not quite happy that I was, because he said there had been evictions in that part of the country and things were rather disturbed there; but as my hostess did not hunt, being decidedly stout, and as I was not bringing my riding habit and I wanted to meet Holman, he agreed to let me go.

I arrived in time for tea. Holman and my hostess were sitting by the fire. Presently Holman said he must introduce me to Mrs. Holman; I was surprised when, from a wooden case, he took out his great 'cello wrapped in fine silk veils.

"See what care I take of her," he said. The beautiful silk veils were, I learned, a present from Mrs. R. They were a lovely blue colour and came from Liberty's. I wound them round my head. Mrs. R. took her place at the piano and we had a lovely time till the dressing-gong sounded. Holman played wild Russian music and Mrs. R. sang well. She sang sentimental Italian songs by Tosti. I thought them beautiful.

My host, whom I had never met, was late and Mrs. R. glanced nervously at the clock and said the dinner would be spoiled. At last he appeared, a tall red-faced man with an abrupt manner. He looked a hard drinker and appeared to be in a very bad temper. Introductions over, he offered me his arm and we went into the dining-room. A couple of rather nondescript men who, I gathered, were neighbours, made up the party. My hostess devoted all her attention to Holman and I timidly tried to make conversation with my host who was resolutely eating his dinner and was not inclined to talk, so I addressed myself to my other neighbour and inquired about hunting, that being the most likely subject of interest to him.

"It's very bad in this part of the country," he replied gloomily.

Suddenly our host spoke in a loud voice that startled every-one. "That damned Land League is ruining the country," and once he began, he did not stop.

"Oh Ronny, talk of something else," said his wife beseechingly but quiet uselessly.

"Ah," he went on, "we will see who will hold out the longest. They would stop us hunting, would they, the . . . so and sos. As I was coming home this evening I saw Paddy Ward and his family lying out in a ditch. His wife doesn't look as if she was going to live till the morning. I stopped and told him he would be responsible for her death; I had warned him as to what would happen if he joined the Land League. Now he has no roof to shelter his family and the woman will be dead before to-morrow."

"And you did nothing about it!" I exclaimed.

"Let her die," he answered. "These people must be taught a lesson," and he went on eating his dinner.

Conversation flagged and I was glad when my hostess gave the signal to me to retire with her to the drawing-room.

Hastily, that night, I wrote a telegram and got the maid to give it to the postman in the morning, asking Tommy to send the carriage for me to the station as I was coming home. I told my hostess at breakfast that I had received a wire from Tommy summoning me home. I could not stay any longer in that house for the sake of any ball or even for the sake of listening to Mrs. Holman."

"I understand, young lady," said the Russian, as I went down the hall steps. I was sorry for Mrs. R.; she was an American. I also understood she was trying to console herself with Mr. and Mrs. Holman.

Some days later Tommy and I stood together on the terrace of the Royal Barracks watching a great Land League procession with bands and banners marching up to the Phoenix Park where there was to be a meeting addressed by Michael Davitt, John Dillon and William O'Brien. The troops were all confined to barracks by Tommy's orders; he always tried to avoid any clashes between the soldiers and the people and was often blamed for this by some of the generals.

"They are quite right," said Tommy. "The people have a right to the land," and then he told me he had made up his mind to leave the army and stand as a Home Rule candidate.

"I took this appointment because I thought it would give you girls a chance of seeing life. Would you mind leaving all this?" he asked. "I don't think I can stand it much longer."

I was surprised, for he had never spoken like this before. "Mind leaving Dublin?" I laughed. "Not a bit, I am often

bored to death by all the people we have to be civil to, people
like Mr. R. who would leave a dying woman lying in a ditch;
who speak of the people as if they were less than animals,—
I hate them."

He took me by the arm. "Come and see what I have
written," and together we went into the house and, from a
drawer in his writing table, he took a manuscript and began
reading it to me; it was an election address.

"Oh, Tommy, how lovely! You are going into Parliament
as a Home Ruler. Where are you going to stand for?"

"I don't know; nothing is arranged. I have not sent in my
resignation from the army yet. I was hesitating because I
don't know if it will be good for you. It would make a great
difference in your position."

"But I would love it. I would help you. It would be wonderful. I am tired of this life; I hate it, don't you see I hate it?"

He put his arm round me "Life is interesting anywhere;
—say nothing of this till I have sent in my resignation."

We were all going to stay at the Canes', at St. Wolestens,
the country house Claude Cane had inherited from a rich
uncle who had recently died; but next morning Tommy
said he was not feeling well and had not been able to get
through his work. He said Kathleen and I were to go and he
would join us the following day. But next day Eva got a telegram saying he had to put off coming as he was still unwell.
When we returned to Dublin, we found Tommy in bed. Nurse
said she was worried because he would not see a doctor and
he was very feverish. I wanted to send for the doctor who was
in the barracks, but Tommy said no. At last I persuaded him
to send for a civilian doctor whom he knew. The doctor came
but didn't seem alarmed. "A few days' rest and he will be
all right."

"There," said Tommy. "What was the use of sending for a
doctor?"

Next day he was worse. That night I dreamt I was standing on the terrace of the barracks just as I had stood when we had watched the Land League procession going up to the Park. Another procession was passing, but it was going in the opposite direction; it was going down the quays. There were bands too, but they were military bands and they were playing the Dead March. I saw it was a great funeral procession. In the curious way dreams have of ignoring limitations of space, though I seemed to be standing on the terrace of the barracks, I was able to follow that procession winding its way right down to the sea. All the small shops along the quays had their shutters closed in mourning. I saw a coffin lifted from a gun carriage and hoisted onto the boat at the North Wall. It was a strange dream, for I had never seen anything of the sort. Ten days after, the exact procession I had seen in dream passed down the quays materially. In the coffin hoisted onto the boat was Tommy's body leaving Ireland to lie beside Mama in Tongham churchyard and the second marble cross was no longer without its inscription.

Yet when I had that dream I had not connected it at all with Tommy; I was not even seriously alarmed about his health,—the doctor had not yet then spoken the words, "typhoid fever." The dream was vivid; when nurse brought me tea, I asked her what it meant to dream of a funeral. "Dreams go by contrary," she said cheerfully. "You will hear of a wedding."

CHAPTER IV

UNCLE WILLIAM

TOMMY HAD MADE his Will long ago when he was going to India with his regiment and Kathleen and I were contentedly playing in the heather that grew so tall and strong on Howth Summit.

He had left his eldest brother William our guardian, executor and trustee. Uncle William had grown rich, old and crusty, but not as mellow as the port wine in which he traded as his father and grandfather had done before him in the City of London.

After the funeral he said: "My house will be your home," and had taken us there.

Breakfast was at nine o'clock and the gong sounded before nurse had finished fastening up our black crape dresses. "Your uncle reads family prayers, so you won't be late for breakfast," she said, kissing the back of my neck as she fastened the last button. Kathleen and I waited outside the dining-room till the footman opened the door for the servants to file out.

Uncle William sat at the head of the table making tea from a big silver urn, just like Aunt Augusta's. "Good morning," he said, as we went and dutifuly kissed his blue-red cheek and sat down on each side of the table. "You are very late; I expect you to be down in time for prayers." I murmured something about not knowing about family prayers being before breakfast.

"No," said Uncle William, "I fear my poor brother brought you up very badly. I suppose he never read family prayers."

He looked at the clock and said: "It is nearly a quarter past nine. You must learn to be punctual; punctuality is most necessary in life." He was right, but I felt rebellious and exchanged glances across the table with Kathleen, very white and quiet, who was demurely eating her eggs and bacon.

Conversation flagged. "I hope you both slept well," said Uncle William, "and found your room comfortable."

We assured him we had and he told us his housekeeper was a very good careful person who looked after everything very well and had had new curtains put up. We had not noticed them, but Kathleen politely said: "They are pretty."

We ate in silence. A big black cat asleep before the fire rose and stretched itself. I poured milk for it in a saucer. Uncle William looked displeased. "You need not give milk to the cat, it is very wasteful. My housekeeper buys a penny's worth of cat's meat for her daily; a very little milk is all that is required then."

Once more conversation flagged. Uncle William rose and said grace and looked out of the window at the falling rain. "A nasty morning, but the church is not far off. You will be ready at a quarter to eleven and I will take you."

"I am afraid I can't go out this morning," I said, "I have a bad cold and our winter black coats have not arrived."

"Your cold is not bad enough to prevent you from going to church; you can put on a coloured coat. It is more important not to miss church than to wear mourning."

Uncle William was right, but I felt rebellious.

"I will wait for you in the hall at a quarter to eleven and don't be late. Have you set your watches to London time? There is twenty minutes difference between London and Dublin. London is first of course," said Uncle William.

"He is an old devil," I whispered to Kathleen, as our arms round each other, we walked up the stairs to the cold drawing-room where the careful housekeeper did not have the fire lit till after lunch.

I had coughed all night; with savage satisfaction I refused to put on my coloured coat and met Uncle William in the hall at a quarter to eleven in my black dress draped only in my long crape veil. Kathleen had been more sensible, but I was very tired and very unhappy, and vaguely at the bottom of my mind was the thought: "If I could only die and join Tommy!" But for that, I would have refused to go to church, knowing that Uncle William could not force me.

That night, nurse sat up making linseed and mustard poultices and in the morning the doctor was sent for. He talked of pneumonia as with his stethoscope he went downstairs to report to Uncle William.

It was some weeks before I was well enough for the edification of hearing Uncle William read family prayers before breakfast.

There were family conclaves. Uncle William, Aunt Augusta, Aunt Mary and another brother of Tommy's, Uncle Charlie who came up from Ascot to attend them. He brought his two daughters, Chotie and May, who had often stayed with us in Dublin; and, round my bed, the black cat and the four of us also held conclaves.

The chief subjects being how Kathleen and I were to be rescued from Uncle William; and how the young could emancipate themselves, for our cousins also had several grievances. Nurse was a sympathetic listener, she had made up her mind that my life depended on getting out of that dreary house and she considered Uncle William a criminal to have taken us to church in the rain and loudly said so. We decided that a close study of our elders would be useful in dealing with them and a copy-book was bought to record family history and the characteristics of aunts and uncles. May and I were the readiest writers and May's brother Arthur was invited to collaborate with pen-and-ink sketches. He was a clever caricaturist and his drawing of Uncle William, who hated to be reminded that he was Irish but had a typically Irish face, as the O'Gonne of Ballygonne Castle waving a shillelah, was such a work of art that later I could not resist cutting it out of the book and sending it to him as a Xmas card.

It was decided before the cousins returned to take Aunt Lizzie into the immediate rescue plot because her daughters averred that she herself was somewhat a victim of the family and would be sure to help. She must ask us to stay with them.

Looking very tall and very thin in my loose-fitting black clothes, I went with Kathleen one morning to family prayers.

Uncle William expressed pleasure at my return to health and at breakfast was solicitous in pressing me to eat, though he added: "I think people generally eat too much. It is not good for the digestion." He had the gift of saying things incontestably true which, when he said them, you wanted to contradict. After breakfast he went to the writing-table and said: "You must want some pocket money," and opening a drawer he took out two little account books and two half-crowns. "I don't suppose you have ever kept any accounts; my poor brother brought you up very badly; I am going to teach you now. I will give you 2s. 6d. a week," and he wrote down "2s. 6d." at the ruled space on one side of the page of each book. "You will write down how you spend it on the opposite page; and on Saturday morning you will bring me the books and I will give you another half-crown."

"Oh thank you, uncle, how generous of you." I said without laughing.

"If you find it is not enough to cover all your little expenses you can tell me next week when you bring the accounts. But I do not like waste. Please be sure to put everything down."

"Certainly," I replied. "Old devil," said Kathleen, as we went upstairs to the drawing-room where nurse had come to an understanding with the housekeeper and there was a blazing fire.

"What are you doing?" said Kathleen from the hearth-rug to me at the writing table.

"Accounts, of course," I answered. "I might forget if I didn't do them at once, so I am doing them for the month."

On Saturday Uncle William expressed himself pleased with the neat way we had entered our accounts and handed us our two half-crowns, telling us to enter them in ourselves. I was sorry he did not turn the page and see the items written in advance. Kathleen was glad for she hated rows.

He was in a great hurry. All the week he had been very perturbed over the progress of socialism and the marches of the unemployed. What was England coming to? The previous day ladies had been taken out of their carriages going to Hyde Park and been made to walk. "Your Aunt Augusta is afraid to go for her drive. She only just escaped yesterday." I thought of the yellow chariot and wished she had been one of the ladies forced to walk. It would have been so funny and so good for her.

"You must neither of you go out to-day. The streets are not safe. I am going to enrol as a special constable instead of going to the City and I have wired to your boy cousins to come up from Ascot to do likewise. Good-bye, and neither of you are to go outside the house. Good-bye." He put on his coat in the hall like a warrior going out to battle; I waved him farewell and ran upstairs to get my hat. Kathleen was immersed in a book on Italian art she had just received from a boy friend of hers in Dublin who was very much in love with her. She wouldn't come out and advised me not to go. She hated crowds. I was not sorry she didn't want to come,—I felt freer alone. I gathered that Trafalgar Square was the storm centre and climbed into a bus to get there.

The square was black with people. There was going to be a meeting. I have always got on well with crowds and have always found them curiously kind and anxious to prevent one being hurt. Perhaps it was my deep mourning dress and delicate appearance that made that London crowd kind to me. I was soon talking to some workmen on the outside, asking them about the speakers. "Here, Miss," said one strong-looking fellow, "You would be much less crushed and safer up by the platform. There may be rushes here. Come with me"; and, shouldering his way through the dense throng, he got me to the base of the lions and sheltered me with his arm from the pressing surging throng. He was not satisfied with this. Catching the eye of one of the stewards on the platform, he called: "Can you make room for this lady? She is getting crushed here"; and before I knew I was lifted up on to the platform and stood leaning against the lion. A young man with a foreign accent was speaking and speaking well. He was calling on the people to resist oppression and stand firm. I applauded vigorously. Tom Mann was on the platform and came and shook hands with me and asked me if I belonged to the movement. I said I was from Ireland where people also were oppressed and wanted to be free. He said:—"You may speak of Ireland here if you like." But I had never spoken and shook my head. "The people are strong if they realise their strength," he said, and went forward to make his speech.

It was a marvellous throng. All united with the same enthusiasm, cheering wildly. It was long before Tom Mann and his chairman could get them silent to listen to the speech.

I don't remember the speech. But I remember the excite-ment. I felt too excited myself to remember much. Then a strange thing happened. The crowd parted; a body of police advanced; they had their batons drawn. On the other side of the square more police appeared. To me they did not look a very large body compared to that huge crowd. The speakers on the platform tried to rally the people to stand. It was useless. They seemed to melt, going in all directions. I couldn't understand. The speaker with the foreign accent said hopelessly: "An English crowd is always like this." They were drifting away down every opening from the square; some forming in processions; others just going.

That evening, Cousin Harry, who had answered Uncle William's appeal to come to the rescue of law and order, was at dinner and the talk was about the necessity of maintaining it and about the laziness of the hunger-marchers who expected industrious people to keep them without work.

I couldn't resist the temptation to say I had watched both of them patrolling the south side of Trafalgar Square (not quite the truth; my workman friend had pointed me out special constables, but they were not Harry or Uncle William). However they had been there all right, for Uncle William sat up straighter than usual; he always looked as if he had swallowed a poker. Harry said; "Why, wherever were you?"—"On the platform with the Lions listening to Tom Mann." Both were too astonished for words; then Harry almost choked with suppressed laughter, but Uncle William did not laugh; his complexion turned dark purple and the butler nearly dropped the dish he was handing.

Some days after this as I opened the drawing-room door I heard Uncle William's voice, very hard and precise, saying: "I tell you, my good woman, I don't believe you. That letter is no proof that the child was his." He was standing with his back to the fire looking stiffer than the poker. A young woman in black was sitting in a chair; she was crying. I had come down to pour out the tea as I always did at five o'clock for Uncle William on his return from the city.

"Please go at once," he continued addressing the young woman. "Can't you see how improper your presence is here?"

She looked up desperately. She looked at me; she was very pale and rather beautiful, if her face had not been disfigured with tears.

"Oh! Miss Gonne, won't you help me?"

"If I can," I said quietly, going over to her. "Are you Mrs. Robbins?"

I don't know if she or Uncle William were more astonished when I said her name. I had addressed an envelope to her from my father the day before he died. There was a cheque in it; I made it out and held his hand for the signature,—he was too ill to write. The Bank returned it next day because the signature was illegible. I told the bank it was all right and to cash it. My voice was shaking for I was crying too as I remembered the last days in Tommy's room. He was delirious nearly all the time and spoke mostly in French and Spanish. I could make little sense of what he said. He was restless and wanted to get out of bed to go to the country and was quiet only when I sat beside him holding his hand or stroking his hair and I hardly left him night and day. That last day he asked plainly for his cheque book. The hospital nurse told me not to mind because he was raving; but when he asked again I got it for him, if only to quiet him, but he was too ill to write and it fell from his hand and he fumbled for it; so I said; "Tell me and I will write it." He made a terrible effort and said the name of Eleanor Robbins and the figure, and I filled it in and held his hand for the signature and put it in an envelope and he muttered an address which I wrote. He was quiet then and seemed to sleep. I told the nurse to get the letter posted; she didn't want to, but I insisted. I had never thought of it again except to tell the Bank to cash it, for I was too stunned with grief for curiosity.

Mrs. Robbins was speaking now,

"I wouldn't be troubling you, Miss, only the baby and I have no money."

"Maud, this is no affair of yours; I will deal with the matter," said Uncle William, very agitated. But I had heard the word "baby", Tommy's baby. I was sitting on the arm of Mrs. Robbins' chair.

"Where is the baby?" I whispered. She looked at me in a curious frightened and half-hostile way, as a dog looks when you lift its puppies.

"She is safe, no one shall take her from me."

"But you will show her to me. What is her name?"

"Daphne. I wouldn't come here at all, but I have no money and I don't know what to do."

"Of course you were right to come," I said soothingly. "Tommy would have wished it. But you must take me to see Daphne. Where are you staying?" She told me an address in the Edgeware Road.

"Maud," interrupted Uncle William, "this is most improper. Please respect your father's memory, even if you have no sense." Mrs. Robbins looked up indignantly.

"I am not one who tells lies. I want nothing from you but enough to keep the child till I can get work. I never asked a penny from anyone and reared my son myself when my husband deserted us. My son is at sea now; but I have been ill and I can't get work and I can't let the child starve. The Colonel was good; he would never have left us unprovided."

"He certainly would not," I replied. "How old is Daphne?"

"Six weeks. The Colonel never saw her. He was dead when I came out of hospital."

"This talk can't go on. Once more I must ask you to go or I shall have to ring for the servants to put you out," said Uncle William, more and more agitated. "You must never come here again or try to see my nieces."

I was furious but helpless; the half-crown pocket money would be no use and I had no other money. So, keeping my temper with difficulty, I went over to Uncle William and took his arm and whispered:

"Please, Uncle, give her money at once! Can't you see she is desperate? We can't let her go like that; Tommy sent her a cheque; it must be gone now. Tommy would wish us to help her; perhaps she has not got money for her lodgings."

It ended by Uncle William handing out five sovereigns and promising to call on her. I did not promise, but I called next day at her lodgings to see Daphne, and Mrs. Robbins and I made friends. She was inclined to be jealous about Daphne and didn't want to give me any claims on her and I think was rather relieved to find I was not one of those born baby-lovers who find charm and beauty in all new-borns and want to hug them. I can't see beauty in fledglings till their feathers appear or in kittens or puppies till their eyes are open, or in babies till their eyes have expression and colour and their complexion grows flowerlike, but I was quite determined that Daphne should want for nothing, because Tommy would not have let her and I was interested in Mrs. Robbins herself and wanted to help her to do whatever she wished. She was a brave woman and life had been unkind to her.

I told her not to worry, for what I had said about that cheque would oblige Uncle William to provide for Daphne and though I had no money at the moment I would have one day and she could count on my friendship and must keep in touch with me. She had the mother-instinct very strong; her one ambition was to work and save money to make a little home for her son and Daphne some day. I helped her to get a post to teach English in a Russian family, by saying she had been my companion.

Russians are nice, human people to those they like, and even under the old Czarist regime treated governesses as human beings. She grew as fond of the children she taught as if they had been her own, and they loved her. She remained

twenty years in that family, but her dream of a home with
her own children was never realised. Her son was killed in the
Great War, and Daphne,—whom, when my old nurse retired
to a little house of her own, I persuaded Mrs. Robbins to place
under her care,—got married in France and has a big family
of her own. Mrs. Robbins gave her gorgeous wedding presents
and quite a handsome dowry.

My uncles and aunts were scandalised; but I felt Tommy
approved and that was all I cared about.

Aunt Lizzie had carried out her part of the rescue plan
arranged at the youth conclave and Cousin Harry had come
to London to escort Kathleen, me and nurse to Ascot next day.
As Uncle William bade us farewell, he held £2 in his hand
and asked for the account books. To save sending the money
by post, he was going to enter eight half-crowns on eight
successive pages, so that we would not be tempted to spend
the pound all at once. It was then that he found that I had also
four week's accounts written in advance. He said in a trembling
voice: "Maud, I am very much displeased; I shall have to
consider how to deal with you." How he did, I found later,
was by telling a lie that good might come of it, and perhaps it
did, but not what Uncle William thought good; things don't
always turn out as one expects.

Spring was just beginning and crocuses raising golden
cups to the sun and incredible almond branches shivering
pink in the wind, and Tommy, who had loved these things so
much, was lying by Mama in the dark ground; it didn't bear
thinking of, and then I would feel he was very near me, and
once I heard his voice telling me not to be unhappy.

Aunt Lizzie was Scotch and very kind, and herself timidly
rebellious; we sometimes thought she should be allowed to
join the conclave of youth, but after all she was not of our
generation, which rendered her inadmissible; we compromised

however by reading her carefully selected passages from the copybook of family records and showing her Arthur's work of art, the portrait of the O'Gonne, at which she laughed heartily.

In London, this redoubtable head of the Clan had been presiding at conclaves of the old, in which my appearance on the socialist platform, my sympathy for Irish rebels and that little matter of the account books were extensively dealt with. One day when Aunt Lizzie was out driving, Kathleen and I were summoned by the butler to the drawing-room. "Mr. Gonne has arrived and wishes to speak to you two young ladies alone." After a frigid greeting, he said: "It is my duty to tell you that my poor brother's affairs are in a bad way. There will be very little money coming to you, not enough to live on. You will have to earn your own living; unfortunately he brought you up very badly and never taught you the value of money; he did not educate you properly, so you cannot become governesses. Nothing would remain for you but to go out as lady companions, a very unhappy position; but your Aunt Augusta has most generously come forward and offers to adopt you both."

Very softly and in equally precise language, I replied: "Uncle William, Tommy did not bring us up badly, and I must ask you never to say that again in my presence. I quite agree with you that we have not the qualifications for governesses, neither have we the desire to become governesses or lady companions. We will be obliged if you will thank Aunt Augusta for her kind offer of adoption; but tell her that we decline it."

"That is foolish talk; you have no alternative but to accept."

"I shall not accept, and I shall earn our living."

"What do you mean?"

"Just what I say."

"But how are you going to earn your living, you foolish girl?"

"That, Uncle, is my own affair and you need not worry." And seeing that Kathleen was crying silently, and not wishing Uncle William to notice it, I put my arm round her and together we left the room to summon a conclave of the young.

The boys seldom attended these; they were mostly away at college, and when they did attend, they treated them less seriously than we did, though sometimes, when in scrapes, they were very glad of our support and made occasional valuable contributions to the family records. On this occasion Chotie and Kathleen were against a complete break with the family. May and I had quite made up our minds that the family, at least our family, meant stagnation, and we were determined to get out of it.

Chotie was the gentlest and most selfless person that I have ever met; she found excuses for the sins of everybody, even for Uncle William; we nicknamed her "the friend of sinners". She adored the family, collectively and individually, and sacrificed her life completely to it, and seemed happy in doing so, though I often wondered if the terrible headaches she suffered from, without apparent physical cause, did not come from some inward conflict, and from her determination not to see wrong in anyone and to take both sides at once, which resulted in tearing her own nerves. For instance, when later, there was a family ukase against seeing me, she always ignored it, but would never admit that the family was wrong in making it.

May was more of a rebel and had fiery red hair and some of the fire of Irish and Scotch ancestors but lacked the staying power for successful rebellion.

Kathleen had none of the rebel at all. She had a passion for beauty, and was herself very beautiful. She would have made a fine artist, if she had not been distracted by marriage and children, and then she concentrated the small will-power she had on living beauty. Beauty was the standard by which she measured all actions. Disputes and rows were ugly, therefore she avoided them. I often think that I was very bad for her, because I fought her childhood's battles for her, which prevented her developing her will. If she heard, she certainly never heeded Tommy's words, that the power of will enables one to do anything. She seldom succeeded in doing any of the things she wanted to do and yet she did succeed in keeping her ideal, for no one can ever say she did an unbeautiful action. She died, a faded white lily, after the son who came nearest to her ideal of beauty, and whom as a child she called her little golden lion, was killed uselessly in the Great War, trying to carry out an impossible order. He, and the whole company he was leading, were shot down; Kathleen's "Golden Lion" was dead, and Kathleen faded away. I was shut up in Holloway Jail at the time this happened, but though I saved her life many times by sheer strength of will and vitality when she was very unhappy and had lost the desire to live, I do not think, if I had been with her, I could have done so then, or even that it would have been well to have tried. She would have suffered so with the unavoidable ugliness of old age. She took no interest in politics and though I was always on the side that all her surroundings were against, we never once in our lives had the shadow of a quarrel.

May and I had already determined to escape from the family. Secretly we had written to the Charing Cross Nursing Institute and secretly, when on a shopping expedition to London with Aunt Lizzie, we had attended a preliminary examination at the Charing Cross Hospital. A medical certificate of Health was essential. May had got hers; mine was refused because of lung weakness. May thought she would like nursing as a profession, I wanted to learn it only because I had felt so hopelessly inadequate when Tommy was ill, and thought everyone should know the elements of nursing.

The stage requires no medical certificate. I had acted in Dublin in some amateur performance for a Charity at the Royal Hospital. Herman Vezin, a well-known London actor, had been present at the Show and told me I would have a great stage career if I wanted it. "If you ever do come to me," he had said. I loved acting and had taken elocution lessons from an old Dublin actor, Granby, who, in the days when Dublin had a repertory theatre, enjoyed a certain popularity, and also from Chancellor Tisdale, a Protestant Divine with a passion for the theatre. So at that conclave we decided that I would go on the stage; that Kathleen would study art at the Slade school of painting and that Chotie would break to Aunt Lizzie the news of May's determination to be a nurse.

Next day, Nurse and I went to London ostensibly to consult a dentist, in reality for me to visit Herman Vezin, and for Nurse to draw out some of her savings, as she wouldn't hear of me taking Mama's jewels to the pawnship to supply the immediate sinews of war for the campaign of earning our living. Uncle William had certainly succeeded in producing unexpected family changes.

Aunt Lizzie persuaded Uncle Charlie that it was quite a sensible idea for May to learn nursing, that she would probably get married and not take it up as a profession (which happened); but, not waiting to be far away from any of her chicks, she also persuaded him that a house in London would be better for his health than Ascot, and that both Chotie and Kathleen could attend the Slade school together.

In four months, I had the satisfaction of addressing to the O'Gonne, a six foot poster, with my name a foot high on it, containing the information that Maud Gonne was leading lady in a theatrical touring company playing an abominable melodrama and *Heartsease*, an English version of *Adrienne Lecouvreur* which I had induced the Manager to produce, to take away from me the bad taste of the abominable melodrama. It has always been a grief to me that I was not there to see Uncle William, behind his silver urn, unroll that poster; it provoked a letter from him begging me at least to spare the family disgrace by taking a stage name, to which I replied that the name belonged to me and I thought I was honouring it by earning my bread.

Then disaster overtook me. I had worked very hard at voice production and spent nights and days rehearsing in drafty, dismal, dusty halls and theatres. The day I was to have started on tour found me lying weakly in bed, after a hæmorrhage of the lungs, in Aunt Mary's little red plush house in Chelsea, and owing a large sum for breach of contract to the director of that ramshackle touring company, which I did not know how to pay, but which, Aunt Mary told me, I was not to worry about.

Was it really a disaster? Things have a way of turning out so differently from what one expects. I know that it seemed to me, lying there, as though it was the end of everything. I had worked so hard and overcome so many obstacles. Would I have the strength to begin again? If I had gone on the stage, it would have taken me away from Ireland.

Once more the conclave of youth assembled round my bed, but I was too flattened out by disaster to make any contribution to its counsels. May was looking remarkably well in nurse's uniform. A probationer's life is hard, but the sense of acquired freedom from the family made her happy. Chotie and Kathleen, art students, had added an amusing story to the family record books, of a visit paid by Aunt Augusta in her yellow chariot to the Slade school to judge the progress they were making; a glimpse caught through an open door of a nude model had so shocked and horrified her that she had fled without seeing them. It was obvious none of us were earning our living. Aunt Mary came in and broke up the conclave by saying I was not to talk, and that, thank God, there was no need for any of us to earn our living, that dear William had been very foolish to make up such a story. He did it for the best, poor man, and was so upset when he heard from her of my illness, that he had declared he would leave the question of our allowances in her hands, and divulged the fact that, when we came of age, we would really be quite well off, not rich but with enough to live on.

CHAPTER V

THE ALLIANCE

The air was sultry when, with Aunt Mary and Kathleen, I arrived at Royat in Auvergne where the doctor had advised I should take a cure.

The Puy de Dôme stood in a white shimmering haze of heat; I was tired but felt strangely excited.

"Something tremendous is going to happen to me," I said to Kathleen. "I don't know if it is good or bad."

"It is the ominous feeling before a thunder storm," said Kathleen.

"No, it is more than that." We were sitting under the trees on the promenade listening to the band. Not a leaf stirred.

The wife of a French general, Madame Feline a friend of Aunt Mary and her daughter Berthe who was also taking the cure, came and sat with us. People were slowly walking up and down.

"It is too hot to go to the play at the Casino to-night," said Aunt Mary.

"There is a storm coming up," said Madame la Générale. "I hate thunder storms and they are terrible in Auvergne." We sat fanning ourselves with the great black fans women carried in those days.

A couple of Frenchmen came up and there were introductions. One of these men I was certain I had met before. He was a tall man of between thirty and forty and looked ill; he was also at Royat for his health. I kept wondering where I had met him before. At last I asked him. "But no, mademoiselle, it is impossible; I would never have forgotten if I had met you." "But you have," I repeated. "Somewhere, some time, but it is too hot to think."

A few heavy drops of rain began to fall; Aunt Mary rose and said it would be well to go in before the storm. The two Frenchmen accompanied us to our hotel; as we reached it the storm broke in a great flash of lightning, a crash of thunder and torrents of rain. Aunt Mary asked the men to come in and wait till the storm abated. The blinds and curtains of the windows in the salon were drawn and the gas light was turned on to keep out the sight of the storm; but the thunder shook the place. Aunt Mary's secretary started playing the piano; he played well, but I wanted to see the storm; I loved storms. So I slipped quietly through the thick curtains out on to the roofed-in terrace. The rain was coming down in a deluge and an intoxicatingly sweet smell arose from the reeking earth where the petals of the roses in the garden were being dashed to pieces by the storm. The lightning was almost continuous and the thunder unceasing, rolling back in echoes from the mountains. It was the most wonderful storm I had ever seen. I longed to go down into the garden amid the havoc of roses. It would be such a lovely showerbath, but the thought of a new hat and dress restrained me, so I only stretched out my bare arms to the rain.

Presently a voice behind me said: "Mademoiselle, your aunt has sent me to look for you and to tell you to come in. It was M. Millevoye, the very tall Frenchman.

"But how can one leave a storm like this?"

"Yes," he said. "it is much better here than inside if you are not afraid of the storm. Are you afraid of anything?"

I shook my head. "One must never be afraid of anything, not even of death. Tell me, where have we met before? I have met you, try and remember."

Because he was a Frenchman, he took this as an invitation and put his arm around me and kissed my dripping wet arm.

I turned away. "Let us go in, Aunt Mary will be anxious. You don't understand; we speak a different language." And we went into the hot hotel salon.

Every day at the springs and at the promenades I met M. Millevoye and we walked together. He was the grandson of the poet Millevoye. He told me the whole ambition of his life was to win back Alsace-Lorraine for France. "A nation who relinquishes one inch of its territory is unworthy and decadent till it regains it," and he spoke bitterly of the compromise and corruption of the politicians of the modern Republic. He came of a Bonapartist family and he hero-worshipped Napoleon, but had no beliefs in hereditary rights of kings or emperors: "At times, the genius of a nation incarnates itself in a man; outstanding genius alone gives the right to rule despotically. The greatness of nations depends on their willingness to recognise this."

One day he said: "If only you were French, together we would win back Alsace-Lorraine for France. With the help of a woman like you, a man could accomplish anything."

I shook my head. "I am Irish and the whole of my country is enslaved and even your Napoleon could not liberate her."

"He would have freed Ireland as he freed the other nations if he had not been defeated. He thought he was striking a blow at the heart of the English when he went to Egypt; perhaps that was his mistake,—he should have gone to Ireland."

Millevoye loathed the English because they had vanquished Napoleon. Another day he said:

"Why don't you free Ireland as Joan of Arc freed France? You don't understand your own power. To hear a woman like you talking of going on the stage is infamous. Yes, you might become a great *actrice ;* but if you became as great an *actrice* as Sara Bernhardt, what of it? An *actrice* is only imitating other people's emotions; that is not living; that is only being a *cabotine*, nothing else. Have a more worthy ambition, free your own country, free Ireland."

I was silent. I was thinking of Tommy's words, "Will is such an incalculable force that if, as a boy, I had said I would be the Pope of Rome, I would have been Pope."

Millevoye continued: "Let us make an alliance. I will help you to free Ireland. You will help me to regain Alsace-Lorraine."

"But we have different enemies," I said. "How can we eat up England and Germany at once?"

"They are not so different," he answered, "the Teutons and the Anglo-Saxons. England defeated Napoleon and his whole dream of a liberated Europe. England encouraged Bismarck in order to keep France and Germany at enmity. Germany is only the incidental, England is the hereditary enemy of France."

I stopped and took both his hands. "Now we speak the same language. I accept this alliance, an alliance against the British Empire and it is a pact to death."

General Boulanger was at Clermont-Ferrand; he was forming a political party. Paul Déroulède with his ligue des Patriotes and Lucien Millevoye with his wonderful power of oratory, were his chief supporters. He wanted to see Millevoye but not publicly. Millevoye wanted me to meet Boulanger and planned a dinner at a little country mill house which later became a famous meeting place for the friends of the General, "la Boulange" as their enemies called them.

This mill was owned by a very attractive country woman who wore the national costume of Auvergne with its big ribbon bow coiffure like that of the women of Alsace. She was very intelligent and a great admirer of the general and of the woman he loved, Madame de Bonnemain, a woman of great beauty and charm and very influential in royalist circles in France. I think later they often met at that old millhouse.

"La Belle Meunière" had given up the milling business when her father died and had turned the mill into a restaurant celebrated for its trout fished in the stream which used to turn the mill and for the brioches that "la Belle Meunière" was so expert in baking.

Some diplomacy had to be exercised to avoid Aunt Mary being invited to the dinner. A lucky excursion in the mountains, planned by Madame la Générale Féline, to which we were invited, provided the occasion; I said the excursion was too tiring for me and Aunt Mary never heard of the dinner at "la Belle Meunière's" and of my meeting General Boulanger.

The general was good-looking with fair hair and clear steady grey eyes. He had great charm of manner; but even at that first meeting I doubted if he had the hard ruthlessness required for the rôle his party hoped he would play. I said this afterwards to Millevoye who replied: "It depends on Madame de Bonnemains. If she is strong enough for the rôle, all will be well; he is crazy about her."

Alas Madame de Bonnemains died a few years later and General Boulanger could not live without her. He shot himself on her tomb in the cemetery of Ixelles near Brussels and wrecked the hopes of his party. He was not the Napoleon they had looked for.

I was just regaining health and on leaving Royat I was going to Constantinople on a visit to Lilla White the daughter of the British Ambassador.

Sir William White in his early days had been a great friend of Tommy's. He had married a German whose somewhat exaggerated clinging to youth made her resentful of a grown-up daughter. Lilla had often stayed with us and had shared sometimes the instruction of Mademoiselle. When she heard of my illness she had written asking me to come and stay with her, as her mother was going away for several months and her father, who adored Lilla, thought we would be happy together.

Millevoye had been addressing a series of meetings in the south of France and came to see me off at Marseilles. He knew the town well and we had a marvellous day visiting Vieux Port, eating "bouillabaisse" in a queer little sailor's restaurant in which was the cleverest parrot I ever met. It sang correctly the words and music of the Marseillaise; its other language was lurid; all the houses had strange birds and pets brought by sailors from distant lands and there were many animal shops. In one of these I bought a little marmoset monkey which I christened my Chaperone; it was only by considerable strategy and a few lies that I managed to get this free day at Marseilles and I said that, in respect for convention, I needed a chaperone.

Marseilles seemed such a happy place. Even the poorest looked gay; all the women had their hair beautifully waved and elaborately dressed; I learned that even the market women went to the coiffeur each morning and paid a few pence to have it properly done.

Millevoye went to an armourer and spent much time trying and selecting a small revolver. I wondered what it was for, as he had a good one which he always carried. When he left me at the boat he put it into my hand and made me promise always to carry it. "It is to protect our alliance," he said. "No woman should ever travel without a revolver."

"I will not forget our alliance; I shall be away only for a month and I will see you before I return to Ireland."

The sea was of a deep, deep blue, thousands of oranges were floating on its surface; I thought some boat laden with oranges must have been sunk, but the captain said, no, it was when there were too many oranges to be sold on the market they were dumped into the sea by the merchants to get rid of them. I thought of Aunt Augusta's words: "Fruit is an expensive luxury and should be indulged in sparingly." Why were not all these oranges given away to children who loved them instead of being sent floating away on the blue sea? They looked lovely, but it seemed a pity. In spite of the blue sea, the wind was strong and the boat rolled and I and my little chaperone retired to the cabin. I lay and watched her antics as she climbed up and helped herself to water from the drinking bottle fastened to the wall. It got rougher and rougher; I decided I didn't like storms at sea. My chaperone didn't seem to mind it at all; I couldn't keep my mind from the fact that it would take six whole days and nights to reach Constantinople, a very different matter from the few hours crossing to Holyhead. I was very miserable and when the stewardess came to announce dinner, I said I wouldn't go to it and she needn't trouble to bring me any. Next morning, though it was still very rough, I began to think I was wasting life by remaining within the four walls of my tiny cabin, so I staggered up on deck. A whole lot of lovely little swallows had been overcome by the storm and many lay, draggled and forlorn, on the wet decks. I picked up one or two and tried to warm and dry them; they revived a little and a dear little girl from the second class (who was going to be a nun), and I tried to feed them with bread and milk, but without success; they died that evening, and the girl and I threw their tiny bodies into the sea, and she cried and I gave her an old silver rosary beads to console her; it was very depressing, and at dinner I asked the Captain when we should arrive at Syra in Greece which was our first stopping place. "To-morrow, but the storm has made us late; we shall only stay for coaling." And, seeing my eagerness, he added: "You mustn't go ashore. It isn't at all safe for ladies. Some very unpleasant things have happened at Syra and I have been obliged to forbid all lady passengers going ashore there."

The second in command was a bearded Corsican who looked like a brigand, had fine eyes and was very attentive to me. Leaning over the rail in the darkness we discussed Napoleon whose memory he worshipped and I ventured to ask him about landing at Syra; for the one thing I longed for was to be on land. People talk of the glorious sense of freedom on the sea. I always feel in prison on a ship, even in fine weather. He shook his head: "No, no, Mademoiselle, the captain's orders are absolute and he is right; no ladies may land, and you are too beautiful. If I could take you . . . But that is impossible; we are all too busy, no one may go ashore." There was no help to be got even from a bearded Corsican who looked like a brigand and was so ready to make love that I retired early to my cabin with my chaperone and the little girl who was an Armenian orphan brought up by French nuns and was going out to another convent of the Order to teach French. She had never been outside the convent before. She was not more than fifteen years of age.

Next morning the sun was shining brightly, but no land in sight. I was longing for land, longing for it with all my might. An old Turk with a long grey beard was strolling on the deck. He was a person of consequence, and on the deck a large canvas awning had been arranged behind which the ladies of his harem were sheltered from indiscreet gaze. I didn't think he would help me to land, but I thought it would be amusing to meet the ladies of his harem. He looked at me gravely, even kindly, as he passed and we spoke a little and I told him I was going on a visit to the daughter of the British Ambassador; but I didn't ask him about landing at Syra or about visiting his wives; for this last enterprise I thought the stewardess would be the best approach and it seemed to me that the advance should come from the ladies themselves. That could wait; there were still four days before we were to arrive at Constantinople and we were just approaching Syra.

It was five o'clock when the ship stopped and was at once surrounded by crowds of boats and chattering Levantines selling all sorts of things to the passengers who were all on deck. The coaling barge was busy at one end. I heard it would take about two or three hours before the ship would start again.

A Greek selling various trinkets and souvenirs smiled at me ingratiatingly and offered me his wares. He spoke a little Italian. I showed him a fifty-franc note and pointed to the shore and managed to strike a bargain with him to row me there and back for it, and, in the crowd, unnoticed, I slipped down the ladder into his boat and was soon on shore. My little chaperone was sitting on my shoulder sheltered in my veil and my revolver was in my pocket.

It was great to be on land again. I went to the post office and sent off postcards and wandered happily among the shops in dark, narrow streets, bought Turkish delight and pots of rose-leaf jam and cigarettes and flowers, the Greek acting as cicerone; I was glad to get rid of him at last at a café on the harbour where I could keep an eye on our ship and on the time while I drank coffee and ate strange cakes.

The boats were getting thin round our ship and I had been two hours on land. My Greek guide had not returned. I thought he must be drinking wine somewhere and I tried to enquire of the waiter as I paid my bill, but he spoke only Greek and was of no help; so I decided to go down to the place where I had landed and the Greek had left his boat. He was not paid; so I felt he was sure to turn up. He was there all right with two other sailor-men sitting in the boat. I got in and told him to start. He seemed in no hurry and said there was lots of time. I told him to start at once and he said something to the sailors who lazily began rowing. It was a marvellous evening. The lights on the sea were enchanting and the town looked white and fairy-like. I was very happy. Then I noticed the sailors were rowing in an opposite direction from that of the ship. My guide was not rowing this time, but sitting on the seat facing me; I pointed to the ship and told him to tell them to go there. He smiled and explained they were going to show me a beautiful point of view. I got angry and told him to turn the boat at once. He only laughed and the men rowed quicker. Suddenly I stood up with my revolver pointed straight at him and said: "Obey, or I fire." The men stopped rowing and there was some quick talk in Greek and the boat turned and rowed to the ship. I sat down, but I kept my revolver pointed but as much hidden as I could. I never took my eyes off my guide till we were at the ship's side and I tossed him the fifty-franc note and scrambled up the ladder while the sailors passed up my many parcels. My Corsican friend was at the ladder. "Mademoiselle, you almost missed the boat. The Captain knows; he is very angry." I thought it wiser to say nothing about the difficulty I had had in catching it, and when, at dinner, the Captain was coldly severe about my disregard of his orders. I pleaded that I, not being a sailor like himself, had such a terrible nostalgia to be on land that I could not expect men who were used to the sea to understand; it was my first voyage, and I was all alone and he must forgive; which he did with good grace, for he could do nothing else, merely remarking I was very young and didn't understand the danger, but he hoped I would not try it again at Smyrna which was our next place of call, or if I did land, for we would make a longer stop there as he had cargo to discharge, I would find a proper escort. "None of these ports are safe for young women alone."

I next turned my attention to getting inside the harem of the old Turk and asked the stewardess who was admitted there to tell the ladies about my marmoset chaperone. This worked, for the next day she brought an invitation from the ladies to visit them and bring the marmoset. The awning was lifted by the Turk himself. Inside were seated on many cushions his two wives and his mother, a very old woman. His wives spoke French and were in ecstasies over the marmoset. One of the wives was old and fat, the other very young and timid, —neither were beautiful. I had brought a box of Turkish delight and some of the flowers I had purchased at Syra. The old Turk made lemon sherbets from fresh lemons in a silver bowl. The talk was limited and strictly conventional and chiefly between myself and the Turk. They had a house in Marseilles where he carried on business, but were returning to Turkey because his mother wanted to go home (to die, I imagined, although this was not said). "We are all glad to go home," said the first wife, "though France is a very nice country."

It was on the whole a dull visit. I knew I would get no chance of talking with the women while the old Turk so courteously insisted on playing the host.

"You must come again and sit with us," he said when I was leaving to dress for dinner. "It is more agreeable under the awning than in the ship saloon; we live here; there is more air than in the cabins."

"Do you never take a walk on deck?" I asked the first wife.

"No. Why should we? It is pleasanter here. We see the sea, we have the air; come back and see us and bring the marmoset."

Next morning the stewardess brought me a box of French chocolates, a present from the Turkish ladies, and an invitation to visit them again; but we were nearing Smyrna and I had to see about landing. Not wishing for unpleasant adventures, I decided to accept the captain's suggestion and the escort of two young German commercial travellers who had already been in Smyrna and knew the town. While one of them attended to business, the other escorted me through the bazaar and we all met at lunch.

The restaurant selected by the young Germans evidently catered for tourists. There was nothing Eastern about it. They told me they were careful where they would take a lady; they were very conventional young men; but they said there was a sight full of local colour and very interesting to be seen at the gates of Smyrna where the heads of six brigands, executed the week before, were nailed on posts to put the fear of God or man into the heart of other brigands. So they suggested, after lunch, hiring a carriage to go and see them. I have a horror of ugly sights, though, if they have to be faced, my nerves never play me false, as I found out a few years later in a famine typhus epidemic in Ireland and, much later, in French war hospitals. But to look for ugly horror unnecessarily, never! So I declined this suggestion, and my German friends, though I think they were disappointed, thoroughly approved of what they called my feminine shrinking and admired me the more for it; at least one of them did and filled in the time till we had to return to the boat by taking me to buy Rahat Lokoum in a Turkish shop where we could also eat a sweet sort of cheese made, he said, from mare's milk and served on fig leaves and, from somewhere, he produced a bunch of roses which he presented to me with a stiff bow and some embarrassment while his friend went off to look at the brigands' heads. I appreciated his real unselfishness and sense of duty in not going to see the horrid sight, so as not to leave me alone. He told me a lot about his business and about the rivalry between his firm and a British firm selling the same goods and was triumphant about a big order he had secured for Germany. He had spent a year in England learning English, so necessary in commerce, and he liked the English although he was always up against them in trade. He was a very ordinary young man, but I was not bored. I can never understand boredom. Every human being is interesting and has a story to tell.

I was glad to arrive at Constantinople and glad to meet Lilla who, accompanied by a young secretary from the Embassy and preceded by a gorgeous person of barbaric splendour who jostled all and sundry, who stood in the way, with a big staff, met me when the boat stopped; but I was really sad to say good-bye to the French Captain, the Corsican brigand, the stately old Turk and his wives, the German commercial travellers and the little Armenian girl.

I passed a happy month in Constantinople with Lilla, sailing on the Bosphorus and riding in the lovely surrounding country with young people from the Austrian, Italian and German Embassies, visiting royal palaces, where each chair and table was a work of art and where we were ceremoniously received by State officials who served us with Turkish coffee in tiny wonderfully beautiful china cups, each standing in filigree silver stands, and rose-jam in cut crystal bowls; and on Fridays we drove to the Sweet Waters where the Turkish ladies, closely veiled in thin yashmaks, used to drive. But, interested and enterprising as I was, I never succeeded in getting to know any of the Turks. I met a few Turkish men at the parties occasionally given at the Embassies; they were courteous and could discuss modern literature, but an invisible barrier existed which never for a moment was lowered. Lilla, who had lived in Constantinople for several years, I found was quite as much a stranger to them as I was. She and her mother, she told me, had been received by the ladies in one or two of the great harems, but had got to know the ladies even less than I had got to know the Turkish family on the boat. This didn't seem to worry her. She wasn't interested.

She had just become engaged to a young Scandinavian in the diplomatic service and was very happy; and, being of a sweet nature, was very anxious to find a fiancé for me among the many young secretaries of the Embassies who seemed to

have nothing to do except to entertain us. But marriage was
the last thing I was thinking about. "You are such a strange
girl," she would say. Sometimes Lilla and I went for walks,
but always preceded by a Kavass in gorgeous uniform with a
long staff who pushed people off the footpaths before us if
they didn't move off quick enough. They would scowl and
mutter and I hated it.

"Why can't we go out without him?" I asked.

"No, it is the custom here," she answered. "Father wouldn't
like us to go out without a Kavass."

I asked Sir William about it at dinner. He told me: "It is
the custom and foreigners are not liked here."

"No wonder," I answered, "if they have a Kavass with
them." It was impossible to escape the Kavass, for there were
always one or two standing in the hall ready to accompany
us. One tall fellow was particularly arrogant and used his
staff most vigorously and unnecessarily. He, I learned, was
an Albanian and the most trusted servant in the Embassy.

It was only when I made friends with the wife of a German
professor of archaeology who was living in Constantinople
that I discovered a way of circumventing the Kavass. I used
to get him to accompany me to her house and say that I was
spending the day with her and that she would see me home.
She, I found, went about unaccompanied and without any
trouble. She knew Constantinople well and laughed at the
idea that a Kavass was necessary. "But I am only a humble
person," she said, laughing. She took me to visit the bazaars
and the eastern part of the city and we never had any adventures; but even she, though she had learned Turkish and
was giving German and English lessons to several Turkish
ladies, never penetrated the real life of the East. We made
friends, however, with the dogs who lived in packs and acted
as scavengers in the different quarters of the town, each pack
having its own streets and never venturing into the territory

belonging to another pack. They were friendly beasts and I was terribly tempted to annex a puppy, for they looked very intelligent. One old dog, the leader of a pack, got to know me and would come when he saw me and accompany us to the limit of his own territory, but never beyond it. No Turk would kill a dog. I read later that when the young Turks introduced more modern methods of street-scavenging and decided to get rid of the dogs, they were all captured and left on a desert island to starve. To amuse ourselves Lilla and I used to dress up as Turkish ladies and wander in the Embassy gardens; I had almost persuaded her to go out costumed to make a surprise visit to some of our friends, but Sir William, when he heard of it, very seriously forbade it. "If you were taken for Turkish women and did anything outside the very carefully prescribed etiquette, any Turk would have the right to arrest you and hand you over to the police." And he made me give my word I would not try it, so Lilla and I had to be content to play at being Turkish princesses in the Embassy gardens, till one day that also was stopped by Sir William, laughingly telling us we were creating a serious scandal for him, as it was being whispered in Embassy circles that the English Ambassador was secretly keeping a harem.

It was all great fun, but I wanted to do something beyond play; so, regretfully, I said good-bye to Lilla and was seen off on a boat for Naples by many of our friends.

At Naples I found a telegram waiting for me from Millevoye asking if I could come to Paris at once, and an invitation from Madame Juliette Adam asking me to come at once to her house which was in a street bearing her name.

She was a remarkable woman, a great Republican, and had been the friend of Gambetta and had played a great part in setting up the Republic. Like Millavoye she distrusted England and Germany. She thought that England aimed at the isolation of France and that, although an alliance with Czarist

Russia seemed an unnatural thing for a Republic, it was a necessity for the safety of France and the only means for France of regaining Alsace-Lorraine.

The Boulangiste party and the Ligue des Patriotes were becoming a powerful force in France and were very much watched and suspected by the French Government which was greatly under English influence. They had certain proposals for a treaty with Russia which they wanted taken secretly to St. Petersburg and delivered to Popodonotzeff, head of the Holy Synod in Russia. He was the Czar's chief adviser. They dared not trust the post and it was very urgent it should be delivered at once. Would I undertake the mission? It was certainly against the whole of English diplomacy, so I did not hesitate and that night I started for St. Petersburg with the documents sewn into my dress. "It is your first work for our alliance against the British Empire," said Millevoye as he saw me off on the train for Russia.

At Berlin, on the platform, I noticed a man carrying an attaché case which he seemed so careful not to let out of his hands that I decided it was a diplomatic valise. He joined the train and passed up and down the corridor several times looking at me and always grasping his valise. I suppose I looked unusual, for I had the habit when travelling of wearing instead of a hat a long black veil to keep the dust off my hair, which gave me a nun-like appearance. He told me later he thought I belonged to some foreign religious order and so did not dare to come into my compartment or speak to me. In the morning we arrived at Wirballen, the frontier station where all passports were examined. Everyone got out of the train for this. I had an English passport which I had got before going to Constantinople but, as I had been met there by the British Embassy people, my passport had never been examined and in those days no passports were needed in other European countries. Russia alone insisted on passports. At

Wirballen I produced mine confidently and was quite unprepared for the Russian official saying in bad French that it was not "en règle", as it had not been counter-signed in Paris as it should have been and that I could not enter Russia till it was. What was I to do? The papers stitched into my dress had to be delivered the next day. Madame Adam had particularly insisted on this because it seemed that counter-proposals were being sent from Berlin and it was of urgent importance the French ones should arrive first.

I saw the man with the precious valise passing freely through the door-way from which I was debarred. I saw him being saluted by the man who was examining passports as though he was a well-known person. I saw him pause at the door-way of the office and look at me; I smiled at him and beckoned him to come back and I asked him if he would have the great kindness to explain to me what this passport official was saying as I could not understand. This he most obligingly did. "Oh, thank you," I said. "It means that I will have to wait here in Wirballen four days till my passport is sent back to Paris and returned with a vise." He nodded and then said it was most unfortunate for Wirballen was a small place and I would find it uncomfortable. I smiled brightly and said I did not mind at all, I was in no hurry and only travelling to see Russia and it would be quite amusing to see the life of a little frontier town, and as for discomfort I was too used to travelling to mind that. "I shall be very well amused, Monsieur; I have only one regret, that I shall not have the pleasure of travelling the rest of the journey to St. Petersburg with so courteous a gentleman as yourself." And I turned away towards the door leading out of the station as if to look for a porter I heard the Russian talking hard to the passport officer and through the corner of my eye I saw him open the precious valise and take from it certain papers showing him to be from the Russian Embassy in Berlin.

The passport officer looked duly impressed; then the Russian came over to me and said he and the passport officer were telegraphing to St. Petersburg to the Foreign Office for permission for me to come without my passport. The train was kept waiting an hour and the permission came. I believe I was the first foreigner to get into Russia without a passport. I was overjoyed, but I also found that my difficulties were beginning because the obliging officials had reserved a special carriage for me and the Russian, and before the train was out of the station he was on his knees telling me of his great joy in meeting such a beautiful and wonderful lady. I had my revolver in my pocket, but that young Russian was altogether too nice and too sympathetic for me to wish to do anything so rude as to produce it. Instead I took his hand and told him I too was happy to meet a Russian like him, who, I felt, would understand an Irish girl; that I had always believed that Russians were understanding people and not like others, English or Frenchmen, who looked on women in a vulgar way; that in my country women were very free because friendship between men and women could be beautiful and not commonplace. The appeal to the national honour worked. He got up from his knees and, though we still held hands, we talked of Ireland and of Russia quite happily till we arrived in St. Petersburg and next day he brought his wife to visit me at the Hotel de l'Europe where I was staying.

In his valise were the very papers from Schuvaloff, Russian ambassador in Berlin, of which Madame Adam had spoken, but hers were delivered first into the hands of grim old Popodonotzeff head of the Holy Synod.

I stayed a fortnight in St. Petersburg, for I had introductions from Madame Adam to Princess Catherine Radziwill, a charming and beautiful Pole who dabbled a little in politics and, in spite of being the mother of eight children, looked amazingly young. We liked each other and she took me to parties with her. It was in her salon that I met the English journalist Stead.

Stead was a curious type. An English journalist with more than ordinary force and vitality, but little culture or literary background. He wrote vigorously in a way interesting to the general public. Princess Radziwill was very anxious to know just why he was in Russia; so I talked with him much to find out. He was a man with puritanical beliefs constantly warring with a sensual temperament, which induced in him a sex obsession. Obsession is the only word to describe it. He could talk of nothing else and introduced it in every conversation, on whatever subject; it made him rather repellent to a girl who hated such talk and I told him so, which led him to write to me a very foolish and very amorous letter, endeavouring to explain. Undecided as to answering the letter, I left it in my writing-case on the table in my room.

Returning one afternoon from a drive in a three-horse droshky with a Russian who years ago had been great friends with Tommy when he was military attaché at the British Embassy in St. Petersburg and who, in memory of that friendship, had offered to show me the sights of that cold, stately squalid city, I found Madame Novikoff, a lady I had only casually met at a party.

I knew she lived much in England and I had heard of her and heard her called a Russian spy when I stayed with Aunt Mary. I had also heard Madame Blavatsky, the founder of the Theosophical Society, called a spy. Madame Blavatsky had even been ordered to leave India, because the English officials there could not understand that strange philosophical old woman and the Indians did. It does not mean much to be called a spy in England; the English get a spy mania every time they are afraid of another country and the English were very much afraid of Russia, in regard to India, at that time. The thought that Madame Novikoff might really be a Russian spy made her interesting to me and I was thrilled to find her waiting for me and explaining that she had such a desire to know me, that when she found I was out she decided to wait for my return, and I was very much disappointed, when after a brief, uninteresting talk, she got up, saying she was late for an engagement and departed.

Next morning Stead called. He was in a state of great agitation. "I have not slept all night. I had to come and ask you how you could, you of all people, have done such a cruel horrible thing."

"Done what?" I asked, amazed.

"Laughed at my love for you with Madame Novikoff, showed her my letter to you."

"But you are raving, Stead," I replied. "I hardly know Madame Novikoff."

"Don't deny it, it makes it worse; she told me the very words in that letter, she repeated it." And because he was an emotional person he buried his head in his arms on the table and cried.

I remembered the unexpected visit the previous day and went to my writing-case. The letter was there all right, but Madame Novikoff must have opened the case and read it before I came in. I felt very angry, but seeing Stead so forlorn and crushed, I said laughingly, to comfort him and to soothe his vanity if not his love: "You have nothing to complain of; you should be very happy; you have made a Russian conquest, much better for you than an Irish one, and the lady must love you very much. Isn't jealousy a sign of love? My compliments." And I told him of finding Madame Novikoff alone in my room the evening before. Madame Novikoff was almost old enough to be Stead's mother, but then Figlio was young enough to be Aunt Mary's grandson,—one never knows; or was there a political reason for Madame Novikoff's interest in Stead? She must have wanted to find out something very much to have resorted to such means. She was obviously watching Stead, for she could have no political suspicion of such a butterfly as myself passing like a flash in the gay society of St. Petersburg. No one but Popodonotzeff and Catherine Radziwill could have known that I, without a passport, had carried to Russia the draft of a treaty which, a few years later, was to change the whole of European diplomacy and alliances in an opposite direction from that desired by England, though its principal inspirer, if not its author, General Boulanger, lay dead, not having the courage to live for his party or for France, after the death of the lovely Madame de Bonnesmain.

My curiosity was aroused. I must find out at once, for I was leaving St. Petersburg next day; so, thinking Stead needed some refreshment after his emotional crisis, I rang the bell and ordered tea, for myself in a long glass with lemon, and for Stead à l'Anglaise with a teapot and a cup and milk, for I had noticed that, while he was trying to be enthusiastic over everything Russian, even their treatment of prisoners, he made vain efforts to enjoy the tea in glasses. Stead cheered up under the influence of his national beverage and admitted the possibility of jealousy being the cause of Madame Novikoff's strange behaviour and told me a story which I found deeply interesting, apart even from my present curiosity. He had known Madame Novikoff a long time. He had met her when he was a very young journalist on a provincial paper; probably she was the first cultivated, intelligent woman he had ever met. She recognised his talent and had first made him believe in himself and in the possibility of becoming, through his power of expression, a real power in the affairs of his country. I think he said that it was through her influence he got into one of the London papers and became eventually editor of the *Pall Mall Gazette*. He and she had both liberal ideas; she stood by him in the fight against prostitution which had landed him in jail on an equivocal charge. She wanted to see

English liberal ideas introduced into Russia and wanted the Russian and the English people to become friends and was working for a strong Anglo-Russian alliance. She brought him to Russia and secured him introductions everywhere, for her family was influential in court circles. He told me that the scene with her the night before had been very painful; she felt he had betrayed her by his too evident admiration for me and had tried to turn him against me by saying that I had laughed at him with her, and showed her his letter.

"Well, perhaps she is right in trying to turn you against me and even lying for the purpose and opening other people's lettercases, for I have only one interest in life and that is to free my country from yours. She is certainly right to tell you not to write such letters and if you like you may tell her I say so and now we will light cigarettes with this one,"—and I took it out of the letter case,—"and not talk about it any more, and in return for your story I will tell you of the reasons why I hate your nation, though not individual English people, many of whom I like very much when I can forget they are English," and I told him about the evictions in Ireland. He was very sympathetic and in favour of Home Rule. He knew Michael Davitt and had a great admiration for him and told me much I did not know about him and his early life in an English factory, where he had had his arm torn off in the machinery, and about his Land League activities. He said he was a great man, far greater than Parnell, and that I must meet him. He would have stayed and chatted all night, but I had many farewells to make before my departure and I had to warn Catherine that Madame Novikoff was working for an English alliance and was responsible for Stead. So I bade him farewell and he promised to help me if ever I needed him.

I do not know if he gave my message to Madame Novikoff, whom I met years later at Claridge's Hotel, where we were both staying. We never alluded to the little matter of the open letter-case. She was busy collecting money for the famine victims in Russia and getting small response and I was busy working for the release of the Irish Treason Felony prisoners and Stead was editing the *Review of Reviews*. Stead and I had seriously quarrelled at this time because his puritanical beliefs or his loyalty to the British Empire or both had made him violently anti-Parnellite, and I, who had never been enthusiastic about Parnell, had, when Gladstone ordered the Irish people to go against him, become violently Parnellite, to the point of quarrelling with Stead and Healy and almost, but not quite, with Michael Davitt.

It was after this quarrel that Stead wrote this rather characteristic article on me in the *Review of Reviews*.

". . . The damage thus inflicted upon the cause of Ireland by the suicidal devotion of an Irish faction to the memory of a dead man (Parnell) will not be outdone by the somewhat fantastic mission of Miss Maud Gonne in Paris for the purpose of founding an alliance of the Friends of Irish Freedom among the descendants of Hoche's expedition. Miss Gonne is one of the most beautiful women of the world. She is an Irish heroine, born protestant, who became a buddhist with theories of pre-existence, but who, in all her pilgrimages from shrine to shrine, has never ceased to cherish a passionate devotion to the cause of Irish Independence. She is for the Irish Republic and total separation, peacefully if possible, but if necessary by the sword, that of France and Russia not excepted. She was at St. Petersburg in 1887, having travelled from Constantinople alone. Everywhere her beauty and her enthusiasm naturally makes an impression and although she is hardly likely to be successful where Wolfe Tone failed, her pilgrimage of passion is at least a picturesque incident that relieves the gloom of the political situation."

Review of Reviews,
June 7, 1892.

CHAPTER VI

LOOKING FOR WORK

I wanted to get to work for Ireland quickly. From what Stead had said, I thought Michael Davitt would be the best person to see, so one afternoon I went to the House of Commons. In St. Stephen's great hall a polite policeman told me to fill in a form with the name of the M.P. I wanted, my own name and address and my business. I hesitated about the "business" and finally wrote "Important" and wondered if that was not a slight exaggeration. But after all, fighting the British Empire was important, even though I only wanted to be told how.

I filled in the time of waiting by looking at the groups of people standing round the barriers, waiting like myself to see some M.P. They were very mixed; some well-dressed women but more, rather nondescript; people from the provinces, some evidently on delegations, others standing alone or walking impatiently up and down.

Occasionally young men with portfolios under their arms passed through quickly, obviously secretaries or officials, for the policemen let them through without interrogation. An elderly woman standing near me asked me if I was interested in the Suffrage movement, and gave me leaflets. I knew little about it but quite agreed women should vote. I asked her if one generally had to wait so long to see a member.

"How long have you been waiting?" she inquired.

"About a quarter of an hour."

"That is nothing, I have often waited the whole afternoon and not seen the man I wanted. They do it on purpose when they don't want to see you. Of course sometimes there are divisions and they can't come."

Occasionally a policeman would read a list of returned cards. Just then I caught sight of a thin one-armed figure standing inside the barrier; a policeman called out: "Mr. Michael Davitt." I pushed my way forward and Davitt asked me inside the barrier, and we sat down on one of the stone seats at the side.

I told him I wanted to work for Ireland and was entirely free; I explained that I had been revolted by seeing the conduct of landowners in Ireland, that I knew many people in France and a few in Russia who were sympathetic with Ireland and that I had come to him to know how I could help. He listened to me attentively and said he had been lately in Paris on work connected with the Times Commission, but I gathered he knew only Irish Americans there, and had not come in contact with French people, probably because of the barrier of language. He said publicity abroad might be useful; the English Government was trying to identify the Irish Party with crime and outrage.

Unwisely, I said: "But that doesn't matter, for with England's treatment of Ireland, whatever an Irishman may do in retaliation, should not be considered a crime. What England calls outrages, are acts of war and perfectly justified. Foreigners could be made to see things in that light."

"No," answered Davitt; "outrages are stupid; they will defeat Home Rule and on Home Rule the future of the thousands of evicted tenants depends. The English Government would invent outrages to create disunion and turn the masses of the English people against Home Rule and destroy the Union of Hearts."

It was the first time I heard that phrase "Union of Hearts" and it didn't appeal to me. I was to hear it often enough in the coming years, used by politicians with their tongues in their cheeks, but Michael Davitt, whose family had been evicted, had been brought up in England. In his youth he had worked among English people in Lancashire, almost as poor and exploited as the Irish people, and he sincerely believed in them and kept his faith in them even during the years he had suffered imprisonment at the hands of their Government. He didn't know me. I noticed a shade come into his keen, kindly eyes when I had spoken condoning outrages.

Abruptly he rose and offered me a ticket for the Ladies' gallery. Years after, when we became friends, we laughed over that first interview and he admitted he had thought I might be a spy. I accepted the ticket but very soon got bored sitting in the gallery listening to rough, old Joe Biggar, with his strong Northern accent (whom later I got to know and respect) reading out interminable reports from Blue Books to empty benches. He was holding up all English business by systematic obstruction.

I had failed in getting useful advice from Davitt as to how I should work for Irish freedom, and decided I would have to find the work by myself in Ireland.

I was almost afraid of returning to Dublin; it would be so lonesome without Tommy! So I gladly accepted Ida Jameson's invitation to stay with her in her beautiful home, Airfield. Her mother and mine had been great friends when they neighboured in Donnybrook. Ida's family were large Whiskey Distillers and her Dad had loved the golden fluid of his famous vats so well that, though he lived on, he had ceased to count among the living and was only occasionally visible in the grounds of Airfield in his wheeled chair, attended by a valet nurse. Ida was the youngest of a large family, all of whom had married,—a strange girl, with a lovely voice and curious psychic faculties. She had known when I was ill in London, though I had not written to her. She wrote to me that she had seen me coming into her room, and knew I

was ill. She could see things invisible to most, and I had
a little of this same gift; it was the basis of our childhood
friendship, for she knew I was not making it up when I spoke
of the dark woman with the sad eyes, who stood by my bed,
and I knew she really had seen the big black dog, with eyes
of fire, said to haunt the Donnybrook Road, and of which
the servants were afraid. Being used to them, we were never
afraid of these things, but as children we were terribly afraid
of being laughed at for speaking of them. Of the dark woman,
so strangely associated with my life, I shall write later; there
came a time when I had to banish her because our wills
clashed and after I joined the Catholic Church I realised that
unless one is very holy, the tearing of the veil which separates
those in the flesh from the inhabitants of the borderland, may
let loose forces dangerous, if uncontrolled, for those we love.

Telepathically, a bond existed between Ida and me. Years
later, when her baby girl died in Dublin, I, in Paris, knew
it, and wrote to her: "I think you are sad, write to me." I
had seen the waxen face of the little dead child.

In the rose garden of Airfield, I told Ida I had come back
to work for Ireland's freedom, and about my disappointing
interview with Michael Davitt. Ida was eager to help; her
family were Unionists. That afternoon, Ida went into town
and ordered two gold rings with Eire engraved on them,
which she said we must both always wear; she also said she
had arranged for us to go to tea next day with a student of
Trinity College, Charles Hubert Oldham who was a Protestant Home-Ruler, and she thought engaged on important
work for Ireland. Her mother must not know about it. Ida
loved to dramatise life, even more than I did.

Oldham must have been amused, for we were both so
ignorant, but he was a great believer in women and their
duty as well as their right to take a share in public life; and,
perhaps a little because we were both attractive young women,

that tea-party led to many others and to a real friendship between Oldham and myself. Ida had just become engaged to the French Vice-Consul, Mr. Boeufvé, and her family were against the marriage, which complication absorbed most of her time.

Oldham said, I must meet the Fenian leader, John O'Leary, and asked me to a meeting of the Contemporary Club, of which he was secretary, and where O'Leary was generally present. In his original way, Oldham introduced me to the Club in this fashion:

"Maud Gonne wants to meet John O'Leary; I thought you would all like to meet Maud Gonne."

I glanced round the cosy room, looking over College Green, where some twelve men were sitting smoking and drinking tea, and I felt a little doubtful about the last part of the introduction, for no women were admitted to the Club; it was only later that a monthly ladies' night was arranged.

A tall, thin, strikingly handsome old man rose from an armchair by the fire, with a puzzled frown on his face (I say old, because when one is twenty, anyone over forty appears old,—John O'Leary was only in middle age). He came towards me. I felt very shy, but taking my courage in both hands, I said in a low voice:

"Mr. O'Leary, I have heard so much about you; you are the leader of revolutionary Ireland, I want to work for Ireland, I want you to show me how."

John O'Leary liked direct talk; the frown vanished from his eyes, which always reminded me of the eyes of a caged eagle. Instead, an eager look came into them as he led me to a sofa, while Mr. Oldham busied himself in supplying me with a cup of tea. I told him my people were all Unionists, that my father was dead and that I had determined to devote my life to working for Ireland, but didn't know how to begin. O'Leary was very interested. I found that along with his hobby, the collection of rare books, his chief interest in life was getting new recruits for Ireland, especially from the Unionist element from which he wanted to form an intellectual backing for the Separatist movement, and I was a possible new recruit. He soon found out, I expect, that I was not intellectual, but I was young and he was hopeful.

"You must read," he said, "read the history of our country, read its literature; I will lend you the books and then you must lecture."

And we arranged that I should have tea with him and his sister Ellen, next day. Meanwhile the Club debate was beginning. I think it was Dr. Sigerson who took the chair; I was invited to remain. They were debating some phase of the Land League, and to my surprise I found that John O'Leary was bitterly opposed to it, especially in its later developments, and was scathingly sarcastic about the Parliamentary leaders and their mock heroics in refusing to wear prison clothes, and also about the so-called "Union of Hearts." In this he was supported by a very brilliant young man with a reddish beard, who, I learnt later, was a barrister, J. F. Taylor. I met him again when I went to tea at John O'Leary's and he and I became great friends. He was, I think, the most brilliant orator I ever heard, and defended revolutionary prisoners with splendid ability and disinterestedness. He succeeded on several occasions in defeating British law, his chief interest being in those whom he knew to be guilty under it.

There were men of all shades of political opinion at the Club, even one or two Unionists, and the debate became very vehement. My kind friend and introducer, Mr. Oldham, was ferociously attacked when he took the side of the Parliamentary Party and defended John Dillon and William O'Brien. I felt sorry for him, but soon realised I need not; attacks, even personal ones, rolled off him like water from a duck's back, as he smilingly put on the kettle and refilled our teacups. Mr. Yeats the artist, father of Willie and Jack Yeats, was a wonderful talker, very tolerant, and kept the debate from getting too fierce, by some amusing anecdote, so well told, that all listened,—though, I fancy, John O'Leary a little impatiently. Several gentlemen, whom I took to be professional and business men, hardly said anything; like myself, they sat, listening silently and thoroughly enjoying it. An old farmer from Donegal, on a visit to Dublin, occasionally threw in a trenchant unanswerable remark in favour of the Land League, and though O'Leary disagreed with him, I saw he respected and liked him. Only once I raised my voice, and ventured to ask about the Ladies' Land League, recently suppressed, and was told by John O'Leary:—"They may not have been right, but they were suppressed because they were honester and more sincere than the men."

In the early hours of the morning, John O'Leary and J. F. Taylor saw me home, but before leaving I received a cordial invitation to attend any meeting of the Club whenever I was in Dublin. I felt very proud of that invitation, and often availed myself of it.

Next day, I went to tea with John O'Leary and his sister, Ellen. She was a charming little lady with the same aquiline features as her brother, only much softer; she was dressed in very unfashionable clothes which suited her, and which I think she must have bought many years before. I was told by Mr. Oldham that she had been engaged to be married to O'Duffy, one of the young Fenian leaders, arrested at the same time as her brother, and who had died in prison. Since his release she had devoted all her life to looking after her brother. There was a curious halo of romance and sadness about her as she presided at the neatly set-out tea table, looking after everyone's wants so quietly, one hardly noticed her. I found out from John O'Leary that she had written some quite good poetry, and later, the year before her death, Mr. Oldham and I succeeded in getting a little volume of it published. I think getting it together, and revising the proofs with her brother, really gave her some pleasure. The room was filled with book-cases, carefully arranged and dusted. "John's treasures" she called them. After tea, Mr. O'Leary selected a number of books, chiefly Young Ireland literature, which Willie Yeats helped me to carry home. He was certainly John O'Leary's most hopeful recruit, though at that time he was a student in the School of Art, intending to follow his father's profession. John O'Leary was anxious he should devote all his time to writing, and that evening he read some of his poems.

After that, I saw a great deal of John O'Leary and his little group of friends. Many pleasant evenings we spent together. O'Leary was keenly interested in meeting any of my Unionist friends who had not been offensive, and whom I had not deliberately cut, before they could have the opportunity of cutting me. He was always on the look-out for recruits from that quarter, but I don't think he ever got any, though several of them said: "Nowhere in Dublin do you hear such interesting conversation as among Maud Gonne's rebel friends." I had not O'Leary's patience and soon tired of that slow work of seeking to make converts, and threw myself into Land League activities, much to O'Leary's disgust. I was a disappointment to him, but we never quarrelled except once, when I went down to see New Tipperary.

New Tipperary was the name given to a settlement of houses built adjacent to the town of Tipperary to accommodate the large number of evicted tenants from the estate of a landlord named Smith-Barry. It was a tactical error on the part of the leaders of the Plan of Campaign, to give battle to this particular man, who had a very large fortune invested in England and suffered little inconvenience by having his Tipperary rents witheld. This fight was waged over a long period and exhausted a large amount of the funds of the

Organisation, and resulted in the defeat of the tenants, most of whom never got back to their lands.

In Oldham's room Ida and I organised a concert in aid of the City of Dublin Hospital, whose matron, Miss Beresford, was teaching me nursing, letting me accompany her round the wards and even take an occasional hand in bandaging and dressings. I had told her how I had tried to become a nurse; she agreed with me that all women should understand nursing and kindly helped me. Ida and I decided the Concert was to be an Irish Concert, with nothing but Irish music and poems by Irish authors; this, we said, precluded naturally the playing of *God Save the Queen*. We replaced it by that grand Irish song, "Let Erin Remember". The Concert was a great success, every seat booked out. All my old Dublin friends were there, to welcome Tommy's daughter, and my new friends, John O'Leary, Willie Yeats and the Contemporary Club, and the general public interested in Irish music. From an artistic point of view the concert was irreproachable, for Ida was a born musician and knew all the good artists. She had a lovely voice trained in Italy, and sang Irish ballads exquisitely. I recited Todhunter's lovely poem, "The Banshee and Dark Rosaleen". To the clamorous encores accorded to Ida and myself, who, because of our novelty, were the great attractions, we gave only rebel songs and rebel poems. The gallery was enthusiastic, but I was amused to see, through a hole in the back cloth, the puzzled looks of many in the expensive seats.

Next day we had great Press notices, but letters, and I think, even a leading article in the *Irish Times*, commented indignantly on the omission of *God Save the Queen*, an unheard of thing at any Dublin concert in those days. I replied, and a regular letter controversy arose. Ida's mother was pained, and after that thought me a dangerous companion for her daughter. Ida, Oldham and I were very proud and thought we had done a little thing for Ireland.

I was inundated with requests to recite at Workmen's clubs and Literary societies. I recited some of Davis's poems to illustrate a lecture of Willie Rooney's at the Celtic Literary Society, and I met there Arthur Griffith for the first time. He was a fair, shy boy one would hardly notice, but I was at once attracted to him, I hardly knew why, for he did not speak, and I got to know him well only in 1899 when he and Willie Rooney came to me with the first copy of the *United Irishman*. They had collected £30 and hoped it would be enough to start the paper, and found they had not even enough for the second Number.

The Celtic Literary Society produced a Manuscript Journal *An Seanachie* which I found very interesting. I was so delighted with the Club and its activities, that I told the secretary I wanted to become a member. He looked embarrassed. Willie Rooney was called to explain, as politely as he could, that the rules of the Club excluded women from membership.

Laughingly I told the Committee of the Celtic Literary Society that I would have to start a Women's society and I would get all their sisters and sweethearts into it, and they would have to look to their laurels then.

Arthur Griffith and Willie Rooney both disapproved of the exclusion of women and, when I did actually start *Inghinidhe na hEireann* in 1900, gave me all the help they could, and the Celtic Literary Society generously lent us their rooms for our meetings and classes, till we were big enough to have a house of our own, and run lectures on History and Irish, dancing, singing and drilling classes for children in three halls in Dublin. Later the Celtic Literary Society admitted women to membership.

I felt it was hardly fair to kind, hospitable old Mrs. Jameson to go on staying at Airfield, and, much to Ida's disappointment, I took rooms in the Gresham Hotel, until I could get a flat.

Almost opposite to the Gresham Hotel were the offices of National League. Passing the door, I went in and told the clerk in the outer office I wished to subscribe and to become a member. He ushered me into a large room with a great table down the centre and rows of chairs for meetings; it was rather impressive. From the inner office a secretary appeared, a genial young man called Quinn. He at once congratulated me on my recitations and on my letter in the Press against the playing of the English National Anthem at an Irish Concert and said he was sure his Chief, Mr. Harrington,—who was out,—would like to meet me, and enquired what time I would be in for him to call. I then told him I wanted to join the National League and was ready to do any work suggested. He also looked embarrassed and said:

"There are no ladies in the National League."

"How strange," I replied. "Surely Ireland needs all her children."

Decidedly there was no place for women in the National movement.

Next day, Tim Harrington, weather-beaten and very able, a man to count with, called on me. He was accompanied by two other M.P.s whom he introduced. T. P. Gill, pale and lanky, a typical clerk, and Pat O'Brien, small and companionable. I longed to ask Harrington if he had brought them to chaperone him in an interview with a dangerous lady, but didn't dare.

We had hardly sat down when Pat O'Brien got up softly and opened the door; a waiter, who had his ear to the keyhole, rose hurriedly, saying he was coming in to ask if Miss Gonne needed refreshments.

"You got a good look at him, Pat," said Mr. Gill, "just as well to know the appearance of these rascals."

"That is what you are up against, Miss Gonne, when you join the National Movement,—spies watching everywhere.

We have our Intelligence Service too," said Mr. Harrington. "This is supposed to be a Nationalist hotel and a good many of our friends stay here. Everyone is watched, and, I need hardly tell you, you are an object of much speculation to both sides. It was reported to me the moment you took rooms here."

I laughed and told him I believed Michael Davitt thought I was a spy in London, and I didn't blame him for it.

"Michael would," said Pat O'Brien.

"And why wouldn't he?" I answered. We all laughed, but I don't think O'Brien and Harrington had any doubts of me. Mr. Gill was effusively amiable and said he would have liked his wife to call on me, but she was in London. He was aiming at great respectability, and I impressed him. Later, when he had attained the giddy heights of Plunket House and the Royal Dublin Society, he looked down on Constance Markievicz and myself as foolish misguided women who had left a world into which with such pains he was climbing.

I told Mr. Harrington that at the National League offices I had been informed no women were admitted to membership. Mr. Harrington's blue eyes twinkled merrily as he said:

"The Constitution of the National League does not allow lady members."

"But there used to be a Ladies' Land League and they did splendid work."

"Indeed they did," said Pat O'Brien; "they were great women and kept things lively while we were all in jail."

"We disbanded the Ladies' Land League when we came out," said Harrington, I thought a little bitterly. "They did too good work, and some of us found they could not be controlled."

"But don't you approve of women in politics, Mr. Harrington?" Again his eyes twinkled and he said, with mock solemnity:

"A woman's place is in the home; but don't be afraid,

Miss Gonne, we will find plenty of work for you, if that is what you want."

I was not satisfied, and said so. "I know women can do some things better than men, and men can do some things better than we can; but I don't like this exclusion of women from the National fight, and the fact that they should have to work through back-door influence if they want to get things done."

He looked at me questioningly but kindly. Perhaps he was wondering if I was thinking of a woman who had great influence on his leader Parnell, and who was very much in all their thoughts though her name was rarely mentioned; but I was not,—at that time I had never heard of Mrs. O'Shea (Stephen Gwynn introduced us later on the Terrace of the House of Commons). He said:

"It is no back-stair work I am going to propose you doing. Have you ever seen evictions?"

I told him how I had left a Cavan landlord's house on account of them.

"There have been bad evictions in Donegal and there are going to be more; I suggest you go and see for yourself. You may be able to do publicity work ; in any case your presence will hearten the people, and let them see they have strong friends on their side. I will give you a letter of introduction to the Bishop of Raphoe and a list of hotels to stay in; but warn you travelling is rough in those parts. Call in at the League Office. Quinn will have the letters ready for you."

When they were gone, I sent a long telegram to May, suggesting she should join me on a riding tour round Donegal; I knew she was taking a holiday after passing a nursing examination. I spent the few days till her arrival going to the livery stables, choosing our horses, and in flat-hunting, as I didn't like the atmosphere of the Gresham Hotel. It was full of priests and men from the country talking loudly and eating and drinking more than was seemly, and of obsequious waiters and chambermaids, who might or might not be spies, always forcing attention and trying to get into conversation.

I got rooms over Morrow's Bookshop and Library in Nassau Street, big sparsely furnished rooms with peacefully faded carpets, and not too comfortable armchairs; but when I had induced the landlord to remove from the walls various pictures of British battle-scenes and added a low couch and many coloured cushions and a few tall vases for green branches, they were pleasant enough and convenient to a very pleasant place indeed for reading and writing, the National Library. The Library staff were always extraordinarily kind, efficient and helpful, and seemed to take a real pleasure in finding the books one wanted and advising on others connected with the subject in hand, particularly if the subject was Irish. I think they were all Unionists, but I must pay them this tribute. Willie Yeats introduced me; he spent much of his time there; Arthur Griffith, Willie Rooney, Douglas Hyde, James Connolly, Stephen McKenna, and many others of my friends made great use of it. Many took the habit of dropping in to see me when the Library closed, for we all kept late hours in Dublin in those days, and went home with the milk.

A big black kettle and a tea and coffee pot in a cupboard in the wall supplied our refreshments and our talk was the wine on which we used to get satisfactorily drunk; the shop being underneath, we disturbed no one. Many now famous poems and plays had their first reading in those rooms in Nassau Street, and many plots were hatched in them, plots for plays and plots for real life. Douglas Hyde, a student in Trinity, believed in the language to free Ireland; to me the method seemed too slow; under his tuition I learned a sentence or two with which to begin my speeches, because it was almost a criminal offence to speak Irish and in Gaelic-speaking districts children in the schools were being daily beaten for using it and people prosecuted for writing their names over their shops in Irish, but I could never learn a language except through hearing it constantly spoken and in Dublin no one spoke it and I was too constantly travelling from one place to another trying to spread revolutionary thoughts and acts to sit down to the arduous task of learning a language. So Douglas Hyde never succeeded in making me an Irish speaker any more than I succeeded in making him a revolutionist.

He was writing his great book, the *Literary History of Ireland*, which was an inspiration to M. O'Leary's group of young poets, writers and revolutionists, it supplied the intellectual background of revolt. That corner of Nassau Street and Frederick Street where I had my rooms, soon became suspect to Dublin Castle who posted two stalwart young men belonging to the Special Branch, then known as G. men,—now as C.I.D.,—before the door. The tricks we used to play on those unfortunate sleuths would fill a volume. By far the most ingenious inventor of tricks and torments was the fourteen-year-old page boy, whose duty it was to open and close the shutters of Morrow's library, clean windows and carry up my supply of coal. He found it stimulating to have a good national and patriotic reason for indulging in a boy's natural proclivities for practical jokes.

One day he carried out two diminutive camp-stools and solemnly set them down on the pavement in front of the astonished detectives, who fondly imagined themselves inconspicuous, politely saying that Miss Gonne feared they would get tired standing so long, and then hastily disappeared into the doorway. The disgusted men after a few moments' hesitation moved further up Frederick Street, and the two tiny stools remained for the wonderment of the passers-by. They were later retrieved by Arthur who repeated this proof of Miss Gonne's thoughtful kindness every day, till the exasperated G. men decided on picking them up and carrying them away.

I wrote to Dublin Castle requesting the return of my property, which I had kindly lent, not given, to the Crown. J. F. Taylor, K.C., helped me to draft the letter. The two sleuths were replaced by two others, as like the first pair as sardines out of a tin.

It was the duty of these two G. men never to lose sight of me when I walked abroad. Unlike the Embassy Kavass in Constantinople, who so interfered with my happiness, by preceding me and pushing people off the side-walk with his big staff, the G. men followed me, a few paces behind. They diminished the paces, for once or twice they had lost me in streets where one car, standing alone on a hazard, had enabled me to mount it and wave them a smiling farewell. Once there was a car and a cab on a hazard; I secured the car and made Dagda the Dane jump up on the seat beside me; he usually ran for exercise; but that day I feared the pace might inconvenience him, so insisted on his jumping up, and though he loved running, he obeyed, for he used to read my thoughts. The G. men engaged the growler and an epic race began,— the two jarveys entering into the spirit of it, and shouting appropriate remarks to each other. We dashed round corners and side-streets. I insisted on taking Grafton Street and, having the advantage of the outside car, I was able to point out the growler to any acquaintances we passed on the pavements. Some people even boohed the growler. The outside car was faster and I had to check the impetuous zeal of my driver when a clear road in front gave him unfair advantage, and we really were risking losing the growler and the sleuths. I had to explain that the chase was really for exhibition purpose, as my ultimate destination was home for lunch; but I wanted first to demonstrate to some guests at the Gresham Hotel, the efficient precautions of Dublin Castle for the safety of the British Empire.

We finally drew up at the Gresham, where, as usual, there

were a good many people standing at the door. The porter, who knew me, came out to help me off. The noble breadth of O'Connell Street had given scope to the faster horse, but the growler got there, and I listened to the sleuths haggling with the jarvey over the fare, and was near enough to back the jarvey sweetly in his demand by saying he had done very well, and deserved double fare, for his horse needed a double feed of corn after such effort. Quite a little crowd had collected, to whom I obligingly explained the situation, before I told Dagda he might get down and run. I then climbed back on my car, and told my driver to drive me slowly home to Nassau Street.

A few days later the driver of the growler apologised to me, and assured me if he had thought I really wanted to get away, he would have lost the car, which I believe was quite true, for there was a good spirit among the drivers at that time and they looked on brave old FitzHarris (Skin-the-Goat) who drove the Invincibles to Phoenix Park, and faced imprisonment and death, rather than betray their names,—as a national hero.

Whenever I did really want to get rid of the G. men, I had only to turn down certain poor streets, both on the south and the north side of the city, where the police never ventured after dark, except in force and where the least misfortune that would happen to them would be well-aimed rotten fish or eggs, and possibly something much worse, if they were seen to be after such a popular young woman as Maud Gonne, for the Dublin people always took care of me. Another convenient way,—for I was always a little nervous of geting my poor friends into serious trouble defending me,—was the big shops like Switzer's with several entrances, which two G. men could not possibly cover. After I had given them the slip several times, they took to coming into the shop with me and following me from counter to counter. Sometimes I would then pretend to mistake them for persistent and obtrusive admirers; I would ostentatiously cast disdainful and exasperated glances at them, once I said in a clear, cold voice to one of them: "Young man, as you will insist on following me and you are certainly not ornamental, you and your friend can perhaps make yourselves useful by carrying my parcels." An elderly lady, buying knitting wool, looked at me approvingly. "That is the right way to treat such creatures, my dear." She might not have said it if she had realised they were the upholders of British law and order; I smiled at her and nodded and a magnificent gentleman, known as a shop-walker, came up: "I am sorry if anyone is annoying you, Miss Gonne, I shall see it shall not occur," and following the discomforted G. men he said, "If you, gentlemen, don't want to buy anything, will you please get out. I cannot allow customers to be annoyed, this is not a public thoroughfare." And they went.

On another occasion, seeing my attendant sleuths, I went upstairs to the department reserved for ladies' and babies' garments, which men are supposed to know nothing about, and proceeded to examine corsets. The G. men looked very embarrassed for there was nothing in the show cases they could with propriety appear to be interested in, and in that rarefied atmosphere they could not take out cigarettes and offer them to each other to keep themselves in countenance. All the young ladies serving were looking at them with wonder. I whispered to one of them that she should go and ask the gentlemen what they required. She was about to do so, when the head of the department, a stout lady clad in black satin, took the office on herself, and sending her young asisstant back to the counter, bore down on the G. men with such terrifying majesty that they fled before she could question them.

The choicest of all these little episodes which added colour and gaiety to life was, one day, while I was writing letters in my room; I heard some sort of commotion in the street and, looking out of the bow-window, I saw one of the G. men holding the unfortunate Arthur, and the other cuffing him unmercifully. It appears that, after he had finished cleaning the windows of Morrows', Arthur had suitably disposed of the pail of dirty water by throwing it over the legs of one of the detectives, of course by accident. I was preparing to rush to the rescue, when I saw a respectable old gentleman, on his way to the Kildare Street Club, render my intervention unnecessary. "You great cowards, you bullies, how dare you ill-treat a child! Give me your names and addresses at once!" And he took a note-book from his pocket and a gold pencil case: "I belong to the Society for the Protection of Children and you shall be prosecuted."

I heard Arthur's voice, in a piteous whine, asserting that the pail of water had fallen accidentally, and the old gentleman consoled him with 6d., remarking that anyone could see the pail was too heavy for him, and still insisting on the names and addresses of the two bullies who had disgraced their manhood by, two-to-one, beating an innocent child. I think he must have succeeded in getting their names, true or false, for I never again saw that particular pair of sleuths. Next day they were replaced by two others. Dublin Castle evidently had a large army of them at its disposal. It costs a lot to keep Ireland safe for the British Empire. Arthur was still further consoled with oranges and cakes at my fireside. Ida Jameson dropped in and joined in our talk over the importance and the amusement of fighting that same Empire, and Arthur felt himself a hero.

I am glad to be able to relate that Arthur has prospered and is now the manager of a flourishing Art shop in Nassau Street.

One day as I was selecting a beautiful vase the serious-looking manager asked me if I recognised him. I did not till he reminded me of these episodes and we had a great laugh while he showed me his choicest treasures. He has become more dignified if less heroic.

CHAPTER VII

EVICTIONS

AT LETTERKENNY, COUNTY Donegal, May and I
dined with the Bishop of Raphoe and the Most Rev. Dr.
O'Donnell, the youngest bishop in Ireland, a strikingly
handsome man. A Diocesan conference had just concluded
and he was entertaining a number of priests. It was a strange
experience for us to sit at table with ten clerics, but
Dr. O'Donnell's simple hospitality put everyone at ease.
His sister, a charming girl who kept house for him, would
not sit down at table,—"I am too busy to-night," she whispered
to me, "I will join you later"; and with the maid she helped
to serve at table,—she was also the soul of hospitality. It was
very charming and homely; with the poverty in the country
I thought that that was how a bishop should live. Tim
Harrington writes, "You want to see Donegal and the condition
of its people; I thought this a good chance to introduce you to
a number of priests through whose parishes you will be passing,
they will be able to tell you the places in which to stay, for
travelling is rough in these parts for young ladies like you."
And they mapped out our tour giving names of the inns, and
sometimes of farm houses where they thought we would be
more comfortable. They were all kind and helpful to two
young heretics and made us forget, and, I think, forgot themselves, that we were. I had not joined the Catholic Church
then but I was never made to feel the difference; there is no
intolerance or bigotry naturally in Irish people, it is only
when politics succeed in exploiting religion that its devastating
influence comes in; some years later when I become a catholic

I found the same wide tolerance among my protestant friends; religious difference never cast a shadow on any of my friendships but politics have broken many. Once, after early Mass in a little Mayo church, an old farmer whom I helped to get back his land after a tough fight, which I had forgotten till he reminded me, said: "I walked thirty miles this night just to see you at Mass, to see the answer to my prayer; the family prayed for this every night as the only way we had of repaying you for what you did for us." "You paid royally," I answered, "though you owe me nothing, for there are no debts between those who are fighting for freedom." He would never have told me of those prayers till they had been answered.

Some of the priests at Dr. O'Donnell's table had been educated at *Le Collège Irelandais* in Paris and enjoyed talking with me about France. When I spoke of the evictions I noticed they all became guarded; one said, "Thank God, there have been none in my Parish," another said, in a half-mocking voice I did not like, "It is a pity Father McFadden of Gweedore has gone home, he would have been the man for you, a real firebrand,"—and there was an awkward silence. Father McFadden had figured in a sensational trial in what the Unionist papers called a murder charge. A D.I. going to arrest Father McFadden in his church, on Sunday, had been killed by the infuriated congregation. Father McFadden had been only recently released from jail. I said, "I shall certainly try to meet Father McFadden." Dr. O'Donnell looked grave. "There have been too many evictions," he said.

"Mr. Harrington says that more are threatened," I ventured.

"There have been too many. God help the poor people," said the bishop.

"Will they resist? They can't let themselves be driven out like sheep," I said, greatly daring in a tense atmosphere.

"What can they do with the force that is against them?"

Shoot the landlords, I thought, but dared not say it in such august company and felt a coward because I did not say it.

"There should be some settlement," said an old priest sitting opposite, and then they all began discussing the chances of a Home Rule Bill. It was evident they were all supporters of the Parliamentary Party and, though no one said so, I sensed the hostility to the Land League, though I knew that some of those priests had been presidents of its branches a few years ago.

I was then a child in Rome, with my father, and at the house of an Irish Unionist lady, Melanie Beresford, I had met a catholic gentleman, Mr. Errington, who it was whispered was on an important diplomatic mission. All I knew was that he had given us tickets for a marvellous ceremony at St. Peter's at which my curly hair had to be covered by a black lace veil. I had seen His Holiness Pope Leo XIII, looking like a white flame against the crimson background of hanging damasks, carried on his Golden Sedia through kneeling throngs. The supernatural majesty of the Pope had made me forget Mr. Errington, or even to ask my father later about his diplomatic mission. I remembered him now and I wondered if that far-off event or the Kilmainham Treaty, or the heaviness of middle and of old age, that was creeping on most of the priests present, had effected the change. But Dr. O'Donnell was not old. He was very beautiful and he was the descendant of one of Ireland's great fighting families and he was the most loth to talk; I even felt that, if he had not been there, the others might have talked more. He was our host. I woke from this dream. A priest who sat next me and, except for his talk of France, had taken little part in the conversation, said, "You will be passing through Dunfanaghy, don't forget to call on Father Peter Kelly, he will interest you." He said it in a quiet significant way. Miss O'Donnell came in with the tea, and sat beside me and we talked of Irish music and of the fairies, and some priests told good stories. We had a very pleasant evening. I learned little, but I was flattered when Dr. O'Donnell told me, as we said good-night, and asked his Blessing, to call again on my return and give him my impressions of Donegal.

The sun was shining brightly and the horses and my Dane dog Dagda were in great spirits as we left Letterkenny next morning for Falcarragh. Muckish, the great mountain of the pig, loomed black and (I tried to think) looked protecting, but a cold wind blew through the pass; it blew cruelly over the sandhills of Dunfanaghy, and when we came near the sea the rain began to fall. We could not ride as fast as we would have liked because Dagda seemed tired and lagged behind; the sharp stones had cut his feet. I got a cobbler in Sligo to make boots for him later, which he always wore afterwards when we went long journeys. We were nearly frozen when we pulled up before Father Peter Kelly's house in the main street of Dunfanaghy. The groom knocked at the door which was opened by Father Kelly: "Come in, come in, you must be perished," he said as he helped me off my horse without waiting to know who we were. I was so cold I could hardly walk or speak. May stood the cold better than I did. Father Kelly ordered tea, but before it was ready he brought us stiff glasses of hot rum and water: "Nothing like it," he said, for preventing colds, and he made me sit in his own big armchair by the fire. "You don't look fit for riding a day like this, young lady," he said. I noticed that his room was nearly as full of books as John O'Leary's. When I felt better I introduced myself and May. We found Father Kelly knew John O'Leary and J. F. Taylor; his sympathies were with the Fenians, and he had no hesitation in saying so; he knew and loved O'Donovan Rossa. "A great and good man the nation should honour." I think Father Peter Kelly felt that as a priest, handling the Blessed Sacrament, he could not shoulder a gun. Morally he would always support the right and fear or self-interest would never make him waver. He wanted Ireland completely free but had lost hope of seeing it in his lifetime. Unlike John O'Leary he supported the Land League; he did not admire the Parliamentary party and had little faith in Home Rule. He thought the Parliamentary Party were exploiting the people; the people had no chance unless organised on a physical force basis; encouraging them to refuse to pay rent and getting them evicted and at the same time repudiating violence, appeared to him illogical. "How many of the evicted tenants will get back their land you will see for yourself; you cannot free the people without freeing Ireland. A robber won't stop robbing for the asking." With a woman's intuitive logic I agreed with him. I spoke of Father McFadden. "You will meet him yourself soon," he said, and for the first time I felt a shade of the reticence I had felt so strongly at the dinner at the Bishop's. I asked him if he thought the people should resist eviction. "Yes, but not unless they are organised to resist and their leaders ready to stand over the resistance whatever the consequence," he answered. "Stones and boiling water are no match for guns."

Father McFadden of Gweedore and I became good friends. He was the peasant type of fighting priests. A constitutionalist at heart, more interested in the land than in the national issue. Astute as a lawyer, he had given Olpherts much trouble, but when he failed in law he organised the resistance of his parishioners, and encouraged the use of boiling water and sticks and stones.

He was a great supporter of the Parliamentary Party and of William O'Brien's plan of campaign and told me that, when he had to read the Pope's denunciation of it (obtained by Errington), he read it in Latin rejoicing that none of the congregation understood it.

Since his imprisonment on a murder charge he was a little afraid of his Bishop who had stood by him loyally till the dignity of the Church was vindicated by his acquittal, but I fancy had reprimanded him privately and intimated he wanted no more trouble in that Parish.

Father Stephens, Father McFadden's curate at Falcarragh, a tall thin young man with dark anxious eyes dressed in a shiny black raincoat, called on us at the Hotel in Falcarragh while May and I were having a late breakfast in an uncomfortable sitting-room by a turf fire which smoked and did not heat, in a grate not meant to burn turf. "You want to see the conditions here. Would it interest you to see how justice is administered? There is a Court to-day, and some of our people are to be tried for stealing turf." It was Fair Day in Falcarragh, the main street was crowded with cattle and country carts full of screaming pigs. We picked our way through the mud and dung to the Courthouse, a solid stone building, and Father Stephens cleared a way for us through a crowd of women in shawls, and man and boys in ragged frieze coats, round the door. Inside the Court a large force of Royal Irish Constabulary kept the people well at the back, but our clothes being a passport at once made way for us and the Sergeant obligingly offered us chairs at the side of a table where an elderly clerk was sitting pen in hand before a big ledger and a Bible. On a raised Dais behind the clerk's table the majesty of the law was represented by a florid gentleman of military appearance in tweeds and leggings. He looked at us inquiringly, and smiled, and bowed, but seeing Father Stephens, the smile turned into a scowl. Opposite us in a wooden pen, between two fine young policemen, were six mountainy men and boys, the accused, their rough fair hair and grey eyes contrasting strangely with their thin weather-tanned faces. A foxy-looking gentleman in riding breeches was reading from a note-book. He had seen the accused on the mountain where they had no right to be; it was the property of Colonel Olpherts; some were cutting turf and some were carrying it away in creels on their backs. A policeman raised the Bible to his lips and gave evidence of having arrested them at their homes. The magistrate asked what the accused had to say; they took no notice, and one of the policemen prodded the oldest, standing next him,—"Answer his honour." The man looked puzzled and said something to the policeman in Irish. The policeman explained that none of the prisoners spoke English. That did not seem to worry the magistrate, he was talking to the foxy gentleman. How much turf did they cut, how much had been carried away, what was its value? When this was established he pronounced sentence. The men would have to pay the value of the turf and a fine of 10s. each, they would have a month to pay or in default go to prison for one month. The clerk wrote in the ledger, a policeman who spoke Irish translated the sentence to the prisoners who were pushed out of the pen and mingled with their friends at the back of the court. The Court was over. I asked Father Stephens who was the magistrate. "Colonel Olpherts, and the man who gave evidence is his agent. Olpherts is judge and plaintiff in the case."

"Will they go to prison?"

"Probably, unless they can borrow the money. They have no turf on their holdings and they must get firing for their families to keep the life in them. They used to get it from a neighbour who had turbary rights with his holding, as the price of their labour in cutting it for him, but he was evicted by Olpherts a year ago, and of course no one will rent his land. Last week another lot of men went to jail for gathering seaweed for manure. All the seashore belongs to Olpherts; there is nothing free in Ireland but the air." I thought of the story of Dean Swift when an English lady politely remarked on the sweetness of Irish air: "Madam, for God's sake don't say that or the English will tax it."

I was back in Donegal to keep the promise I made to Father McFadden to return for the Evictions. Father Stephens was thinner and looking more anxious than ever. What would become of his people? Over 150 Eviction decrees; that meant a thousand people homeless. We were in his little sitting-room, talking to two reporters from English papers. Paddy, the son of a widow woman under eviction notice who had attached himself to me,—always at hand to help me over perilous bogs or pull stones out of walls for me,—put his tousled head through the door; his face was white and tense and he made vigorous signs,—he wanted to speak to me. I went out into the dark stairway leaving Father Stephens with the newspapermen.

"There won't be any evictions to-morrow, we have killed the bailiff," he whispered. I drew in my breath.

"Paddy, will anyone get into trouble?" He shook his head. "I don't think so. Michael got stuff from the Cow Doctor; we put it in his drink. We didn't mean to kill him, only to make him very ill; but he's dead." Paddy was trembling. "My God, it's terrible." A girl with a shawl almost concealing her face pushed the front door open. "Is Father Stephens there?" "He's upstairs." I went into the street with Paddy. "She's come to fetch the priest to him," said Paddy. In a few moments Father Stephens came out followed by the girl who went up the street. Seeing me, Father Stephens said, "I've a sick call, it's not far, the night is fine, will you walk a bit of the way with me?" And followed closely by Paddy, I went. "It's the bailiff," said Father Stephen. "I can't refuse a sick call; if he's really ill there will be no evictions to-morrow for there is not another bailiff in this part of the country to do the dirty work; it may take them a week to get one, but it may be only a trick of his wife to get me into her house,—no one will go there."

"Let's hope he's ill," I said cheerfully. "It would be great if the evictions were postponed and all that force of police having to be sent off again, and Colonel Olpherts left to house and feed his twenty Emergency Men. What did the girl say was wrong with him?"

"She said he fell dead at the door of his house; the neighbours wouldn't help his wife carry him in; she had to manage it herself, but the girl consented to go for the priest." We turned down a little lane outside the town. In the doorway of a cottage a big woman was standing almost blocking the light from inside; she came towards Father Stephen. "I was afraid you wouldn't come," I heard her say and through the door I glimpsed an old man lying very still; then I heard a groan. Father Stephens and the big woman went into the house and closed the door. I went over and sat with Paddy on a little wall. "He's not dead," I whispered. "Perhaps the Cow Doctor's medicine was not strong enough." Paddy did not speak. I didn't know what I hoped for. I had no sympathy for the bailiff but I thought of Paddy's mother. He was her only son and I was afraid for Paddy. After what seemed a long time to us waiting there in the moonlight Father Stephens came out and we heard him say to the woman, "He's only very drunk, but drink will kill him one day all right."

"Will there be evictions to-morrow?" I asked when we were in the lane.

"Maybe not, he must have a fearful lot of drink taken; I shouldn't have gone to the house of a drunken bailiff but a priest can't refuse a sick call."

The Cow Doctor's medicine was not strong enough; the next morning, protected by several hundred of the Royal Irish Constabulary, posted strategically to keep a straggling crowd of sympathisers at a distance from the doomed houses, and a party of villainous-looking Emergency Men headed by Olphert's foxy agent, the bailiff appeared leaning on a big stick and looking green and shaky. The passport of my clothes got me through the police cordons, near enough to hear the bailiff read the eviction decree. He had to be sure that every living thing was out of the evicted house or British law was not fulfilled and the eviction was not well and duly carried out.

It was a small two-roomed cottage inhabited by a bed-ridden old woman, her daughter and two children; the man was in Scotland seeking work. There could be no resistance, the door was closed and barred but it was easily smashed in by the Emergency Men; no need for the battering ram,—it remained in a sturdy cart on the road. Father Stephens pushed his way through the broken door with the Emergency Men to see they did not ill-treat the old woman. She was carried out on a mattress clutching in claw-like hands a little statue of the Blessed Virgin and her Rosary beads, her eyes blinked sight-lessly in the light,—she had not been outside the house for years. She and her mattress were deposited on the roadside, and her daughter and the children cried beside her, while their little household goods were pitched out after them by the Emergency Men.

"Where will they go?" I asked Father Stephens.

"The workhouse,"—his dark eyes more anxious than ever and a high colour on his thin cheeks. The bailiff was nailing a plank across the broken door; the eviction was well and duly carried out and the police were already moving across the field to the next house. I noticed the D.I. and the foxy agent and the bailiff were having some discussion and I moved nearer to listen. The old man with the green face was shaking his head; he said he was in pain and must go to bed; the D.I. and the agent were evidently impatient but they were being polite and persuasive; the bailiff was indispensable,—if he failed them the evictions could not proceed. I prayed that the Cow Doctor's medicine would prove potent. After long argument and encouragement the bailiff was hoisted by the Emergency Men on to the cart with the battering ram, and

the procession moved on. This time it was an old couple whose
door was smashed in. They walked out themselves. They had
built the house fifty years ago when they were married. There
were little of their belongings to be smashed by the Emergency
Men; they must have removed them earlier themselves. They
were going to live in their married daughter's crowded tene-
ment room in Derry. They took a last look at the neat little
garden patch they loved and moved slowly across the fields,
two lonely pathetic figures, and the eviction forces moved on
to a cottage close by. Here when the door was smashed in a
woman with a one-day-old baby was carried out by the
Emergency Men on a mattress followed by a crowd of crying
children and a man, his face white and distorted with helpless
rage. Their household goods made a great pile on the road.
"Better knock down the gable or they will go back," said the
foxy man but the D.I. said it would take too long to unload
and erect the ram, there were one hundred and fifty evictions
to be done this week, so they must lose no time, he promised to
post two men to see the people did not get into the house
again, so the Emergency Men only smashed the two windows
and went to the adjoining house, where the bailiff was already
reading the eviction decree. The rain began to pour, a hopeless cold drizzle. I went back to the woman with the one-day-
old baby. Father Stephens was talking to the frantic husband.
"What are you going to do?" She shook her head and only
cried.

"If I could only walk," she sobbed.

"Don't bother about that, we'll get a car. But where are
you going?"

"I don't know. Anyone who takes us in will be evicted."

"But in the village some one will give you shelter."

"Falcarragh belongs to Olpherts too; they dare not." I
turned to Father Stephens.

"Take a room at the hotel in my name. Olpherts cannot

prevent me having the guests I choose, the hotel people need not know till this woman is in bed who my friends are." And Father Stephens went off to carry out these difficult negotiations and to secure a car. With a friendly newspaper man we set the children to light a bon-fire to warm themselves. As a fire, it was not much of a success because of the rain but it kept the children occupied, while I, being still interested in the state of health of the bailiff, went off to watch the eviction party. They had finished that group of houses and the agent was pointing up the mountain and the D.I. was ordering his men. The bailiff was refusing to be hoisted on the cart; he was not going on the mountain road either in the cart or on his legs; he was going nowhere but back to his bed and this time the agent failed to persuade him. Leaning heavily on his stick and stopping occasionally to vomit and groan, his heavy ungainly figure stumped doggedly along the road towards his home. The evictions were over for that day and only six of the one hundred and fifty had been carried out. As I watched the bailiff hobble away I had quite solved the question in my mind the night before. I knew I hoped he would die, and if I could have done anything to contribute to his death I would have done so and would have felt I was committing no sin, since he was an essential cog in the British war machine. I would rather that it should have been Olpherts that was killed, or the Chief Secretary or the Lord Lieutenant or the British Prime Minister because they were more important and more responsible cogs. Just as in all warfare it is counted better to kill generals than private soldiers. I have always hated war and am by nature and philosophy a pacifist, but it is the English who are forcing war on us, and the first principle of war is to kill the enemy. Unfortunately the English have been more successful in killing than we have,—so far.

The one hundred and fifty evictions were carried out, but it took much longer than a week to do it. A thousand Irish men, women and children were left homeless and how many of them died that winter I do not know. It surely went into hundreds, for babies and young children died like flies in the overcrowded workhouses. The D.I. killed trying to arrest Father MacFadden was the only casualty on the British side in that particular Donegal battle, for the bailiff recovered and another bailiff was secured to supplement him.

I left for Dublin to get Mr. Patrick O'Brien, M.P. ("little Pat the builder" he was called, because of the number of Land League huts he had erected) to come and devote his talents to Donegal.

John O'Leary shook his head when he found me entirely engrossed with Pat O'Brien and the building business. I loved Pat O'Brien for his cheerful unselfishness, his whimsical humour and his real love of poetry, but later politics broke that friendship of many years; he remained a parliamentarian when I had ceased all toleration for that compromise, but we built many Land League huts together, not only in Donegal but in many places in Ireland.

Land League huts were at least better than the workhouse. Some of them were better than the miserable cabins from which the people had been driven. They were the co-operative work of the whole countryside; boys and girls vied with each other collecting stones for the walls, strong farmers supplied the straw for the thatch, skilled thatchers and masons worked enthusiastically and for love,—no one asked pay. When the houses were finished a barrel of porter and home-made cakes and a local fiddler and blazing turf torches celebrated the house warmings. Everyone said they were the grandest Ceilidhe that ever were known and I never enjoyed any as much. For a moment, at least, they made the evicted tenants forget their misery, but the misery was there because Ireland was not free, because we had no land and the people no means of living and the caoin (keene) soon replaced the songs, as the emigrant trains, like poison snakes, wound their way continually through the green deserts of derelict farms down to the coasts, where big ships carried away the boys and girls, leaving the old people wearily watching their evicted farms, till the evicted tenants became a nightmare which every politician tried to forget.

I land-leagued a good deal on my own, in many parts of Ireland, but only in isolated cases; and my conscience is clear, for no tenant I ever advised to come out did I ever fail to reinstate back on his land; but I was not dealing in masses, I was only working as a free-lance on the fringe of what had been a great movement,—I could pick and choose cases where weak landlords could be quickly beaten. I owed this caution perhaps to my conversations with Father Peter Kelly and to my woman's sense of responsibility.

The great days of the Land League were when I was a child in France, when it was a real war with all the horrid savagery of war on both sides, when the evictor and his agent never knew from behind which hedge a bullet would come. The landlords, the British Garrison, were on the run then as they were again in 1922.

When I saw those evictions in Donegal the Land League had become a Parliamentary and Constitutional movement, with savagery admissible only on the side of law and order, and the landlords creeping back and everybody denouncing crime and passing pious resolutions condemning murder while deprecating evictions. Even the grabbers of evicted farms were becoming respectable; gradually the evictions were forgotten; John Redmond became England's great recruiting agent and appealed to the sons of those evicted tenants to join the English army and fight for Home Rule in Belgium.

Till Ireland is free her people cannot be free or prosperous. Only in spasmodic moments do the whole people seem to realise this; a minority of them always do and to this minority Ireland as a nation owes her existence.

Perhaps it is a virtue, if only a negative one, that our race cherish the names and memories of some of that minority when they are dead, cherish them and honour them above those of the majority they have acclaimed in life but whom they forget and scorn when they have passed away.

CHAPTER VIII

MY FIRST SPEECH

My Co-operative house-building with Pat O'Brien was to suffer some delay. Tim Harrington called on me one evening in Dublin:

"You said you wanted to work for Ireland; I have some work for you."

"But you don't want women's work. None of the parties in Ireland want women; the National League, the Fenians, the Celtic Literary Society, the Contemporary Club, have all refused me membership because they accept no women members, so I have to work all by my lone, till I can form a women's organisation." I laughed; Harrington laughed too.

"Well, I have some work for you now. There is a by-election at Barrow-in-Furness in Lancashire. It is such a Conservative stronghold that the Liberal Party have refused to fight it. The Irish will fight it on the evictions and Home Rule issue." I shook my head:

"That's not the work I want. I know nothing and care less about English elections. It is in Ireland the work must be done. I am going back to Donegal to help Father MacFadden and Pat O'Brien build houses."

"This election is different from others," argued Harrington; "the Liberal Party doesn't want it contested. We want to show our independence of them. It will only mean one week's hard work and you can go back then to Donegal. You have just come from those evictions; you would be a great help."

I knew John O'Leary would not approve, but I let myself be persuaded. I liked Tim Harrington. I feebly insisted that

I would be of no use as I was not a speaker, but Harrington said I would be good at canvassing and that that was far more essential in winning elections than public speeches.

Next morning Harrington and I were on the boat for Liverpool and little Pat O'Brien waved us good-bye and shook his fist at Harrington for carrying off his "master builder".

Some of the election committee met us at the station and said a meeting was in progress and Harrington was to speak at it. Harrington insisted I should come to the meeting as it would make canvassing easier if I were seen on the platform. I was soon seated on the right hand of the elderly chairman, facing an audience of 1,500 English people. The chairman asked if I would speak next. "I am not a speaker, I have only come to help canvass." I did not know it, but he was stone-deaf, and to my horror I heard him announce in a loud voice: "Miss Gonne, a young Irish lady, will now address you." Harrington, sitting immediately behind me, gave me a poke in the back. "Go on, you'll have to speak now." I got up: "Ladies and Gentlemen," my voice, owing to my stage train-ing, rang out alarmingly clear, then I stopped. "Tell them about the evictions you have seen," prompted Harrington, and I began. It was easy telling a straightforward story of the scenes which I had witnessed and which were so terribly in my mind. I told of the old couple driven out of the house they had built fifty years ago; of the woman with her one-day-old baby left on the roadside, of the little children trying in vain to kindle a fire in the rain; of the desolation of the overcrowded workhouse and the separated families. I forgot where I was and then suddenly I remembered and I became aware of a dead silence, of thousands of eyes looking at me and my mind a complete blank. I stopped in the middle of a sentence, my knees began to shake and I sat down and began to cry; I would have given worlds to hide, to disappear. I was too confused for a long time to know what was happening and vaguely thought the meeting was breaking up because I had made a fool of myself. I did not realise that, after the intense silence which had startled me, the audience had risen to its feet and was applauding me. When I recovered enough to take my nose out of my handkerchief Harrington was speaking. The chairman patted me on the shoulder protectingly. "My dear young lady, you were wonderful, but you must be very tired."

"I am sorry to have made such a fool of myself." He was deaf, so did not hear my apologies. At the end of the meeting a cab was got to take me out of a crowd all wanting to shake hands.

Over eggs and bacon at breakfast next morning Harrington read me the local papers full of my speech, all interpreting my stage-fright as evidence of the sincerity of my emotions. "You made a great impression; I have rarely seen an English audience so thrilled," Harrington said.

At the election committee rooms there were demands on all sides for the young Irish lady to speak at the meetings. "I am here to canvass and canvassing is more important than meetings," I repeated Harrington's words, knowing nothing about the matter, but eventually I spoke at five meetings every day.

Harrington was examining the canvass books. He came over to me and said: "The Salvation Army are very strong here. They all voted Conservative at the last election; I want you to call on the Captain," and with a local election worker I started out. The Captain was out; his pretty young wife said he would be in for dinner and asked me to come in and wait in a chilly, marvellously neat sitting-room, crowded with cheap hideous furniture and knick-knacks and the walls covered with photos of leaders and groups of the Salvation Army.

"I will light the fire," she said hospitably. "We don't use this room much; the kitchen is cosier."

"Kitchens are cosy places," I said. "Let me come into yours and we can talk while you are preparing dinner."

"I would have liked to have heard you speak last night; some of our people came in after and said you were better than the men. I always say women are more convincing. They do wonderful work in the Army." She pointed to a very attractive baby playing on the floor of the spotless kitchen: "I used to lead the singing often, but now I can't get out much because of her." We compared notes on stage-fright and I confessed that I had never made a speech till last night. I was curious to hear about the work of the Salvation Army of which I knew nothing; really great work it appeared, and the time passed quickly till a tall, fair, soldierly man, the Captain, arrived. "You are the young woman who spoke last night. If things are as you say, they must be changed. They are a disgrace to England and unchristian." He questioned me closely about the reasons which led to the evictions and then said: "There have been some terrible murders in Ireland."

"I wonder there have not been a great many more; crime begets crime."

"That does not justify it." I looked at the golden-haired baby trying to pull itself up by clutching its father's leg and I said: "Captain, if this little home of yours were to be knocked down and all your treasures scattered on the street and you and your wife put in separate wards of a workhouse and that baby taken from you and put in another part of the house which you knew to be unhealthy and overcrowded and it fell ill and neither you nor your wife were allowed to see it or care for it and it died, would you not feel like murdering its murderer,— the landlords in Ireland who, because cattle rearing is more profitable, are destroying homesteads like yours all over the country." He took the baby in his arms and did not answer.

"Might you not feel it your duty to stop such things, this slaughter of the innocent?"

"I hope God would give me strength not to murder," he said. "But I would stop such things. They must be stopped." They asked me to stay to dinner with them but I said I had to meet Mr. Harrington and I think the captain was relieved as there were only two chops. "We have a unit of the Army in Ireland," said the Captain. "Some of them are returning here next week; if their report agrees with what you have told me, it will be the duty of the Army to vote against the Government."

I remembered seeing a small, jeering crowd in Dublin surrounding a Salvation Army meeting in Foster Place and I rather hoped the return of the members of that unit would be delayed till after the election.

As the Captain's wife said good-bye to me on the door-step, she whispered: "It's all right; they'll vote to stop evictions." They did and we won the election.

Harrington was triumphant. "You won the election for us." "The Salvation Army Captain's baby won it," I replied as, after the declaration of the poll, we were in the night train on our way to London.

The Conservative newspapers, trying to palliate the political significance of the defeat, had headlines about the election being won by the beauty of a woman, etc., and momentarily I became the fashion in London. The newspapers dug out old clichés of photos taken in Dublin in my court dress by Chancellor and Lafayette. London photographers invited me to sit for my pictures. Invitations for parties at the houses of the big hostesses of the Liberal Party, people I had never met, poured in. My aunts looked on me with less disapproval; Aunt Mary particularly was enthusiastic; Uncle William still shook his head. I doubt whether, even if the invitation had come from Conservatives, he would have forgiven the poster of Maud Gonne as *Adrienne Lecouvreur* or the stories of Maud

Gonne at the evictions which he had read of in the papers;
he did not know which had the more disgraced the family
name.

I went to one or two of the parties, looking for people who
could help to release the prisoners, both the Land League and
Treason Felony prisoners, for I was always one-idea'd and I
had promised a mother and a wife in Donegal that their sons
and husband would be returned to them. I found some sympathy for the Land League prisoners; none for the "Dynamit-
ards" who had planned to blow up the House of Commons,
and had made a big hole in London Bridge.

An elderly baronet, who was a Liberal M.P., Sir John ——,
proposed to me. He had conceived the idea that I would make
an ideal hostess for a Liberal salon. I told him I could never
look at an Englishman without seeing prison-bars and he
eagerly talked of freeing Land League prisoners and with real
indignation over the imprisonment of members of Parliament
like William O'Brien and John Dillon, but shook his grey
head sadly when I said *all* Irish prisoners must be released and
that I was most concerned over the life-sentenced prisoners.
I knew he would do nothing.

I was more hopeful of help from a young barrister, Mr.
Morton, with a remarkable gift of speech, who had a real
love of justice coupled with a passing love for myself. In this
I was not mistaken, for as secretary to John Morley when the
Liberal Government came into office, he obtained the release
of the Donegal life-sentenced men and materially aided in
hastening the release of the Treason Felony prisoners. His
devotion to me lasted some years and I fear was bad for his
own career, but I had to encourage it for the sake of the
prisoners.

I wanted to get back to house-building for evicted tenants
in Ireland but stayed in London long enough to get in touch
with the London Amnesty Association.

They had an office in Chancery Lane. Dr. Mark Ryan was chairman, Dr. Anthony MacBride secretary. Willie Yeats took me to the committee meeting; most of the members belonged to the I.R.B. of which Willie Yeats was also a member. An old Fenian, Mr. Sheridan, described his visit to one of the prisoners and the horrible conditions of their treatment in Portland. The prison regulations permitted visits of twenty minutes once every four months, but as the Irish prisoners' homes were in Ireland, Scotland and America, only very few, such as John Daly, James Egan and Thomas Clarke ever got visits; distance and the poverty of the families prevented. There were twenty-seven prisoners, the majority of whom had been ten years in prison without a visit. Mr. Sheridan had obtained a permit to see one of these by saying he was a cousin. He said to me, "You should try to get a permit and see for yourself. We have been able to get no publicity. By the will of the English and unhappily by the will of the Irish Parliamentary Party they are forgotten men."

I doubted if I could establish family relationship with any of them to satisfy the authorities, but having obtained a sheet of Uncle William's best writing paper with his crest and address on it I wrote to the Home Secretary as a lady distressed that the benevolent intentions of the prison authorities to keep prisoners in touch with their families, because of the good moral effect on them, should be frustrated by distance and poverty; that, having come across the families of some of the prisoners, I proposed to visit them and bring them news of their homes, and I asked for permits to see eight. I signed the letter Edith Gonne; Edith is one of my Christian names I never used, and I trusted the official who received the letter would not connect it with the Maud Gonne of Barrow election fame. I got the eight permits each admitting two visitors. I was accompanied by an English journalist who wanted to see Portland, and who, Dr. Ryan suggested, should accompany me. We arrived at the prison at two o'clock. On the way up the hill from the station we saw gangs of convicts harnessed like horses to great carts of stones; they were all dressed in hideous yellow clothes decorated with broad arrows in black. Uniformed warders stood by each gang directing operations.

We were asked to wait in a little office inside the prison gate. Two uniformed men inspected the permit and looked curiously at us. I was hardly the sort of visitor they expected. Then one said: "Will you please sign this, Miss," and held out a paper. It was a written undertaking on official paper to the effect that I would use the visit for no ulterior purpose.

"What does it mean?" I enquired, standing by the desk, pen in hand. "In my letter to the Home Office I stated my purpose, to keep the prisoners in touch with their families."

"That's all right. I don't rightly know why you are to sign this; it's not customary, but the governor said you must. I suppose it means you are not to try and arrange escapes, but," and he smiled grimly, "it seems unnecessary; no one ever escapes from Portland. Or it may mean that you are not to tell the prisoners anything they shouldn't know; but you needn't worry about that as I am there to see you don't." I signed and passed the paper to Mr. Smith who signed it.

When later I wrote and spoke about the prisoners in France and America I was accused by England of having broken a written undertaking.

"You won't be able to see the second prisoner on your list. He misbehaved and is in punishment and has forfeited his visit, but seven visits will take long enough; you'll be tired."

"What has he done?"

"I can't answer that question." I discovered later that what he had done was to become insane.

We were taken along a passage and shown into a cage which contained two chairs. It was exactly like the cage of wild animals at the zoo, with iron bars in front giving onto a passage about four feet wide. A similar cage with its iron bars faced us. The warder who had examined the permits took his stand in this and another warder leading a prisoner came into it from a door at the side. As the door opened with much clanging and jangling of keys I saw a third warder in control of this door. The warders carried revolvers. The prisoner was dressed in faded yellow with broad arrows. He looked at me inquiringly and suspiciously. To break the awkward silence I said: "Your friends asked me to visit you. I have just come from Ireland and am returning there; I want to tell them about you."

"There is nothing to tell about me," was the sullen answer; he was very suspicious. I tried again.

"I thought a visit, even from someone you don't know, would break the monotony. I am Irish too." The prisoner kept his puzzled eyes on my face but did not speak. I was thinking hard what to say to gain his confidence and the warder, to try and help me out, said: "I am sure it is very good of the young lady to take so much interest." I shook my head impatiently: "It is not good at all. It is quite natural that Irish people should be thinking of you and of what you are undergoing for Ireland."

This seemed to reach him, for an eager look came into his eyes, and he said: "Tell me how are things there now. Is Parnell going to get Home Rule?"

"You mustn't answer that question," said the warder, "that is political." Wanting to keep things pleasant I smiled at the warder and asked the prisoner:

"Tell me how is Dr. Gallagher."

"He mustn't answer that question," said the warder, "that concerns the prison."

"I am sorry, but his friends have heard that Dr. Gallagher is ill and asked me to enquire" (we had heard that Dr. Gallagher was insane).

"Perhaps you will be able to give me news of him if a prisoner mustn't. I wanted to visit him for his sister, but didn't get a permit," I said to the warder.

"No," said the warder, "only the governor can give information about prisoners' healths." Still addressing the warder, I said sweetly:

"I see conversation isn't easy here. Please tell me what we may talk about." "The weather," said Mr. Smith under his breath.

"Oh, anything except politics and prison affairs," replied the warder.

"I will try and be careful," and turning to my companion I said: "Mr. Smith, you remember what your father said (I didn't know if Mr. Smith had a father) when Mr. Gladstone was defeated,—he said that when he took up the Home Rule question he would get into power and be dependent on the Irish vote and would win. There are likely to be elections this year." And with Mr. Smith I began discussing current political affairs. I saw the wisdom of the suggestion of the Amnesty Association that I should have a companion for the visit. The prisoner was listening eagerly. The warder was looking worried, but as I was not speaking to the prisoner nor he to me, it was difficult to interfere. "Time up," said the chief warder.

"Thank you for coming," said the prisoner, "God bless you."

"Keep up your heart and remember your friends are thinking of you and hoping to have you with them soon." The keys rattled and as he disappeared his last look at me was less suspicious.

Another prisoner and warder were standing in the front of the cage.

It was all very unsatisfactory. I felt the horror of the place and the sufferings of the prisoners deeply affecting me, almost paralysing my thoughts. The next prisoner looked apathetic and had great difficulty in articulating. He was almost unintelligible, as if he had forgotten how to speak,—the silent system has this effect on some. I was glad when the chief warder said: "Time up," and felt guilty for being glad. The prisoner didn't want to go; he got out the words: "Will you help us?" as the door clanged on him.

God, what these men had suffered and were suffering for Ireland and the struggle against the British Empire. And the people outside had forgotten them. It was a nightmare. More and more I found it hard to concentrate my thoughts. "I wish you would do some of the talking," I whispered irritably to Mr. Smith. "I don't know what to say to them," he answered.

The prisoner now standing in the cage was a tall, rough-looking man with blood-shot eyes and a strong Northern accent. He wasted no time in thinking who or what I was. "I have lost the sight of one eye and the sight of the other is going. The doctor here says the injured eye should be taken out but he can't do it here, so I'm to be let go blind; they are not content with having destroyed one of my eyes. . . ." The Chief warder broke in: "Stop that, O'Callaghan, you are not to speak of the accident." "But I will, and you shan't stop me." "Another word and I will stop the visit." The prisoner gripped the iron bars with his strong hands. "I will say what has been done to me. I don't care how you punish me after. You may kill me but I will tell her. I can't be in any more pain than I am for anything you can do to me." The door clanged open. The warder gripped him by the shoulders. "Come on now," but Callaghan clung on to the bars. The chief warder seized him by the other shoulder; a third warder came in from behind.

I rose from my chair and shouted: "O'Callaghan, don't trouble to tell me; I know what happened and I am here to arrange for an oculist to be sent to you." The struggle ceased; prisoners and warders stared at me astonished.

"Go quietly," I said; "you shall see an oculist as soon as I can arrange it and in six months you will be a free man." He relaxed his hold on the bars. "See he is not roughly treated," I said to the chief warder; "he is in great pain." "Good-bye, O'Callaghan, go quietly now; I will see you again soon." And I sat down feeling more and more in a horrible dream and another prisoner and warder were standing before me:

I don't remember what I said after that; but in the train on the return journey to London, as I sat silent and very tired in the corner of the carriage, Mr. Smith said: "Miss Gonne, may I ask you something? I know you did it because you felt sorry for them; but wasn't it a dreadful thing to have promised life-sentenced prisoners that they will be released in a definite space of time?"

"What do you mean?" I asked.

"Why, you told the man with the bad eye he would be free in six months. You told others they would be released in two years, in three years. It is cruel to raise hopes you can't realise."

"Did I tell them the time?" I said. "I don't remember. but if I did, they will be. Something spoke through me, something stronger than myself."

And they were released within the time and in the order I had told them.

CHAPTER IX

THE WOMAN OF THE SIDHE

I WAS IN DONEGAL again.

A council of war held in Father McFadden's study with its neat pigeon-holed walls and files. Pat O'Brien, Father McFadden and Father Stephens. I sat and listened, feeling I had not sufficient knowledge to advise on matters involving the life and death of many people, but trying to make up my mind as to my own conduct.

With all his local influence and intimate knowledge of the affairs, temporal and spiritual, of every one of his parishioners, Father McFadden had been unable to secure a rood more of land in the wide, desolate stretches of his parish on which we could with any security build Land League huts for the evicted. Colonel Olpherts and his friends owned everything. The few huts we had built were shockingly overcrowded;—two or three big families in each; hardly floor space for them to lie down at night. Many evicted families were sheltering under hedges, or in the heather on the mountains, and the winter was coming on. The rule of the estate against sheltering evicted families must be broken down. Those tenants who had broken away from the tenants' League and secretly scraped up money and paid their rents to avoid eviction must be induced to risk eviction and shelter the evicted. In the outlying farms it could be done more or less secretly. Pat O'Brien was confident that the agitation in the English Parliament about the evictions was growing and would soon make it hard for the Conservative Government to allow the use of police and military to protect the landlords' agents and Emergency Men on wholesale eviction campaigns and without this outside force the local constabulary would be powerless to do so; the priests were certain the people would be able to defend themselves against the Emergency Men and the bailiff. The great thing was to hold the people on the land and to prevent them from drifting to the towns and the emigration ships. Publicity must be kept up against evictions and Pat O'Brien said Miss Gonne must go on a lecture tour through England. I shook my head. I did not want to become completely identified with the parliamentary Home-Rule campaign. I hated English towns, I hated the alliance growing daily more and more complete with the English Liberal Party. This sentimental talk of the Union of Hearts sickened me. The Liberals were just as imperialist as the Conservatives.

"No, I will stay in Donegal and help Father McFadden to reinstate the people and if necessary take a pot shot at Olpherts. You must build me a little house in the mountains, Pat," I said laughing.

"We will do that surely, and a big house too," said Father McFadden, "but Pat is right. After your success in the Lancashire election you will have to go on that lecture tour first."

"Much good that election did," I answered. "The Liberal candidate we put in, Duncan, won't even help me release the Treason Felony prisoners." I had already come to judge of the sincerity of politicians by their attitude to political prisoners.

"Duncan may be a dud candidate," said O'Brien, "but your effectiveness in telling of evictions to the working people in England is worth while."

I still shook my head. I would not go. "John Dillon and William O'Brien can do that lecture business," I said. "The English Liberals love them. If I lecture anywhere it will be in France against the British Empire."

It didn't sound practical politics to any of them. Finally it was decided that, in order to get the constabulary reinforcements withdrawn, the excitement in Donegal was to be allowed to die down. No more resistance was to be offered at the remaining evictions and nothing said openly about keeping the people together for reinstatement. Pat O'Brien, and especially myself, as the storm centre, were to disappear and return only when Father McFadden sent for us.

"How disappointed all the English visitors will be. No more eviction fights," I said. The hotels in Falcarragh and Gweedore and even Griffith's farm where I was staying were packed with English sympathisers. I found it hard to be civil to them, though I had to admit that some of them were quite sincere, good, worthy people, doing what they felt was their duty, seeing for themselves the wicked things the Conservative Government was doing. They had come to sympathise with the Irish and they sympathised earnestly and continuously. They hero-worshipped John Dillon and William O'Brien, especially the ladies, and were fulsome in their praise. They would, I think, have been quite ready to put me in a niche too for worship but for the tactless remarks I occasionally made in answer to their reiterated assurances of the determination of the Liberal Party to right the century-long wrongs of Ireland. "By clearing out of Ireland, I hope!"

"My dear, Ireland can never stand alone. England has her responsibilities; she must undo her wrongs and make you all love us; there must be no more hate, etc."

It was no use arguing with them, so I followed my natural inclination of avoiding them, but it was difficult to do.

I tried getting up very early so as to be out before they were stirring. Only once I was able to look wonderingly at the big serviceable boots of the English ladies outside their bedroom doors, for they were early risers and before I had got my tea in the little farm parlour they were up and ready; so I tried, instead, getting up very late and asked kind, overworked Mrs. Griffiths to bring me breakfast in bed; but, following Mrs. Griffiths and the tray, came a stout lady and her bouncing daughter, with anxious enquiries about my health and a box of cough lozenges. They insisted on sitting on my bed and telling me I did not eat enough and that my shoes were too light for the rough walking we had to do. I got rid of them only by telling them they would be late for the evictions, that I did not know in which direction they would take place and that it was urgent that they should find out; so they bustled off to interview the officer in charge of the police. In the evenings there was no escape from their questions and their overflowing sympathy.

I said I would leave next day for Dublin with Pat O'Brien. "No," said Father McFadden, "Before you go I want you to come round the farms with me and put some spirit into those who are to shelter the evicted families. They will do anything for Maud Gonne." And he and Father Stephens laughed. "They are saying you are a woman of the Sidhe who rode into Donegal on a white horse surrounded by birds to bring victory. No one can resist this woman; she confabbed with the Bishop, she releases prisoners, even the police can't stand against her."

For the first time I heard of the legend that was growing. It had small foundation, but it explained why Irish-speaking women who could not understand a word I said kissed my hand after meetings and boys and old men looked at me with adoration. I had attributed this to their astonishment at seeing on their side a woman better dressed and much more triumphant-looking than Olphert's ladies and I was always careful to say that Ireland would win, Ireland could not be defeated. Once when I was going through a mountain glen with young Paddy, we had come upon a group of police guarding four prisoners arrested for defending their home; a sergeant was in charge; they were waiting for the police car. I had noted that my good clothes impressed the police, always respectful to ascendency.

Even the D.I. made way for me and sergeants would willingly have helped me on or off my car if I had let them.

I went up to the sergeant and asked him why he had arrested these boys, and speaking in a tone of authority told him it was a stupid mistake as I was interested in them and knew them to be good, honest fellows. "Let them go now; I take full responsibility," and I waved to the prisoners to go. They went. The police made no move, and with a careless nod to the sergeant, I walked on as if nothing unusual had happened, followed by the astonished Paddy, while the prisoners disappeared up the mountain. The bluff had worked. How the young sergeant explained matters to his superiors I do not know. Many of the police were half-hearted and hated eviction duty. Young Paddy had spread this tale and it had helped the legend; next day it was to be further illuminated.

Pat O'Brien said he would wait another day or two for the pleasure of travelling with me to Dublin. The following day on Father McFadden's car we made an early start. The wind was blowing so cold and hard from the sea that I resisted Father McFadden's suggestion that we should go a little out of our way to see a spot where the waves, mountain-high, were dashing over the cliffs. "As grand a sight as Niagara," said Father McFadden. These Donegal men were so hardy they didn't seem to feel the wind, and they were so proud of their wild and lovely country. The wind took my breath away and made me feel dizzy and stupid. As a child, on the hill of Howth, I had loved to run with the wind and called it my playmate; and on a windy day, walking with my governess in Hyde Park, I had been happy because I thought my playmate had come to London to find me. But now I was afraid of the wind which took my breath when I wanted to keep it for fighting the landlords. The whole of the previous night, in my tiny bedroom at Griffith's farm, I had had to sit upright fighting against suffocation and coughing little streaks of blood; but I told no one; it would not do for the Triumphant One to be ill or subject to human infirmities; but I was not going to waste any of my strength sight-seeing. Pat O'Brien, sitting next to me on the car, felt my reluctance. He was, as he often said, stifled by the smoky air of London and would have loved that wonderful sea-drive, but, kind and thoughtful always for me, he said: "Miss Gonne is right; we have a lot to do. Don't let's waste time"; so the car was turned inland by the short road to the townland we were to visit. The road became worse and worse; the driver got down and led the horse; soon we all had to get down and walk over the bog to the houses. Young Paddy turned up, as by magic he always did, to help me over the hard places. I was exhausted when we got to the first house and gladly sat down by the turf fire, while the tousled-haired Ban na Tigh poured me out a strong cup of tea and Father McFadden and Pat O'Brien talked to the men outside. In an incredibly short time the news of our arrival had spread to neighbouring farms and there was quite a crowd outside and children posted as sentries to give warning if police cars were coming. A scout ran in and announced two cars coming along the road from Gweedore—not police cars. Soon they were visible from the hill we were on. "English sympathisers," I said wearily. But how had they found us out? They should have been attending evictions the other side of Falcarragh. On the first car, beside the driver, there was a strange-looking bundle of fur; on the second two men, one with a wide felt hat which the wind succeeded in grabbing and which some of our ragged scouts were dexterously endeavouring to recapture. Some of the men went down to the road to help the visitors; I returned to the fire. The woman of the house was showing me an ejectment notice her husband had just received. It was a big house with out-buildings, which we had hoped would shelter several evicted families.

Father McFadden came in with a tall old gentleman who had

unrolled himself from the fur rug on the car but was still protected by a fur-lined coat with fur collar. He was explaining that, being a Member of Parliament, he thought it his duty to see the evictions which were being so much debated in Westminster. I recognised Sir John —. The boys had evidently recaptured the hat of the man on the other car for its owner was taking it off, bowing ceremoniously and presenting me with a letter of introduction from Millevoye. He was a French journalist who could not speak a word of English but had picked up an interpreter in Dublin and wanted to know all about the eviction campaign. At this juncture Sir John importantly announced he wanted to speak with Miss Gonne alone. Tactfully Father McFadden drew everybody out of the crowded cottage to an impromptu meeting outside at which he said Sir John would speak after he had rested a few moments.

"I went to Dublin to see you and hearing you were in Donegal decided to come and follow you here and renew our conversation. I want you to see how, if you listen to me, you will really be able to do far more for Ireland than by wasting your time on the bogs in this impossible climate." He was pursuing his idea that, as his wife, I would make an ideal hostess for a great Liberal salon in London. To show my aptitude as a hostess I suggested to the tousled-haired hostess of the house that Sir John would enjoy a cup of tea, and I was amused watching his disgusted refusal. He brought out from his pocket a little neat parcel which he handed to me. Astonished, I unwrapped it and, still more astonished, I disclosed a big diamond pendant. "It is not beautiful enough for you, but I got it in Dublin. I will get you something much more beautiful in London." My amusement was turning to anger. Did he imagine I could be bought by such a bauble?

"I don't care for jewellery, Sir John. But I thank you for the gracious thought and your kindness shall not be wasted. This jewel will save this family from eviction." And calling to the woman, who with her husband was standing in the doorway, trying to hear what Father McFadden was saying and at the same time what the strangers in her home were saying, I put the diamond pendant in her hand: "Sell this and pay your rent. You need not fear eviction now and you can shelter the others. This kind gentleman has brought it for you."

"Michael, look at it," said the woman.

"But we can't take this," said the man. "It would not be right."

"Oh, but you can. Have no fear; it will bring you luck. Put it in your pocket and come and hear what Father McFadden is saying. Sir John, they are waiting outside for you to speak," and I went out into the cold. Sir John wouldn't speak. He left early next morning. The legend had grown. When I returned to Donegal the people were saying the woman of the Sidhe scattered jewels which brought luck and stopped evictions.

Next day Father McFadden was raging. He had heard the story. "And the mean hound," he said, "went back later to the cottage and bought his diamond from Michael for the exact sum he owed for the rent. Michael didn't know the value and was glad to let it go. Why didn't you tell me, Miss Gonne? If I had known, he wouldn't have got it back and we would have had money to help all the people." I laughed. "How could I have thought of that?"

"It is hard to be up to the English," he said.

At Griffith's farm the English sympathisers looked curiously and coldly at the French journalist. I spent the evenings enlightening him and, being the only one who spoke French fluently, had it all my own way.

Word was brought me from Dunfanaghy that another Frenchman had arrived and was ill at the hotel there. I felt sorry for him as the hotel was none too comfortable in those days. "Irish beds don't seem made to sleep in," said the French journalist with a wry face. " You must be very tired to sleep at all in them. The unfortunate man probably does not speak any more English than I do and will be very unhappy till he meets you." The post car brought another letter for me in Millevoye's handwriting. Another letter of introduction, I thought, opening it. To my consternation it was not a letter of introduction but a letter saying he had come himself to Donegal to see what I was doing so long in this wild country neglecting all the work of our alliance and that he had ridden from Derry and had fallen ill in Dunfanaghy and couldn't proceed any further.

I was surprised and rather annoyed. I didn't like being followed, even by a great friend, without being consulted; but the thought of him alone, ill, in that Spartan hotel, unable to make anyone understand him, decided me. I must go to Dunfanaghy at once; I could just catch the return mail car and I told the young Frenchman it was clearly his duty to a compatriot to accompany me. It was dark when we arrived. "The priest is with the French gentleman, I sent for him," said the mistress of the inn, as, with some hesitation, she showed me up the dark staircase. My heart stood still. Father Kelly reassured me when I opened the door. "No. I am not here in my priestly capacity, but the Frenchman speaks no English and no one here speaks French, nor do I; but we both speak Latin and can understand each other fairly well. I have sent for the doctor. Now you are here you will be able to translate better than I can."

Millevoye was propped up with pillows in a bed that was much too short; his hand was burning,—he had evidently a high temperature.

"I don't know what I should have done but for Father Kelly," said Millevoye. "He is a great doctor."

"I gave him the same remedy I gave you when you and your cousin arrived frozen at my door, but unluckily I didn't give it to him in time. It was only to-day they sent for me. But I think he will be all right."

Pat O'Brien had to go to Dublin without me for I stayed a week in Dunfanaghy and with Father Kelly nursed Millevoye till the doctor said he might safely continue his journey; he just escaped pneumonia. We quarrelled seriously, for he tried to persuade me to leave Donegal and come and work against the British Empire in France. He said things that, because of the truth there was in them, made me angry. I was killing myself and only fighting a side-issue. If I succeeded in ruining Olpherts, what had I achieved? The British Empire would not be shaken. I would be doing more, stirring up indignation abroad and securing allies for Ireland. "Leave this work for others. You are the only one who can do the more important work abroad."

I thought of the hopeless families sheltering in the bare mountains, of the joy of reinstating them in their houses. I could think of nothing else and I was annoyed that Millevoye had come to take me away from this work. So, though I had my plans made to travel to Dublin, I refused to travel with him and, after seeing him safely in a covered carriage of which Father Kelly had got the loan to drive to Derry, I went back to Falcarragh to collect my belongings and take the train for Dublin the following day. I was to wait there till Father McFadden reported the departure of the police reinforcements.

In Dublin Doctor Sigerson shook his head over me. We had become great friends. He was preparing his big compendium of Irish poetry, *The Songs of the Gael and the Gall*, and used to drop into my rooms in Nassau Street and read me gems of his translations. My rooms were a meeting place for many of the literary men O'Leary had gathered round him.

Dr. Sigerson noticed my cough and was anxious. More than once he had sent all my guests away early when he saw I was getting tired; once he sat up all night putting on poultices for me. "I think Father loves you even more than he loves us," said his beautiful, dreamy-eyed daughter Dora to me one day.

"That is because he is interested in me as a patient," I said, "though I am a very bad patient and refuse to do anything I am told. A short life and a merry one is my motto."

That was the day after Dr. Sigerson had stayed up all night nursing me; I had obeyed him in not getting up. My bed had been moved into the sitting-room because the fire in my bedroom smoked. I was half asleep with a high temperature when the door of my room opened and an old workman who had been to all my meetings for prisoners put his head in at the door. The service arrangements in my digs were somewhat erratic; people often could walk in at will.

"Oh, Miss Gonne, I didn't know you were ill," he exclaimed. "I came to ask you if you would speak for our club next week."

"The doctor won't let me," I answered. "I am pretty ill and I mustn't talk."

I suppose I looked ill, for the old man suddenly came forward. "Oh, Miss Gonne, my darlin', don't say you are going to die on us. What would we do without you and the hope you bring!" His voice shook; then suddenly: "I mustn't stay and tire you, but dear heart, I promise you this, if you die we will give you the biggest funeral anyone has ever seen in Dublin." And he vanished.

I shook with laughter till it made me cough and that night when Dr. Sigerson came to see me I was really better; I told him the old man's visit had cheered me up. True to Tommy's teaching I was never afraid of death. Because of this indifference I think I lived on.

Another patient of Dr. Sigerson, and one whom I think he loved as much as he loved me and cared for even more assiduously, for she obeyed him better, was Rose Kavanagh, the poetess who edited the childrens' page of a Catholic magazine. She and I were great friends and were both in much the same condition of health. Dr. Sigerson was a believer in a new treatment of consumption by injections and wanted us

both to undergo the cure. I refused resolutely; Rose consented.
I was too much of a fatalist to believe in the efficacy of any cure;
besides I had just heard from Father MacFadden that the last
of the extra constabulary had departed; so I was arranging to
return to Donegal and reinstate the tenants. I did not dare tell
Dr. Sigerson, but when he called next day he found me gone,
leaving a little note of thanks to him and saying that the joy
of seeing the people in their homes again would certainly cure
me if anything could.

The woman who brought luck was back in Falcarragh. One
by one the priests and I reinstated the evicted and collected the
neighbours to rebuild the gables and put in the broken window
panes. The honour of tearing down the wooden planks nailed
across broken doors by the bailiffs was left to me. It was even
more fun than building Land-League huts and much quicker.
The local police looked on helplessly; they could do little against
the general enthusiasm of the people and, to be fair to them,
they much preferred not being spoil-sports. Olpherts and his
foxy agent, with the few Emergency Men he still kept round his
place, remained safely out of sight. Many of the short sentence
prisoners had returned. We welcomed them with a torchlight
procession and they took part in these house-warming rejoicings.
I thought of the life-sentenced prisoners and breezily promised
they should be released. I had no idea how it should be done,
but I had convinced myself as well as the people that we were
invincible.

One night Pat O'Brien arrived. In reply to my joyous welcome he looked very grave. "Miss Gonne, I have come to take
you away. There is a warrant out for your arrest. In your state
of health, six months in jail in winter is a death sentence. When
I heard in Dublin through our intelligence service that the
warrant for your arrest was signed, I took the train at once; I
have all arrangements made,—you must leave to-night for
France."

I was inclined to refuse. "Are there any more warrants signed?" I asked.

"As far as I have heard, there is only one, for you. They don't want to arrest the priests on account of trouble with the Church. Olpherts has been pulling strings in Dublin Castle. They hold you responsible for the reinstatements which have undone the eviction campaign here. With luck they won't start evicting the people again; they will have now to bring actions against them in the courts; Father MacFadden can be trusted to cause legal delays; it will take a long time and a general election may come in time to save them. You must leave to-night."

Father MacFadden was equally insistent. "It will spoil everything and dishearten the people if you are taken," he said. I hated running away but I knew that jail would be the end of everything and before I died I wanted to get the prisoners released, I wanted to see Millevoye and I wanted to begin the fight against the British Empire in international affairs.

Pat O'Brien's arrangements were complete; I had just time to pack my bags and get on his waiting car. In the darkening evening we drove to a lonely place where the night train passed over the wild moorland on its way to Stranorlar. There was no station but it slowed down and stopped; the guard helped me in to an empty carriage; Pat O'Brien threw in my bags and the train went on. The guard had my ticket for Larne in his hand. "It's all arranged. You will be met at Stranraer and taken safe to the boat at Larne," said Pat O'Brien. "From Stranraer to London, don't stop till you are in France. Wire me from there. Good-bye. Good luck."

The lucky woman departed mysteriously and suddenly as she had come. Shortly after, the bishop visited Falcarragh and Gweedore. I am sure he was glad to see so many people back in their houses. Even though they had received court summons for illegal possession of the houses they and their fathers had built. He had long talks with Father McFadden, enjoining caution and no violence. The excitement in that wild northern land died down and the people returned to their drab lives of hopeless toil and privations, feeding calves on the milk their children needed and selling eggs they all required to scrape up the money for Olpherts' foxy agent in order to avoid eviction, and pinning their hopes on Land-Purchase Acts which, when they came, left them little better off. I heard all the news in 1897 when in America I met Father MacFadden who was on a lecture tour collecting money to build the cathedral in Letterkenny. "Those were the days," he said to me with a merry twinkle in his grey eyes.

I was not in Donegal again till 1919 when the British military were trying some sort of food blockade to starve the already starving people and prevent them supporting the Irish Republican Army. I was organising the feeding of the school children for the White Cross. Many whom I had known in the old days were dead, but old people would still come out from the little cottages with welcomes and blessings. They seemed to me no better off and I believe never will be till Ireland's freedom is established.

CHAPTER X

THE BLUE MOUNTAIN

DR. GRANCHER LOOKED at me with his fine thoughtful grey eyes. He had made a thorough examination with a stethoscope in absolute silence, and the nurse had buttoned up the back of my black dress, I sat down at the opposite side of his great desk-table in his rather magnificent consulting room.

At last he said: "Mademoiselle, from all I hear of you, you are one to whom one can speak with entire frankness. You would rather hear the truth?"

"Oh, yes, Doctor, you needn't mind telling me the truth,—I am not afraid of death; a little sooner or later, what does it matter? I have dear friends on both sides of the door," and I thought of Tommy, and smiled.

"If you go on as at present, you will be the other side of the door in six months, and it is a pity; you are too young; the disease might be stopped,—it is worth trying."

"Do you mean I could be quite cured, or only patched up, and how long would it take? I won't have an invalid's life; I would much rather go at once than that."

"If," he said, "the disease can be checked, you would be stronger than you have ever been, but there is a big 'if' and it depends a great deal on yourself. It is worth a six months' trial. Life will be short, but not merry much longer, if you don't take care, for you are nearly at the end of your resistance."

"I can't go back to Ireland and my work till the Conservative Government in England is out of power, so I may as well try. What have I to do?"

"Nothing very hard. Live as merrily as you can, but live out of doors in the sunshine all the time. I suggest you go to the south of France to a little place that is very beautiful and hardly known,—among pine trees, St. Raphael. There is no casino; nothing to tempt you out in the evenings. You will go out after breakfast in the sunshine and you will stay out in the pine trees all day while the sun is up, then you will light a little creosote lamp I will give you, in your room, and let it burn all night till you go out again next day. If you have friends to play with in the pine woods, so much the better, for you must be happy or the cure won't work. Take lots of books and a paint box. It is so lovely there I wish I could get away from Paris to the sunshine," he said wistfully.

St. Raphael in those days was all Dr. Grancher had said, a little fishing village on the blue Mediterranean, with one or two new hotels, with hardly anyone in them. I lived in an atmosphere of creosote, but got so used to it I didn't even notice the smell, though everyone who came near me did. I reeked of it. There was a market where peasant women sold all sorts of vegetables and fruit, grapes and purple aubergines, and great yellow pumpkins that reminded me of fairy tales. The boats brought in coloured fish with fantastic heads and fins and shell-fish called sea-urchins, which have a strong sweet taste when one learns how to get off the shaggy prickles which cover them. One old fisherman used to eat them, prickles and all, to my great amusement, but opened and prepared them carefully for me. It was in that market that I learnt to know and appreciate all sorts of wonderful toadstools the people gathered in the woods; but the market soon palled and I took to the woods to search for toadstools myself.

Millevoye came to see me, from the Corrèze, where his father and mother lived and we had wonderful picnics in the woods. Dr. Grancher had sent him also out of Paris for the winter. He and his brother were fond of shooting and there was a lot of game; partridges and "bécassines" in the woods; they brought their shooting-dogs, who at first were very unfriendly with my Great Dane, Dagda. He could have devoured them easily but was benevolently contemptuous and they became great friends.

Millevoye had secured the services of a local poacher, Raymond, who took care of the shooting-dogs and the guns. At first I was not able to do much walking, but Raymond got a little pony trap and used to drive me out to the woods and prepare a fire and roast partridges for the shooting party. I was soon playing merrily in the woods as Dr. Grancher had recommended and only found it hard to remember I must be in before the sun went down. Millevoye bought a light rifle and wanted me to shoot also. I brought down a little bird at the first shot,—a little lark singing high in the air. Raymond was enthusiastic and declared it was a better shot than anyone had made. I was overwhelmed with the horror of my deed when the pointer brought back the tiny lifeless, ruffled body, and after that I never aimed at anything but fir cones and probably would have missed if I had, so I remained with my glory.

I got a letter from Dr. Sigerson,—he had taken Rose Kavanagh to Arcachon, where she was very ill; he was terribly distressed; the injections had not worked and she died there, a few months later.

I was getting steadily better and was greatly amused when Willie Yeats sent me a poem, my epitaph he had written with much feeling:

> "I dreamed that one had died in a strange place
> Near no accustomed hand;
> And they had nailed the boards above her face
> The peasants of that land.

Wondering to lay her in that solitude,
And raised above her mound
A cross they had made out of two bits of wood,
And planted cypress round;
And left her to the indifferent stars above
Until I carved these words:
She was more beautiful than thy first love
But now lies under boards."

There was a blue mountain of the Esterel that I often looked at. "When I am able to climb that, I shall be quite recovered," I said. Millevoye was now staying in St. Raphael and in the evenings we used to read and write a great deal together. He used to do a lot of journalism, chiefly in provincial papers for the Boulangiste cause and suggested I should try writing also about Ireland. I wrote an article called "Un Peuple Opprimé" and he helped me a great deal, for I had never written for the Press. It was a description of the evictions. I sent it to *La Revue Internationale*, edited in Paris by Madame Ratatzi, a great-niece of Napoleon Bonaparte. It was accepted and I began getting letters from all sorts of people, among others from the President of the "Cercle des Etudiante Catholiques", asking whether such appalling things could really be taking place and asking me to let him know when I would be in Paris, and if I would lecture for the students.

Paul Déroulède was organising his "Ligue des Patriotes" in the south of France; he had been speaking in Nice and wanted to see Millevoye. He and Millevoye were General Boulanger's two great lieutenants. I was curious to meet Déroulède, so Millevoye wrote to him to break his journey back to Paris at St. Raphael and he was with us at several of our picnics in the woods.

Like Millevoye he was very tall; he was full of vitality and terribly one-idea'd. He lived for "la Revanche", the re-taking of France's lost provinces, and hated the Germans more than I hated the English. Millevoye also lived for the regaining of Alsace-Lorraine, but looked on the English as being more the hereditary enemy of France than were the Germans. In the woods above St. Raphael, I listened to their talk, and realised that Déroulède was a danger to all I hoped. He would gladly have entered into an alliance with England. Millevoye saw the danger of an expanding nation like Germany, with a growing population, bottled up in a space too small for her and would have liked to encourage her in Colonial enterprise. Like Jules Ferry, he would willingly have given Tonkin in exchange for Alsace-Lorraine. "We in France have everything we want. What do we need with colonies? Let Germany colonise, and take English colonies." But Déroulède saw red. "Strengthen Germany? No! She took Alsace-Lorraine from us by the sword; we must take it back the same way."

I listened and said nothing. I was a foreigner, but I think Déroulède and I felt we were in different camps and mistrusted each other.

Raymond, the poacher, was plucking the partridges, Millevoye was off with his dog and gun; my book bored me; Raymond had lighted a fire of sticks so I should not be cold. He had grown very fond of me, and had faithful eyes like a dog. I looked at the blue mountain and got up:—

"Don't wait lunch for me, if I am late, I am going for a walk."

"Take care you don't get lost in the woods," he said.

"Dagda," I told the Great Dane, "we will go up that mountain to-day and then we will go to Paris,"—and Dagda looked up and laughed as he trotted by my side. The blue mountain looked near but it was very far; Dagda and I would not turn back,—on to that mountain we would go. The sun was shining and melting the thin snow which had fallen in the night. It was very lovely. The sun was sinking behind another hill when we returned and the sudden chill of the Riviera was rising. Raymond's fire was out; he and Millevoye were in different directions searching for me. I was very tired and told Dagda to go and look for them. He soon brought Millevoye back, very angry, because he had been seriously alarmed for me. It was said that the mountains and woods were none too safe and people escaping from justice robbed the unwary, but I never thought of that; I never met any but friendly people and very few of those.

"Where have you been?" he exclaimed.

"Up that mountain,—I always said I would climb it to know I was well. Lucien, I am cured. I can go back to work for our alliance; so don't be vexed. I had to do it."

Next week I was back in Paris. I lectured for the Catholic students in the Luxembourg. The Republican students had also asked me to lecture, but wanted me to lecture for them first:

"We are a bigger association."

"First come, first served," I answered, "the Catholic students asked me first."

There was great rivalry between those two great students' Associations. I made friends with both, and both helped me later on in my campaign for the political prisoners. The students are a real power in France and, unlike the students in Dublin, take a vehement interest both in foreign and home politics.

I was young,—they were young. They adopted me and together we ran lecture tours through France and played tricks on the English.

I took a tiny apartment in l'Avenue de la Grande Armée and had a childish quarrel with an English family living in the apartment underneath mine.

The owner of that apartment, a true Britisher, called on me to ask me to sign a petition to stop omnibuses running up the avenue, because the noise disturbed him. I laughed and refused to sign, and said I was Irish and thought it would be a great impertinence for foreigners to make such complaints. The Britisher glared at me and departed. On St. Patrick's Day I hung from my balcony an Irish and a French flag. In the morning a young French policeman called and asked me politely to take the flags down. I asked why, and he told me the Britisher underneath had called on him to have the flags removed, because it was against French law to beflag one's house except on the French National fête day, the 14th of July, anniversary of the taking of the Bastille. "But the 17th of March is Ireland's national fête day," I said to the policeman. "See, I have hung my flag and your flag side by side as I shall certainly hang them on the 14th of July. Don't you see that is all quite right? Only an Englishman would object. Certainly no Frenchman would." The policeman smiled, and the flags remained and the English family raged. I knew Augusta Holmes well and she often played Irish music; below the English would retaliate with *God Save the Queen.*

One day my landlord told me that the English family had complained that I kept too late hours and disturbed them at night, that all respectable people went to bed at 11 o'clock and the unmarried lady above could be heard walking about, receiving company and playing music till one or two o'clock in the morning. She could not be quite respectable, and it disturbed them. My landlord replied he had no power over the time his tenants went to bed, but had promised to mention the matter to me. The English resolved on drastic action, and the son of the house invested in some sort of hunting horn or cornet and made fearsome sounds with it on the balcony under my bedroom window early in the mornings. Maria, my French maid, was determined that the rest of her demoiselle should not be disturbed and interviewed the young policeman; so next morning, at the first notes of the cornet, he knocked loudly at the Englishman's door to inform him that the French law prohibited the use of a cornet in apartment houses because of the nuisance it created. But I was not long to enjoy morning peace. The daughter was learning the violin and with the window open made ghastly sounds from seven o'clock. My kind policeman could not help me there, as there was no law against violins; so I turned up the hearthrug in the room over the bedroom where Mr. and Mrs. Englishman slept the sleep of respectability at 11 o'clock. I gave them a quarter of an hour to go off to sleep and then I dropped a fire log on the bare space and repeated the operation from time to time till I went to bed myself.

A few days after, my landlord, looking very serious, called on me:—

"Mademoiselle, I have always taken your part against that objectionable Englishman, but this time you are getting me into serious trouble; read this,"—and he produced a legal paper from a "Huissier" which stated that, called in to listen to a nuisance, he had waited in the said apartment till 11 o'clock and heard nothing unusual, but at 11.15 he heard the sound of a hard body fall on the floor above. He waited and the same sound occurred three times at a quarter of an hour's intervals. It was evident that the occupant of the apartment below could not enjoy the rest and sleep he was entitled to, etc.

"Don't worry," I said, "you shall have my legal reply to-morrow." So I sent Maria to ask a young medical student who had just become a practising doctor to come and see me. He duly wrote a medical certificate to the effect that his patient, Mademoiselle Gonne, suffered from a nervous complaint and that whenever her sleep in the morning was disturbed in any way by any musical intrument, the nervous complaint caused her such shakiness of hand that she was apt to drop anything she held, especially towards evening, when she tired.

I sent this to my landlord and everything was all right. The English family gave notice and I sent a message to my student friends that the English family were leaving and had a violin and a cornet for sale. On Sunday afternoon great numbers of students used to pass up l'Avenue de la Grande Armée on their way to the Bois de Boulogne. By hundreds they called on the unfortunate English family with enquiries about violins and cornets or to visit the apartment shortly to be let. The English had to evacuate and leave their apartment. My landlord soon found another tenant; I was triumphant but a little lonely,—it had been fun.

The Conservative Government had been defeated. Pat O'Brien wrote me it would be safe to return; the warrant for my arrest was cancelled. I was completely cured and I went to England to work for the release of the prisoners, but retained my little flat in Paris.

Here is an extract from an article on my work in France, written by Willie Yeats, who in those days used to add to his income by free-lance journalism:

"England has indeed, as Mitchell phrased it, gained the ears of the World and knows right well how to tell foreign nations what tale of Ireland pleases her best. . . .

". . . More than one Irishman has sought in vain to get a hearing. The late Mr. Leonard tried all his life to make the people of Paris listen to the true story of England and Ireland, and with no very noticeable success. But now Miss Maud Gonne, as eloquent with her tongue as 'Speranza' with her pen, has made her voice heard, where so many have failed. Every speech has been a triumph greater than the one that went before it.

"Thousands who come to see this new wonder,—a beautiful woman who makes speeches,—remain to listen with delight to her sincere and simple eloquence.

"Last week at Bordeaux an audience of 1,200 persons rose to its feet, when she had finished, to applaud her with wild enthusiasm. The papers of Russia, France, Germany and even Egypt quote her speeches, and the tale of Irish wrongs has found its way hither and thither to be stored up perhaps in many a memory against the day of need. She is going through France addressing town after town, and besides spreading a better knowledge of Ireland and awakening a wider sympathy for our wrongs, has already, though this is not her main object, gained, I believe, a considerable sum for the evicted tenants.

"It is not, however, to describe her success that I write but to review a Supplement of *La Revue Catholique*, which has just reached me. It is a verbatim report of her long speech at the Catholic University Cercle du Luxembourg, and enables one to judge once for all whether she rules her audiences by the power of beauty alone, or whether she has indeed the genius of the orator.

"I do not think that anyone who reads through these twelve columns of clear and vigorous French will doubt the answer.

"The middle ages in the most sombre period of their history never beheld such misery. Men and women eat the dogs, the rats and the grass of the fields, and some even, when all food was gone, eat the dead bodies.

"Those who died were cast into great ditches so hurriedly opened and badly closed again that the pestilential odours helped to make death travel more rapidly. They were called the pits of the famine, for in them the famine cast its human harvest. Ireland was heroic in her suffering. Whole families, when they had eaten their last crust and understood that they had to die, looked once upon the sun and then closed up the doors of their cabins with stones, that none might look on their death agony. Weeks afterwards men would find their skeletons gathered round the extinguished hearth.

"I do not exaggerate, Gentlemen; I have added nothing to the terrible reality. If you come to my country, every stone will repeat to you this tragic history. It is only fifty years ago;

it still lives in thousands of memories. I have been told it by women who have heard the last sigh of their children without being able to relieve their agony with one drop of milk. It has seemed to me at evening, on those mountains of Ireland, so full of savage majesty, when the winds sighed over the pits of the famine, where thousands of dead enrich the harvests of the future,—it has seemed to me that I heard an avenging voice calling down on our oppressors the execration of men and the justice of God."

CHAPTER XI

WORKING FOR PRISONERS

In London my first visit was to the Committee of the Amnesty Association. I had to give them £20 subscribed after my lecture at *Le Cercle du Luxembourg de Paris* and to report that, being now completely recovered, I was ready to speak at any meetings organised for the prisoners.

The Committee had great news for me. First, as a result of my visit to Portland, and my letters to the Press, O'Callaghan had been removed to a hospital where his injured eye had been taken out; he was in a fair way to recovery and was likely to be released when he could leave the hospital. This gave me great hope. He had left Portland within the six months I had unreasonably promised.

Other great news: the chief of police of Birmingham, Mr. Farndale, having fallen ill, had sent for the chairman of the Watch Committee, Alderman Manton, because his conscience was troubled and he felt he could no longer keep silent. He knew that the dynamite dug up by the police in a raid on the house of James Egan, who kept a hardware shop in Birmingham had been planted there by a member of the Detective Force of Ireland who had come over specially to round up Irish revolutionists in England. John Daly had been staying with Egan shortly before he was arrested in Liverpool. On the evidence of that planted dynamite and his connection with Daly, Egan had been sentenced to twenty years of penal servitude. Alderman Manton, who was a conscientious man, had written at once to the Conservative Home Secretary, who had refused to reopen the case, and he had then given the information to the Amnesty

Association. It was hoped that the Liberal party, now in power, would do justice. John Redmond who, till then, had refused to do anything for the dynamiters, had taken up the matter and had got out a pamphlet based on Farndale's statement.

My next visit was to Pat O'Brien and on the terrace of the House of Commons he told me of a lovely trick he had played on the English and on Mr. Balfour, Secretary of State for Ireland, who denied that British troops were ever engaged on eviction work. Pat O'Brien, who always carried a pocket camera had photographed many eviction scenes. He had hired a barge and a magic lantern and while Mr. Balfour was actually denying the use of British troops, Pat O'Brien was displaying photos, showing the English soldiers surrounding farms while they were being destroyed with the battering ram. The large screen on the barge drawn up on the Thames opposite the terrace of the House of Commons politely gave the lie to the Minister, and the whole House of Commons rushed out to see this novel exhibition. Pat had added some interesting photos of police shadowing priests and he promised me a set of his slides for use in France to illustrate my lectures. We were soon joined by a number of Irish M.P.'s. congratulating me on my recovery; Some had read reports of my first lecture in Paris and were delighted. "What are you going to do now, Miss Gonne?" they asked.

"Work for the release of the Treason Felony Prisoners."

Someone gave me a copy of Mr. Redmond's pamphlet and said it should be possible to get Egan released on that. "*All* must be released," I said, but I realised most of the M.Ps. were not encouraging. "Mr. Field, I have not forgotten your promise to speak for the prisoners."

"Quite right, my dear, I will help you." And he brushed his black locks out of his eyes. Mrs. Crawford, Paris correspondent of the *Daily News*, and Mr. Morton, now private secretary to Mr. Morley, and Spence Watson, a prominent member of the

Liberal Party and treasurer of its funds, though not an M.P., joined us.

One-idea'd as usual, I continued to talk about the Treason Felony Prisoners.

Mrs. Crawford said: "But surely, Miss Gonne, you don't support men who would throw bombs endangering the lives of innocent people? Their motives may be excellent; but no one enquires into the motives of mad dogs."

My anger was rising. "You all seem to forget that there is a perpetual state of war between Ireland and England. Irish homes and lives are being destroyed by Englishmen. Irishmen must hit back how and when they can."

Spence Watson put in soothingly: "We are going to end that war. We are going to stop evictions. I quite agree with Miss Gonne also that there should be an enquiry into prison conditions. Prison reform is necessary everywhere. But I assure you Portland is a paradise compared with the prison of St. Peter and Paul in St. Petersburg," and he began speaking of the atrocities perpetrated on political prisoners under the Czar and invited us all to a meeting of Free Russia, a society of which he was the treasurer and whose principal object was to help the escape of Russian political prisoners. That evening it was to be addressed by a prisoner who had escaped from Siberia. "You must join Free Russia, Miss Gonne; it will give scope for all your generous enthusiasm for prisoners."

"I prefer doing the work to hand. I have seen my own countrymen in Portland and till they are released I have no time to right wrongs in far-off lands. If the English don't release them, I am going to appeal to the French Press to start a campaign against the atrocities in Queen Victoria's prisons, to equal that of the English Press in regard to the Czar's prisons."

Mrs. Crawford laughed sneeringly: "You won't find that easy unless you have a lot of money to back you. I know Paris. The newspapers there do nothing unless for money."

"I know France too and France is the country where money counts least; people are judged, not by their money, but by what they are. I have no money and I will prove you are wrong."

It was lucky a division bell, ringing with urgency, broke up our group. "Keep Miss Gonne till I get back, Morton," said Pat O'Brien, "we must have tea together." And William Field stayed behind the rest of the members to squeeze my arm and say: "You are quite right, my dear, and I will help you."

"Amnesty meetings then, are being held next week at Manchester, Liverpool, Newcastle, Edinburgh and Glasgow. Will you speak at some of them?" I called after him.

"I will," and he did, and paid his own expenses to save our funds, which were small.

Not being an M.P., Mr. Morton could ignore the division bell. "Your Donegal prisoners are safely back in their homes now. I took my present position as Mr. Morley's secretary to ensure that. Are you pleased?"

"Indeed I am and ever so grateful to you. Will you help now about the Treason Felony Prisoners?"

"I will do anything for you, Miss Gonne, but those men...."

"Hush," I interrupted, "don't say a word against them. They are far more interesting than the Donegal prisoners who acted instinctively. The men in Portland deliberately risked their lives and everything for the holy cause of Ireland. They accepted lives of poverty and hardship for Ireland. Many of them could be rich and prosperous in America to-day, and instead they are undergoing worse than death in Portland."

Morton sighed. "Their release is much more difficult. Morley, who is really a great and good man, won't hear of it. Spence Watson is a great personal friend of Morley's. I am going to stay with him soon. I heard you say you were going to Newcastle. Would you stay there too if I can arrange it? You would like Mrs. Watson and she would love you. They are quakers, and quakers are always good about prisoners. If we could get Spence Watson interested he might influence Morley."

I told him the date of the Newcastle meeting and added I would have a few days to spare before going to Glasgow and Edinburgh.

Those Amnesty meetings were a great success. They united all sections of the Irish in England, and Home-rulers and Fenians worked together. Mr. Kennedy, the Irish Protestant, Vicar of Plumpton, acted as chairman for many of them. He was morally, and physically, one of the most courageous men I ever met, as well as being the most kindly. So adored was he by his English parishioners that he was independent of his bishop, and a few years later, during the Boer war, took the chair for me at anti-recruiting meetings in England which had the honour of being the first meetings ever proclaimed in England.

Mr. Morton arranged the invitation to the Spence Watsons and he and I stayed a few days at their lovely home near Newcastle. Spence Watson had not attended my Amnesty meeting on Saturday night, but Mrs. Watson took me to her Quaker meeting on Sunday morning. She was a charming woman and she and her daughters, I thought, looked lovely in their dove-grey dresses which suited their fresh pink-and-white complexions. They addressed each other as "thee" and "thou" in the old Quaker manner.

Everything breathed peace and comfort in the household of the long-golden-bearded Spence Watson, and Mr. Morton and I thoroughly enjoyed our short visit, though, as I remarked to him, a little of that peace and comfort goes a long way with me while there are prisoners in Portland and people starving in Ireland, and it might get very dull. Spence Watson gave me a copy of a pamphlet John Morley had written, before he became minister, on the necessity of releasing Irish political prisoners, but said that John Morley was only referring to such prisoners as John Dillon and William O'Brien.

Encouraged by the enthusiasm displayed at the Amnesty meetings, especially at the meeting in Newcastle, where numbers of English Socialists had attended, I said: "If Mr. Morley does not keep the written promise of his pamphlet to release all Irish prisoners, the Irish might defeat him at the next elections." Morley was M.P. for Newcastle and Spence Watson acted as his election agent.

Morton looked pained and Spence Watson smiled serenely and indulgently at me. "There are not enough of your countrymen here to do that."

A year later I was at Newcastle again, staying in an uncomfortable English hotel, not addressing public meetings, but negotiating with Irish election leaders to support a socialist candidate who had no chance of election, but who, by splitting the Liberal votes, secured Morley's defeat. He and Sir William Harcourt, another Cabinet Minister, were both defeated through the Amnesty Association because they would not release the Treason Felony Prisoners.

This period of my life was one of ceaseless activity and travelling. I rarely spent a month in the same place. In Scotland I visited the place where O'Callaghan, Devany and some of the Treason Felony Prisoners had been arrested and interviewed the lawyers who had defended them in the vague hope of finding legal loopholes on which demand for their release might be based. Organising the Amnesty Association in Scotland and in England; house-building for evicted tenants with Pat O'Brien in many parts of Ireland; seeing my friends in Dublin; holding meetings in France and arranging a sort of Press agency for Ireland in Paris.

My student friends in Paris helped me in more ways than in playing tricks on my British neighbours in the apartment house of *l'Avenue de la Grande Armée*. They arranged lectures for me on Ireland, on the evictions, on British prisons and Irishmen being driven insane in them, in almost every University town in

France. La Société de Géographie, the Catholic Students' clubs, and the Republican Students' clubs, sponsored these lectures and learned professors often took the chair and sometimes the mayors of the towns and the Press of all parties reported. Pat O'Brien's lantern slides were shown wherever a screen and a magic lantern could be arranged. "I like to speak with documents in support. These are my documents," I used to say. At La Rochelle, people were so indignant that they demonstrated after the lecture outside the British Consulate and had to be dispersed by the police.

The wall of silence John Mitchell deplored was broken for the time at least. The "Argus de la Presse," the Press-cutting agency, sent me two thousand cuttings on Ireland in one year till it became so expensive I had to cease my subscription, though I had obtained specially reduced rates, because my bank account was always overdrawn.

A Dutch writer, Mademoiselle Louise Stratenus, had been at one of my French lectures and asked me if I would lecture in Holland and in Belgium. I accepted and again it was chiefly the students who organised the lectures. At Amsterdam and Groningen I was received by a mounted cavalcade of students who accompanied me as a guard of honour. The French Press continued to report with picturesque details, and not only to report; leading articles appeared in many of the big papers. The Paris *Figaro*, the diplomatic paper read in all the chancelleries of Europe at that time, had a front-page article headed: "Les Atrocités dans les Bagnes Anglais."

Millevoye was delighted; the work of our alliance was going well. "Don't you see, your work in Paris is more important to Ireland than anything you can do in Dublin or on those wild mountains of Donegal. You are really helping your people far more this way."

After every meeting subscriptions were collected which I always asked the organisers to send directly, sometimes to the

Amnesty Association, sometimes to the Evicted Tenants' Committee, sometimes to Father McFadden; they were often quite small sums, but in that way the people at home knew I had not forgotten them. I often laughed when I thought of Mrs. Crawford's words, "Money is the only thing which counts with the French Press." I proved her wrong. France is a country of great ideas and great enthusiasms. Because I represented a great cause of human liberty everyone was kind to me and spoilt me; I had invitations and free passes to the Opera and nearly all the theatres. I told myself all this success was luck, destiny, the will of the Gods.

An emissary from the Russian Embassy, asked me if I would agree to go to Russia to visit Russian prisons and write an article showing how much better they were than English prisons. But I declined. "You would only show me the prisons you chose and the good side of them. I could never bring myself to write or speak well of any prisons." I often wondered after if I had been wrong in refusing. If I had gone, I could have proved that, for systematised cold inhumanity, English prisons were really worse than any other prisons where terrible but isolated things happened.

I was going to America where twenty million people of Irish blood should be able to free Ireland and defeat the British Empire. I wanted Ireland to be freed by her own sons.

While I was in America Arthur Lynch had occasion to see the American ambassador in London and told me an amusing story he heard from him. Asquith had sent for John Redmond. On the desk before him were a great number of newspaper cuttings with reports of my lectures and the article of the *Figaro* "Atrocités dans les Bagnes Anglais" on the top.

"Do you think articles like these are helping the Home Rule cause?" said Asquith. "How can you expect concessions being granted to people who are doing their best to injure England? You must stop these articles."

Redmond had truthfully answered he had nothing to do with them and was powerless to stop them. "No one can stop Miss Gonne. She consults no one and acts entirely on her own. Nothing will stop her but the release of the prisoners."

They were released shortly after. The last life-sentenced man was released four years after my visit to Portland and I think that the generous campaign of the French Press had more to do with it than even the defeat of two cabinet ministers at the elections and the huge Amnesty Association we had built up in England and Scotland which must have enrolled at least two hundred thousand people.

The English party in France looked on displeased. Madame Séverine told me that Clemenceau, its leader, had said: "We must break the friendship of Millevoye and Miss Gonne, or break them one through the other."

CHAPTER XII

LA SAINT PATRICE

SHORTLY AFTER MY first lecture to the students of the *Cercle du Luxembourg*, I had received two invitations, one on a big gilt-edged card from l'Association du Saint Patrice to a banquet, and one, only a little less magnificent, to a "bal irlandais" on St. Patrick's Day.

John O'Leary had founded the St. Patrick's Society when he was an exile in France. He and an old Fenian friend of his, Mr. Leonard, also an exile, had industriously sought out and called on all the descendants of the Wild Geese, who had served in the Irish Brigade in France and had got them to join an association in honour of their Irish ancestry. O'Leary hated writing letters and had lost touch with it since he had been able to return home, but he was anxious to get news of his child, so I arranged to be in Paris on the 17th of March.

I was also invited to attend Mass for Ireland under the auspices of La Saint Patrice at the Church of Nôtre Dame des Victoires and had brought a basket of shamrocks to distribute at it. There were masses for Ireland also celebrated at the *Collège Irlandais* and at the English-speaking church in l'Avenue Hoche. There were more French people than Irish at Nôtre Dame des Victoires, but everyone was equally anxious to wear shamrocks and my basket was emptied before I went into the church where the organ was playing Irish airs.

The banquet was small and very select, held in a fashionable restaurant. I, as the guest of honour, sat at the right hand of the President, le Comte O'Neill de Tyrone, a charming courtly old gentleman, and on the other side was the

Vice-president, le Comte d'Abbadie d'Araste, a distinguished Philologist who spoke much about the Gaelic and Basque languages with le Comte d'Arbois de Joubanville, sitting next to him, who was Professor of Celtic literature at the Collège de France; later I got him to take J. M. Synge as his assistant. Opposite me sat le Comte Bonaparte Wyse, whose sister, Madame Ratazzi, had published my first article, "Un Peuple Opprimé" in the *Revue Internationale*, which she edited and le Comte O'Kelly de Galway, le Comte de Crémont and M. de Godre, a writer on a Catholic paper, *L'Univers*, who also acted as secretary to the Association, and others, whose names, pronounced in French, one hardly recognised as of Irish origin, but when written, looked Irish enough. I think the only one there who had been in Ireland, beside myself, was Count Bonaparte Wyse. Most of them were interested in philology and genealogies and many in proving that they were descended from Irish kings. Count O'Kelly de Galway made genealogies his special study and (I think) profession, for he called on me a few days later to offer to trace mine. He was rather shocked when I told him I had no time to waste on hunting up ancestors and left that to Aunt Lizzie who made rather a hobby of it; she said she had discovered that the Gonne family had emigrated in the dim ages to Scotland, and some had returned to Mayo, whence our branch of the family came. But when she said that some of our ancestors had presented loyal addresses to English kings, I lost all interest and even felt they had better be left in oblivion. Later, when I started my little paper *L'Irlande Libre* I could have made it a paying concern, which it never was, if I had consented to accept genealogies proving that those who sent them were descended from some of the Irish kings. I always vetoed these genealogies as of no interest to a Republican paper.

I was the only woman at the banquet; when I asked the reason, I was told that membership of La Saint Patrice was (in true Irish fashion) confined to men. At first they had invited ladies to the yearly banquet, but this had been stopped by decision of the Committee. I indiscreetly asked why, and Count d'Abbadie d'Araste told me: "Because of a regrettable incident." Curiosity got the better of discretion, and from Count Bonaparte Wyse I learnt that a certain member, a distinguished military gentleman, had invited as his guest a lady whom he had introduced as his cousin; but later the Committee had discovered she was not related to him by ties of blood. After that the Committee had decided that no ladies should be invited to the banquet as members could not expose their wives and daughters to the possibility of such contacts. The care these gentlemen took of their ladies equalled that of the old Turk on the boat to Constantinople. The daughter of the Comte O'Neill de Tyrone, who must have been at least fifteen years older than myself, called on me a few days later. She was accompanied by a maid half her age, who sat in the antechamber while she talked with me in the drawing-room. She told me she had never been out of doors unaccompanied in her life. She was so friendly and charming that I refrained from asking her what she thought would have happened to her if she had.

The Secretary told me that, after the speeches of the President and Vice-president, I was expected to speak in reply to the toast of Ireland. I had prepared a tactful little speech on the glorious history of the Irish Brigades in France and on the bonds of sympathy they had created between France and Ireland and had carefully translated a verse out of Davis's "Fontenoy." But while eating *potage Shamrock* and *Poularde Irlandaise* and *Glace Killarney* and drinking varieties of most excellent French wine, I was trying to think of a few things which would bring reality into this very rarefied atmosphere. The President and Vice-president did all the talking necessary about the glories of the Irish Brigades and then launched into abuse of the French Republic, and I felt uncomfortable. I was enjoying the hospitality of France. I am no good at extempore speaking and always prepare my speeches, but on this occasion I decided to forget what I had prepared. After thanking them for their kind reception, I spoke of Ireland's gratitude to the Republican soldiers of Humbert and of their little green graves in Mayo, and then of the evictions and of the Treason Felony Prisoners of to-day; and appealed to them as descendants of Irishmen not to forget that the struggle for freedom was still going on, and that, while we were banquetting in honour of Ireland, Irishmen were suffering unutterable horrors in England's convict jails. There was a real movement of sympathy as I sat down and someone proposed a collection for the evicted tenants; though the Secretary said it was not customary at their banquets, it was made, and twelve or fifteen pounds were handed to me, which I asked the Saint Patrice Association to forward to an address I gave.

I had to leave early, for I was going to the *Bal Irlandais* in a Hall near the Gare de Lyon. I was met at the door by a florid gentleman who smelt strongly of whisky; many had evidently been celebrating St. Patrick in what was called the National drink. This was a more democratic affair, and no one, I gathered, enquired about relationships. Dancing was going on, and I was conducted by members of the Committee to a dais at the end of the hall.

"You will say a few words, Miss, but try and keep off politics; there are many English here; the Jockeys of Maisons Laffitte are the principal supporters of the ball."

"If I speak at all, I speak of Ireland; I cannot speak of Ireland without speaking of evictions and prisoners."

"Well, don't say too much that will hurt English feeling, you understand."

A man wearing shamrock said in an Irish voice: "Let the young lady say what she likes. Ireland for ever, I say." He was in the English army and on leave in Paris.

"I think I won't speak to-night,—people are here to amuse themselves; I have nothing amusing to say. Don't interrupt the dancing."

The florid gentleman, proud of his achievement in getting me here to give tone to the very mixed assembly (most of them had obviously been celebrating) would not be put off, so when the music ceased at the end of a dance, he got up and called for cheers for Ireland's Joan of Arc, which was responded to vociferously. I rose and bowed, and only said in French: "Remember Ireland is not free and Irishmen have to free her. Go on with your dancing. Good-bye," and then, saying I was tired, I left before the supper.

The St. Patrick Society invited me each year to its banquet and whenever I happened to be in Paris I attended. The courtly old Count O'Neill de Tyrone died and was succeeded as President by the Comte de Crémont. He insisted on women being admitted to membership, but many of the old members objected and some left the Association. Comte de Crémont was very proud of his Irish descent, but he was also proud of some former incarnation in which he remembered he had been a tiger and also he recognised me as having been his tigress mother. Being a bit of a poet, he put this imagination into verse and recited it, and severely shocked the faith and morals of Nemours de Godré. I, as a Republican, shocked him even more seriously.

After that first St. Patrick's day experience, I felt that I could count really on useful help for Ireland in France only from French people. The Irish colony, represented by the Old Brigade families in Paris, was so reactionary and hostile to the Republican Government in France, as to be embarrassing, while the Jockey crowd, dependent largely on English money for whisky to toast Ireland and St. Patrick, did not appeal to me. The most hopeful helpers might be the poor gover-nesses I had seen at the Mass at Nôtre Dame des Victoires, some living in French families or in hostels run by English patronage.

There was discontent and home-sickness among those and love of Ireland. But what could they do? A few young Irish priests, both from the Irish college and from the church in l'Avenue Hoche belonging to the Passionist order, came to me at the office of *l'Irlande Libre*, in the *rue des Martyrs* and offered help in collecting and translating articles; but when it was discovered by their superiors, it was discouraged and those who persevered were sent away from Paris.

However, Willie Yeats and I started a branch of the Young Ireland Society, as we felt we ought to try and work with our own people. Arthur Lynch and his wife, Miss Barry O'Delany, Stephen McKenna, Patrick McManus and Synge were its most notable members, but we never did much effective work, except sending votes of congratulation (or the reverse) to political groups in Ireland.

Shortly before one of the annual banquets of La Saint Patrice, a Mr. Teeling, a former employee of the Dublin Corporation, whose boast it was that he had once served in the Papal guard, arrived in Paris, and as descendant of the family of Teeling who had been hanged by the English at Ballina, just before General Humbert drove them out, he applied for a ticket for the banquet of La Saint Patrice, and of course got it. He then called on the Committee to say that he had been sent especially to Paris by the Irish Party to repudiate Miss Gonne, who was the daughter of a Colonel in the English army. Count de Crémont was very angry. His filial tiger heart rose to defend his tigress mother, and having said: "Mademoiselle Gonne requires no credentials from anybody," ordered Mr. Teeling out. Then a note appeared in a little read paper speaking of Teeling's glorious ancestry and Papal connections and again affirming he was sent by the Irish National Party on a mission to Paris to repudiate Miss Gonne.

It was only then I heard of the matter, for de Crémont came to me for the addresses of John O'Leary as head of the Fenians and of Harrington of the National League and of Michael Davitt as representing the anti-Parnellite section of the Parliamentary party. He wrote asking about Teeling, and who had sent him. All three answered that their parties disclaimed all responsibility for Teeling, and that he represented no one but himself, and all gave generous praise to my work for Ireland in France. The letters were duly read at the meeting of the committee of la Saint Patrice. I prevented their publication in the French Press on the grounds that England rules Ireland by fomenting divisions and then bases her propaganda on these divisions, as proof that Irish people are too quarrelsome to govern themselves, so it is unwise ever to refer to Irish dissensions in the foreign Press, especially on so unimportant a matter as this. I was at the height of my popularity in France and it would have taken a great deal more than that to have shaken it, so I laughed at the whole matter. I learnt later from Count d'Alton O'Shea, who, with Capitaine Patrice Mahon, were the only Republicans I had met among the descendants of the Irish Brigade, that the reason for Teeling's extraordinary attack was that he considered me responsible for inviting Amilcari Cipriani, the friend of Garibaldi, to the '98 Centenary Commemoration. He claimed to have fought against Garibaldi and looked on it as a personal matter.

Like Stephen McKenna who was living in Paris, Cipriani had gone to fight in Greece against the Turks. I had done my best to dissuade both of them, for I had no use for fighting except for the land which God has given us, or, if one is an Irishman or an Indian or an Egyptian, against the British Empire anywhere, but I had not succeeded. Cipriani was badly wounded and came back on crutches. Stephen McKenna came back so disillusioned by the modern Greeks that he hated talking of it. Cipriani was a noble, picturesque figure, and he got a great reception in Ireland when he came.

De Crémont's survival of filial sentiment had been too strong to allow him even to enquire into the motive of Teeling's attack on me. He had ordered him out with scant ceremony; if he had heard him out, he might possibly have shared his disapproval of Cipriani for he was a staunch supporter of throne and altar. "Throne" with a capital letter, but nothing could have shaken his loyalty to his tigress mother. It was also unfortunate that he and other members differed as to who was the rightful heir to the throne of France.

I was invited one day to a reception of L'Association du Saint Patrice in the salon of the Countess de Crémont. I noticed that many of the notable old members were not present. At the end of the salon there was a small dais draped in red; on it was a golden throne and several gilt chairs. My white-haired tiger son offered me his arm and led me to the dais and suggested I was to take a golden seat next the throne; His Royal Highness would shortly arrive and had consented to preside. I asked who His Royal Highness was, but I regret to say, after all these years, I no longer remember if his name was Jean or Louis. Being a Republican, I declined, and went off to eat delicious cakes in the dining-room with de Crémont's young daughter, whom I met in Dublin recently, as the charming wife of the French Ambassador to the Free State.

Pretenders to thrones were as plentiful in Paris at that time as the blackberries in the fields of the Howth of my childhood. I met three who, I was told by small groups of faithful adherents, were the legitimate rightful heirs of Saint Louis; a fourth who claimed that Alfonso of Spain had usurped his throne and a fifth who said he had the rightful claim to the allegiance of the Serbian people. Even Willie Yeats' friend McGregor, the famous oculist, I think had a throne-pretender for Scotland up his sleeve, though whether on the terrestrial or astral plane, I don't quite remember. Everybody laughed at them, but they all added interest and colour to the lives of charming but small groups of ladies and gentlemen who had leisure to occupy, and gave real thrills to American travellers lucky enough to get invitations to meet them.

I set my face against establishing Irish genealogies; I had no wish to discover rightful, legitimate or illegitimate heirs to the Ard-Rig-ship of Ireland or even to the kingship of one of her provinces. After the truce of 1921, when in Paris I attended the Irish Race Convention in the gilded salon of the Grand Hotel, I got a shock when I again saw a red-draped dais, a gilded throne and a blazoned coat of arms surmounting it and learnt that it was to be occupied by the great Duke of Tetuan, a descendent of the O'Donnells who had consented to preside. He knew nothing of Ireland except its horses and had bought some good ones for the Spanish Government. It hardly seemed to me or to Constance Markiewicz sufficient reason for erecting a throne in his honour to preside over what we hoped would be an assembly of Irish men and women whose object was to discuss the help all the scattered millions of the Irish race could give to the Republic established by the blood and sacrifices of so many young and gallant lives. I had laughed gaily at the gilded throne in de Crémont's drawing-room; I could not laugh at that throne in the Grand Hotel, and the sneers and mockery of the reporters of the French newspapers ("Voilà les Républicains Irlandais!") worried me. De Valera seemed quite content; he was a charming host. At that very time, our Republic was being bartered in Hans Place in London.

But to return to these earlier years. I was really touched by those generous letters of praise from Harrington and Michael Davitt, for I had at that time openly opposed them on several occasions. I differed from them in policy and the difference was ever widening as I realised the futility of Parliamentarianism.

A robber will not give up his spoil for the asking unless the demand is backed by force. Once a constitutional party turns its back on physical force, because, not being able to control it, it finds it embarrassing, its days of usefulness are over. It may linger on, but, being unable to deliver the goods, it falls shamelessly into the corruption of its environment.

Corruption must be buried in the purifying earth or it poisons the air; the less noble look out for themselves and use the movement to secure jobs before it finally collapses. Tim Harrington, Michael Davitt and little Pat O'Brien and some others of the Parliamentary party were great generous-hearted Irishmen and had given good, unselfish service to Ireland. It was not their fault that the movement they had worked so hard to build up had grown old and effete. Few men realise that organisations, like the human beings who compose them, follow the universal law of age and decay. Too honest to accept the many chances of personal fortune offered them if they deserted, too intent and earnest in working for Ireland and the people to spare time to use their splendid ability to work for personal gain, such men always live and die poor. Perhaps money never meant more to them than it did to me. The tragedy comes when ever-moving life, creating new life out of death, causes the nation not only to forget but to kick aside the little white stones over the dark bog where the feet of the Queen have rested on her march to freedom. The people do forget and are often unjust, yet it is not ingratitude but only life itself in its eternal movement that makes them seem forgetful. A funeral is always tragic. The funeral of the Parliamentary party should have taken place when its leader Parnell was lowered into the grave at Glasnevin in October 1891.

He had failed when he had repudiated acts of violence. He was never a physical-force man himself, but he had walked hand in hand with physical force in the early days when luck and the spiritual forces of Ireland were with him, so that even

ordinary words from his lips became charged with great significance and power. Luck deserted him when he deserted the
force which had made his movement great.

I was inclined to think he had been murdered. I had dined
with him at Dr. Kenny's house a week or two before his death;
he had just finished a highly successful tour through Ireland.
There had been horrid indecent opposition at his meetings,
led by Tim Healy, but on the whole he was triumphing; the
people were coming back to him, and once more he had the
backing of the physical-force Party who had begun to support
him, from the moment that Gladstone ordered Ireland to give
him up, and that is the Party the English always fear.

By chance I was on the boat that bore his dead body back to
Ireland, for I had not thought to attend his funeral. There was
a terrible storm and all the day of burial it rained as if nature
mourned for him. Some said Parnell was not in the coffin and
would appear again; more said he had been murdered. Colonel
O'Kelly and Pat O'Brien, his devoted friends, had rushed from
London to Brighton when they heard of his death. Neither of
them were allowed to look on the face of their dead leader
though they arrived but a few hours after his death. The coffin
was closed.

I stood in the thick mud of Glasnevin among a dense and
silent throng. Dusk was coming on. As the thud of the earth
sounded on the coffin, a rift in the leaden sky parted the clouds
and a bright falling star was seen. Hundreds of others saw it
as I did. The Parliamentary Party was dead before Parnell,
and should have been buried with him. It is an ungracious task
to kick about a corpse; it is what Griffith and Sinn Fein had to
do and I helped because its leaders refused to bury it.

I never ceased to love my old friends, only their movement
had to die that the young might live.

Life out of death, life out of death eternally.

CHAPTER XIII

COUNTERING A PLOT

IT HAD BEEN one of our late nights in my rooms over Morrow's Library, for Anna Johnson and Alice Milligan from Belfast were staying in Dublin and Anna had read us some of her poems and we were full of almost envious admiration of some numbers of the *Shan Van Voght*, the daring little paper Anna and Alice were editing. They were so different but worked so well together,—Anna, tall and romantic with her long face and tender dreamy eyes,—Alice small, aggressive and full of observant curiosity. I thought Dublin would have to look to its laurels if it were not to be outdone in literary journalism by Belfast. Willie Yeats had read his play, *The Countess Kathleen*; he wanted to have it produced in Dublin and he wanted me to play in it. He said he had written the part of the Countess Kathleen for me and I *must* act it. I was severely tempted, for the play fascinated me and I loved acting, but just because I loved the stage so much I had made the stern resolve never to act. I was afraid it would absorb me too much to the detriment of my work. I knew my own weakness, and how, when I got interested in anything, I was capable of forgetting everything else,—house-building, evicted tenants, political prisoners, even the fight against the British Empire, might all disappear in the glamour of the stage; it was the only form of self-discipline I consciously practised. "I am a horse that has to wear blinkers to prevent being side-tracked,—I must not look to the right or the left." Later, in 1900, when I started *Inghinidhe na hEireann* we had a dramatic class and I used to teach in it all I had learnt in my short-lived stage adventure that had so enraged Uncle William, but I would never act myself in any of the plays we used to produce. Sally and Mary Algood, the beautiful Maire ni Shulaigh and Mary Quinn, all members of the Dramatic Class and of *Inighinidhe na hEireann*, often wondered at my unshakable resolve. The only exception I ever made was when I played Cathleen ni Houlihan, and I did it because it was only on that condition that Willie Yeats would give us the right of producing his play, and I felt that play would have great importance for the National movement.

That evening Willie Yeats was sad and tried hard to persuade me to act the part of Countess Kathleen. "I wrote it for you and if you don't act it we shall have to get an actress from London to take the part," which eventually he did with no marked success.

Edward Martyn was writing his first plays and had promised to finance production: Willie Yeats and George Moore were determined to have their plays given in Dublin and we were all anxious to help. It was part of the movement for capturing the intellectual life of Ireland for the National cause.

John O'Leary and J. F. Taylor both approved of my refusal to act. They probably understood my character and my fear of an absorption which would be detrimental to my work, in which they were interested, especially in its French side, that was beginning to be of real importance to the National struggle.

Taylor was often inclined to be impatient with Willie Yeats; he wanted more directness. His own contribution to the literary movement was a brilliant *Life of Owen Roe O'Neil*; but his real genius lay in his oratory and penetrating intellect. If he had lived, he would have been famous; even his honesty in politics couldn't have prevented it. He disliked the mists of the Celtic Twilight which shrouded with auras many weak effusions, just as fairies and the ancient gods protected George Russell's bad paintings. But in the case of Willie Yeats he was entirely unjust in his criticism, for neither fairies nor ancient

gods had ever cause to complain of the new clothes Willie put
on them and in which, round 1900, they became the fashion.
Douglas Hyde, devoted to the revival of the Irish language,
would have had more cause for complaint on the score that the
materials for these rainbow garments were not entirely of Irish
weave, but he never did. I used to say to Taylor: "Everyone
must work according to his temperament." It was my philosophy of life applied to art and politics. I never willingly discouraged either a Dynamiter or a constitutionalist, a realist or a
lyrical writer. My chief preoccupation was how their work
could help forward the Irish Separatist movement.

The dawn was approaching before the last of my friends went
and the unfortunate sleuths, standing in Frederick Street, were
able to go home and I and Dagda retired upstairs to our
beds.

I was asleep when, at 9 o'clock, the maid brought me my tea
and the daily papers, which I would hardly rouse myself to
open. When I did, I became very wide-awake, for in big
headings I read: "Irish and Nihilist Plot to Assassinate the
Czar," and lower down, in the text I saw that Irishmen had
been arrested in France, in Holland and in England.

What could it mean? Only a few days before I had come from
Paris where preparations for decorating the streets for the Czar's
visit were in progress and the great new bridge over the Sein
that was to be named Le Pont Alexandre was to be opened on
the occasion in honour of the Alliance which would secure
France from the haunting obsession of German invasion. Even
the French socialists, though not enthusiastic, were silent.
French diplomacy had triumphed over British; the Alliance,
planned by General Boulanger, was an accomplished fact. If
anything interfered with the Czar's visit, all would be undone
and the Socialist opposition would flare into life at the insult
of unwanted decorations and the unnamed bridge. The anti-
British party would suffer a terrible set-back. France could not

remain isolated and would seek a British Alliance. But what had Ireland to do with this? Why were Irishmen arrested? It could only be the work of the British Secret Service.

Leaving my breakfast tray untouched on the bed I dressed hastily and Dagda and I, followed by the two G. men already standing at the hall-door, walked quickly to J. F. Taylor's lodgings in Ely Place. He was on the doorstep preparing to go to the Law Library where barristers spend their mornings. "You, out so early! Have you another legal letter to write about stolen property?" he laughed.

"I have sacrificed sleep and breakfast to catch you, and if you have time, and there is any tea left in your teapot, you shall give it to me and we can talk out of ear-shot of these two followers of mine."

Taylor had read the morning papers but was inclined to discount a newspaper scare.

"It is more than that; it is the British Secret Service at work. Irishmen arrested in France, Holland, and England. I am crossing to-night to prevent extraditions. You have promised to defend any prisoner I am interested in. I am terribly interested in this unknown Bell arrested in England. He may be an honest fool, or he may be a knave. But through him we may get to the bottom of this mystery." And I outlined the possible diplomatic consequence involved and convinced Taylor of the urgency of the situation. "The Irish cause in France is ruined if the Irishmen are convicted. You must stop their conviction."

Generous as ever, Taylor put aside his own work and that night we crossed to England together. After breakfast at the Euston Hotel we went to Dr. Mark Ryan's house in Gower Street and found the doctor in his consulting room very perturbed and in very bad humour. When I said: "There is another prisoner arrested and Mr. Taylor has promised to defend him," he answered:

"Indeed, we will not defend him. If the Irish Americans have got themselves into the mess, they will have to get themselves out of it. I will have nothing to do with the matter."

"But I will," I said softly and then sat back and let Taylor and Dr. Ryan talk it out. With his clear, trained mind, Taylor was trying to find out exactly what Dr. Ryan knew and to what extent, if any, the Irish revolutionary organisation was involved. From the doctor's genuine indignation, I think we both were satisfied that the organisation of which he was the head knew nothing and had not been even consulted or warned of any activity of the *Clan-na-Gael*, the American organisation, in Europe.

"If Miss Gonne's theory is correct and this is a British Secret Service job to upset French diplomatic relations and injure Ireland, the more we find out about it the better," said Taylor.

"I will have nothing to do with it," repeated the doctor, but when he saw that we were both determined, he became more amenable, only objecting that there was no money available for the defence.

"As far as I am concerned," said Mr. Taylor, "that doesn't matter. I practise at the English as well as at the Irish bar. But a solicitor will be necessary. I doubt if any good man will undertake the case without a provision of £100."

"We have no money," repeated Dr. Ryan.

"The Irish American organisation has," said Taylor.

"Yes and they should pay, as it is their own men who are involved, but it will take time to get into communication."

"And time," said Taylor, "is what we can't afford or the English will be planting a lawyer of their own to defend Bell and have things all their own way."

"Well, we have no money."

"I can raise money at once," I said, and both Dr. Ryan and Taylor protested.

"I will see that the Clan refunds if you do," said the doctor, for which I was thankful, for my own account was always overdrawn, but I never let want of money prevent me from doing anything I really wanted and I felt the bank who held my trust securities and where many of my family had accounts would not refuse me an extra overdraft of £100. If they did, I reflected, I still had some jewelry to pawn, but I said nothing of this and only asked who was the best solicitor to engage. Taylor thought that the firm of Charles Russell, who was fresh from the triumph of exposing the Pigott forgeries, would be the best if it could be persuaded to take up the case, which was doubtful, as the Russells had little love for revolutionaries. Taylor, I think, secured some sort of I.R.B. credentials from Dr. Ryan to show Bell so that he would not hesitate to entrust his case to him, and we departed, Taylor to seek an interview with Bell and I, first to Cox's Bank to arrange for an overdraft and then to Charles Russell's office.

I had a long time to wait as I would not confide my business to any of his clerks or leave a message. At last Charles Russell Junior arrived; he recognised me though we had never met and we talked of Irish affairs and of mutual friends and then I told him my business. He did not look pleased. "But who is behind this?"

"I am, Mr. Russell," and I showed him my cheque for £100.

"But who is behind you? For whom are you acting? That is a fair question for any lawyer to ask before taking up a case."

"I am acting for myself as member of the Amnesty Association. We find it easier to stop a man getting into prison than to get him out when he has been convicted," and with that he had to be content. As he seemed to be still hesitating and asked me who gave me his address, I added that I had come to him because, since his experience of the British Secret Service in the Pigott Forgery Case, I thought he would not be surprised at any mean despicable thing the English would do to injure

Ireland's reputation, and that I was certain this was another case of the sort.

He undertook the case. I gave him the London address of Mr. Taylor whose name was familiar to him and whom he praised. I had just time to go and see Kathleen before meeting Taylor at the Grosvenor Hotel. As he had anticipated, a strange lawyer had already seen Bell whose real name was Ivory and was offering to defend him, but on seeing Mr. Taylor's credentials the prisoner at once promised to have nothing to do with the other lawyer and gladly accepted his services. "He is a decent poor fellow," said Taylor. "You were right, he knows nothing about a plot against the Czar, but I am afraid there is damning evidence against him about a dynamite plot in England."

I wired Millevoye and Arthur Lynch who was on the staff of the Paris *Journal* that I would be in Paris next morning and asked them to meet me at the Gare du Nord.

"Your Irish Revolutionaries are even worse fools than I took them to be and I beg you will not mix yourself up in this idiotic and wicked affair. You will risk your own popularity here and you will undo all the work you have done to create sympathy for Ireland in France if you do not repudiate them at once," said Millevoye.

We were in the Lynch's apartment in the Rue Chaptal where we had gone from the Gare du Nord to talk matters over. Millevoye was very exasperated and the Press was decidedly bad, full of nasty references to unwanted revolutionists from other countries, etc.

"How you go on, my friend," I replied. "And you know nothing of what you are talking about, any more than the Irish Revolutionists know about a plot to assassinate the Czar! All I ask you to do is to prevent the extradition of Tynan; hold him in jail as long as you like till the truth is proved, but don't hand him over to the English. Holland is sure to follow

France's example about the men. Don't set a bad example by handing over a political prisoner. My friends, the Irish revolutionists, may have been arranging a little dynamite plot in England,—more power to them!—though whether they chose their time wisely is another matter; but the whole story about the plot against the Czar is an invention of the British Secret Service, and for God's sake don't you also walk into the trap by extraditing Tynan, so that they can go on inventing whatever suits them. I certainly will *not* repudiate them; but I have come to Paris to say that I know for certain that this talk of a plot against the Czar, as far as Irishmen are concerned, is an English lie."

Millevoye was hard to convince; the arrests in France and Holland had given colour to the tale. The French police would not have acted without some evidence. He was only concerned in keeping my name clear of the whole affair. I could have hit Arthur Lynch when he put in that Tynan was No. 1 of the Invincibles and that, even if he did believe the Czar was a tyrant who should be exterminated, he ought to be released at once in France, the country of Liberty.

I turned on him ruthlessly and rudely: "Lynch, you don't know Tynan and you don't know anything about Irish revolutionists. We don't know even if Tynan is the No. 1 you talk about. The English papers say so, which is a reason for thinking he probably is not. Whether he is No. 1 or not, he has evidently walked into a trap and deserves a little prison for having been so stupid. But I do care that he should not be extradited, which would make it so much more difficult for us to get at the truth. I am not asking Millevoye to do anything but stop his extradition, to use all his influence with the magistrates and with the police to prevent that," and turning to Millevoye, I whispered: "I ask that in the name of our alliance."

I got the promise and then I asked Millevoye to help to draw up some interviews for me to sign which Arthur Lynch would take round to the French papers. "*Only, remember, no repudiation of my friends the Irish Revolutionaries.*" I was almost too tired to think and my nerves were at breaking point. I had not been in bed for two nights and ever since I had read those headlines in the Dublin papers I had been working at high tension to counter the British plot. Annie Lynch, coming in, said I looked so tired and with her usual kindness wanted to put me to bed in her room, but I wanted to go to my own flat for I knew I would sleep for twenty-four hours without waking.

Tynan was not extradited, and two months later, when I was again in Paris, Arthur Lynch triumphantly brought him to call on me. He said he wanted to thank me for his release. Remembering my calm remarks about not caring how long he remained in the French jail I felt the thanks were undeserved and that Arthur Lynch had been generous in not repeating them to Tynan, who was really the No. 1 of the Invincibles, a brave good Irishman who remained my friend and until his death in 1936 always sent me Xmas greetings and often small subscriptions for the young I.R.A. prisoners in Ireland for whom I am still working.

I did sleep eighteen hours without waking and my post brought me a big card of invitation with the City of Paris Arms emblazoned on it, for the reception at the *Hotel de Ville* in honour of the Czar and Czarina of all the Russians.

On the raised dais in the magnificent hall I had an opportunity of looking closely at that dreamy-eyed potentate the Czar, strikingly resembling his cousin George, afterwards George the fifth of England, except for those dreamy far-away-looking eyes, and at his flushed, nervous-looking wife, the Czarina.

The American Ambassador to London told me later that Queen Victoria had herself done her best to prevent the Czar and Czarina from coming to Paris by urging the danger. "My police have unearthed one plot; they may not always be able to protect you." And how the Czar had smilingly replied:

"I am not afraid to go to France, and as for the Irish, why should they be my enemies? They can have no quarrel with me."

As I looked at the Czar and the tired Czarina, soon to become a mother, in all that glare of splendour, they seemed to me marked out for a tragic destiny and I was not the only one who felt that strange overshadowing gloom.

I did not go to Ivory's trial at the Old Bailey. For some reason Taylor did not want me there, but he told me about it afterwards. We had talked over the case, which he had very much at heart. He had gone himself to Holland to gather evidence and had interviewed the two Irishmen released by the Dutch authorities at the same time as Tynan was released in France. There had been a third man with them, a leader, they said, but he had vanished before they were arrested. Taylor was convinced he was the link with Scotland Yard.

Taylor had taken a great liking to Ivory. "He is a sincere man and very brave." He told me the English were afraid of the case and would have liked to drop it if they could. They had offered Ivory, if he would plead guilty, to give him a comparatively light sentence and to release him on grounds of health within a year, when the sensation was forgotten. Yet the evidence against him was damning, as far as a dynamite plot in England was concerned, for the police had captured documents. "Except for not finding the dynamite actually in his possession, they have material enough to get him a life-sentence. I had to tell him this," said Taylor, "when he asked me to advise him what he should do about the offer made to him by the police. He asked me which would be the best for Ireland and I had to say to refuse to plead guilty and let the case go on, but I would not urge him to do it. He replied that he was an Irishman who had pledged himself to fight for Ireland's freedom. He had come from America prepared to sacrifice his life and he would go on." Taylor was terribly moved. "I have one chance to save him. I admit that it is slight; even to you, I don't want to say more now. It is not eloquence which will save him. I will leave that to my American colleague." The *Clan-na-Gael* had sent over a lawyer to defend Ivory and I gathered he and Taylor were not pulling too well together and I don't think Taylor confided to him what he said he would not confide to me.

The days before the trial, the English papers sailed near the wind in regard to contempt of court and prejudicing the case against the prisoner by demanding exemplary punishment for dynamiters and terrorists who did not hesitate to wage their nefarious war on crowned heads and on peaceful English people. I thought of the thousands of peaceful Irish homes being destroyed by battering rams and fire. There must always be war till Ireland is free.

I read the account of the commencement of the trial in the early evening papers and my heart sank. But on returning to my hotel, I found a telegram from Taylor: "Ivory free sailing America."

I heard about it later from Taylor. At the lunch adjournment, Taylor had stood up and asked the judge kindly to tell Inspector X. to be sure to have the note-book with notes of interviews he had had in Belgium on two separate dates which Taylor named. The judge looked intently at Taylor; "Is that necessary?"

"Your Lordship, it is; my whole cross-examination will be on it."

"Very well," replied the judge.

Taylor had shot his bolt and few in court had even noticed it. He had no evidence; he had only intuition. The suspense of that lunch hour must have been worse on Taylor than on the prisoner who had accepted his doom.

When the court resumed, to the amazement of everybody and the wild indignation of the British public, freely expressed in leading articles next day, the Crown Prosecutor announced a Nolle Prosequi on the grounds of insufficient evidence.

The judge read Ivory a pious sermon and said, as he had evidently been keeping bad and dangerous company and as he was an American citizen, he would order him to be put on a boat and sent back to America.

But he went as a free man, thanks to the unsparing and unselfish work of J. F. Taylor and his courage in acting on intuition. As for Taylor, the reaction after the strain and anxiety made him ill. I was frightened by his appearance. Though I did not know it, he was already suffering from the illness of which he died shortly after. "I will be all right when I have had a little rest; I am going to a nursing home for a bit. I will prepare notes on the case and we may be able to have it exposed in the English Parliament if some of the Irish M.P.s. will take it up." I suggested that Michael Davitt would do it, but Taylor thought a lawyer would be able to bring out the points better and decided he would give his notes to Tim Healy. I hardly knew Tim except from reading his witty satirical speeches, and was satisfied.

I have since often reproached myself for having let the matter rest there; for this case, which might have had real diplomatic reactions against the British Empire, was quietly interred by Tim Healy, as many other things damaging to the British Empire were interred. He certainly earned his Governor-generalship of the Free State!

Later, a well-intentioned Irish back-bencher raised the Ivory case from a wrong angle and asked about the injustice of arresting an innocent American citizen merely because he was of Irish origin. It was Ivory's guilt (from an English point of view) that should have been brought out in asking the reason of his release, shewing how the whole case had broken down because England dared not risk the exposure of how Scotland Yard had engineered a bogus plot on the Czar in order to discover it, a bogus plot grafted onto a real Irish plot shepherded by an agent provocateur.

CHAPTER XIV

SPIES

At a reception given by Madame Ratazzi, the great-niece of Napoleon, all Paris, literary, political and artistic, had congregated. The great salons were so crowded it was hard to move. A distinguished-looking Frenchman spoke to me:

"Mademoiselle, we French people are very interested in your work for your country."

"French people are very kind to me."

"Those who know you, and those who do not, wish to help you. You are being spied on by the English."

I smiled. "In Ireland, yes. I cannot move without being followed by detectives, but in France I am free."

"You are spied on just as much but more cleverly. Take care; the name of everyone who calls on you is transmitted to the British Embassy and every letter you receive photographed and copies sent to the British."

"We know the Post-office is held by the English," I replied, "so no one in Ireland is foolish enough to send through it any letter they mind being read."

"It is not the Post-office here you have to fear, but spies in your own house, and because they are French, I am authorised to warn you. Look out yourself. I say no more." Then, other people coming up and speaking to me, he was lost in the crowd. A French deputy, who saw me looking as if I would have liked to say more to the man who had passed on, said:

"He is a high official at the Prefecture."

As I let myself into my flat I felt puzzled and worried. Maria sleepily shuffled out of her room. "Does Mademoiselle want anything?"

"No, Maria, go back to bed." In my room I thought hard. My household at that time was composed only of Maria and myself. Maria was the maid of all work I had engaged when I first took my little flat in Paris four years ago, an elderly woman, a good cook, very efficient and I thought very devoted to me. Dagda, who slept on a mat in my room, came and put his great head on my knee. Maria was a widow with one son for whom she slaved. I had helped her to get a job for him as accountant in a business house and had given her the servant's room on the sixth floor for him, because I liked to have her sleeping near me. She had been so kind and nursed me so well when I was ill; she said, after her son, she loved Mademoiselle and no one else in the world. It seemed impossible that Maria could be a spy; besides she was nearly illiterate, although she had given her son a good education.

I went to the waste-paper basket and took out the envelopes of the letters I had received by the evening post and examined them very carefully. I could not discover much but by the post marks I should have received them a day earlier. I opened a secret drawer in a small cabinet where I kept a few precious letters of purely personal and not political interest; old letters of Tommy's, a letter to Tommy from my mother, yellow with age, and one or two other recent letters I had been foolish in keeping but had not had the courage to destroy,—these last were missing.

"Dagda, are you the only one I can trust?" I kissed the head of the Great Dane and, feeling rather miserable, got into bed.

Next morning, when Maria was out with her market-basket, I determined to make an examination of the servant's room on the sixth floor. I had no key, but the concierge I guessed had pass-keys to all the rooms. I told her I had to get some things in a hurry that I had stored there, and Maria had just gone out. At first she denied ownership of a pass-key, but I got over her scruple and she went up with me.

A camera stood on a tripod near the window and I picked up a little bit of film with photographed writing on the floor. The concierge watched with interest. I said:

"My letters have been arriving with so much delay, I wondered if you forgot sometimes to bring them up in time."

"Mademoiselle knows well I am punctual and Mademoiselle is very right to find out where the blame lies," she replied stiffly.

We went downstairs. "Say nothing to Maria of this," I said to the concierge and went out on the Avenue de la Grande Armée. I saw Maria with her market-basket and Dagda returning from the market.

"Dagda," I said, "a day in the country will do us both good, come along."

The dog understood and bounded with joy; I just felt incapable of dealing with the situation.

"Oh, Mademoiselle, you are surely not going out before lunch; you said you had invited a gentleman."

It was true and I had forgotten.

"Ask him to eat the lunch but tell him I was called out unexpectedly on important business; I don't know when I will get back."

Dagda and I went off to the Gare de Lyon and took a train to Fontainebleau and wandered the whole day in that marvellous forest, finishing up with supper in the little restaurant near Les Gorges de Franchard. I was fond of Maria and so was Dagda. It seemed so impossible that she was a traitor. I recalled a strange incident to which in my overcrowded life I had not given the attention I should have, but which, though strange enough, still seemed to prove Maria's love for me. I

Maud Gonne in a pale primrose satin brocade dress, *c.* 1885-1886.

Maud Gonne, photograph by Chancellor & Company, Dublin, *c*. 1890-1891. It was used by W.T. Stead in his piece on Maud Gonne in the January 1892 issue of *The Review of Reviews* in which he described her as 'one of the most beautiful women in the world'.

Maud Gonne, a photograph by Chancellor & Company, Dublin, *c.* 1892-1893. This was used on the dust jacket and as the frontispiece of the first edition of *A Servant of the Queen*.

Maud Gonne in her favourite winged hat and wearing her Inghinidhe na hEireann brooch, *c*. 1900-1902.

Maud Gonne wearing her Inghinidhe na hEireann brooch, *c.* 1900-1902.

A photograph of Maud Gonne in the title role in the first production of W.B.
Yeats's play *Cathleen Ní Houlihan* on 2 April 1902, with W.G. Fay as Peter
Gillane, Maire T. Quinn as Bridget Gillane, and J. Dudley Digges as Michael
Gillane. It was performed with AE's play *Deirdre* at St Teresa's Hall,
Clarendon Street, Dublin.

Opposite page, above. The battering ram after it had done its work. Such
rams were used in evictions in C. Donegal and elsewhere. This was, apart
from the author's portrait, the only illustration to appear in the first edition
of this book. Below: 'The Irish Joan of Arc sounds a note of discord': a
cartoon in June 1903 issue of *The Gael* (New York and London), implying
the influence upon Maud Gonne of John MacBride who, because of his anti-
British activities in the Boer War, could not return to Ireland. In a fracas that
became known as the Battle of the Rotunda, Maud had intruded onto the
platform at a meeting there of the Irish Parliamentary party with several
others, including Edward Martyn, to arouse hostility against a proposal to
present a loyal address to King Edward VII, who was about to visit Ireland.

Maud Gonne in France with her two year old son Seán, in 1906.

had returned from the South of France and was only staying in Paris to get a change of clothes and a night's rest on my way to Ireland. Before I was up in the morning, a doctor, whom I had met at the house of a French lady, called with a letter from her, urging me to see him as she was anxious about my health. Not wishing to appear ungrateful, I told Maria to bring him in. Maria continued packing my trunk while he examined me. He looked very grave and told me I could not possibly travel; I might die of haemorrhage if I did. He wanted me to go at once into a nursing home and said he would promise to cure me in ten days or a fortnight at most with a very slight operation. Maria had suddenly rushed across the room and thrown herself on her knees by the bed.

"Mademoiselle, don't listen to him, I implore you. He will kill you. Go and see a doctor in your own country."

I was about to apologise for Maria and explain that I could not delay my journey, when, looking up, I saw the doctor's face livid with rage.

"Get out of this at once, how dare you speak," he shouted to Maria. "It shall be the worse for you." She had risen from her knees and was facing him.

"*You* get out of this; I know you and I will not let you kill Mademoiselle."

It was a strange scene. They evidently knew each other. Both were so excited it was with difficulty I made them listen.

"Maria, get on with my packing; there is much to do. Please, Doctor, you must excuse her great affection for me."

He recovered himself with difficulty, saying: "You are wrong to trust that woman; I am sorry you won't take my advice," and left abruptly.

I tried vainly to get Maria to explain what she had meant by saying: "I know you"; she only kept muttering: "Have

nothing to do with him; he will kill you; he is your enemy."
I had a lot to do before leaving Paris, but in London the
incident worried me and I dropped in on an old doctor of the
family, whom I knew since I was a child, and told him that a
French doctor had said I was in danger of a sudden
haemorrhage and needed an immediate operation. He
examined me and said: "Nothing wrong with you, young
lady, I assure you. My advice to you is to avoid that doctor,
for there are blackguards even in my profession."

I had thought of that incident again when a queer Frenchman, M. de Mondion, who had travelled much in India and
was said to be employed by the Russian Secret Service, told
me there were few houses where he felt safe in dining because
the English Secret Service were trying to poison him.

"They nearly succeeded in India; they may succeed here;
they are still trying. Have they never tried to get rid of you?
You should be careful," he told me.

Two months later he was dead and the woman with whom
he lived came to me and said he had been poisoned and that
the French police had refused to allow a post-mortem examination. She had written to the Minister of Justice without avail;
she was not his wife and had no legal status. She wanted me to
use influence to have the body exhumed. I knew it would be
useless. Dog doesn't eat dog, neither do the international police
forces embarrass each other, where there are diplomatic reasons
against it.

I thought of all those things as Dagda and I ambled through
the forest of Fontainebleau. We got home late that night. I had
decided to deal with the situation and, when Maria brought
my morning coffee, I said abruptly:

"Maria, you are dismissed. You leave to-day. I will give you
a month's wages instead of notice. I know you are a British spy."

She at once flew into incoherent, indignant expostulations
and denials in a loud voice, asserting her innocence and calling

God to witness. The rest of the scene was quite unexpected. There was a rush and a loud scream and Maria lay on the floor with Dagda's great paws on her shoulders; he was growling menacingly.

I sprang from my bed and seized Dagda's collar in one hand, and with the other reached for and turned the key in the bedroom door. In a very quiet voice I said:

"Stop screaming and listen. I will let the dog kill you if you do not answer truthfully. See, I have the key, so no one can save you. You are a filthy spy, but the British Embassy would not receive a disgraceful old cook like you. Where do you or your son deliver the letters he photographs or the papers you steal?"

"It is not the English but M. Clemenceau who has your papers."

I was still not satisfied.

"I don't believe you know M. Clemenceau. Where do you deliver the letters?"

She gave me an address I knew well. It was the house of a Frenchman who was very assiduous in helping me and had organised several of my lectures.

"He does it for Clemenceau, not for the English," gasped Maria.

Dagda was still growling softly. I had got all the information I needed and I pulled him off Maria's shoulders. He had not bitten her, only thrown her down with his great weight, but had acted entirely on his own good sense. He was as interested in the work of Irish freedom as I was. He was the most wonderful friend I ever had. Very shaken, Maria got up.

"Mademoiselle, I will get back the papers for you but don't send me away; I love you."

"Pack and go. I don't want the papers; they have been soiled by your dirty hands. You or Clemenceau can keep them as souvenirs. I give you an hour to clear out."

Tearfully Maria took her leave. I believe she did love me and had risked a good deal when she thought my life in danger. Possibly even she did not know my papers were delivered to the English. Perhaps the Secret Police held her through her son, a vain, weak young man, possibly he may have done some trivial shady act which he was afraid might come to light.

Late that afternoon I was dozing in an armchair, for I had not slept much the night before. I had told the charwoman who replaced Maria that I would see no callers and didn't want to be disturbed. I woke to see Mr. O., the man to whose house Maria had confessed my papers had been delivered, looking at me.

"How did you get in?" I asked him.

"By the door of course," he answered. "Your new maid said you were not at home, but my business is so urgent I disregarded her."

"Get through with it quickly then, for I am in no mood for talk."

He unfolded a newspaper. It announced an interpellation for the following day on the Cornelius Hertz scandal.

"What has that to do with me?"

"You know very well you are the one person who can stop it," he replied. Cornelius Hertz was a big financier, a notorious British agent, who had put the distance of the English Channel between himself and French law. He had financed extravagantly Clemenceau's little-read newspaper, *La Justice*. The interpellation was on that.

"You must make Millevoye withdraw that question. It will be very awkward for you if you don't, because you have lost certain papers and would not wish them published."

"Thank you, Monsieur. Before you spoke I had only a general interest in this question, for I don't meddle in French politics, but now that you show me the connection it has with stolen property of mine, I will urge Mr. Millevoye to push the matter vigorously and ask him to secure me a place in the public gallery to listen to his exposure of British agents; and now, as I don't consort with thieves or spies, you had better go at once or I will ask Dagda to put you out." He left without delay.

Clemenceau, later known as "the Tiger", was the leader of the pro-English Party in France. A man of great cleverness but entirely unscrupulous in political intrigue. The exposure by Millevoye, a few days later, of the vast sums of money paid for advertisement in Clemenceau's small paper, *La Justice*, by Cornelius Hertz, a financier reputed to be an English agent, who had had to seek safety in England, shocked France and caused Clemenceau's defeat in his own constituency to the mocking cries of "Oh yes!" (in English). Some years later he came back into public life through the less popularly controlled senate. When the Entente Cordiale, for which he unceasingly worked, had brought about the Great War, he became one of the dominating figures in the framing of the Versailles Treaty.

The incident had a sequel later. I was warned that an obscure journalist, with no reputation to lose, was to be got to produce those stolen letters of mine. One day, as I was passing the shooting gallery of Gaston Renette on the Champs Elysées, much frequented by duellists and journalists, a sudden impulse came to me to go in. Dagda and I were at once welcomed.

Looking round, I saw the editor of a paper much addicted to publishing sensational news. He had the reputation of being a deadly shot and of having fought a large number of successful duels.

"M. Dreyfus," I said, going up to him, "You are a wonderful shot; I am not a bad one, I challenge you to a match."

He looked vexed, but there was a chorus all round, "You can't refuse a match. Maud Gonne and Camille Dreyfus." The proprietor of the gallery came up to arrange the conditions. Very gallantly, M. Dreyfus proposed a handicap.

"No, equal duelling conditions," I insisted.

The cardboard figures were set up. I had not practised for years since I had learnt revolver shooting with Tommy in Rigby's gallery in Suffolk Street, Dublin, but I knew that day luck was with me.

"Feu! Un, deux, trois." Our six shots rang out, mine each time before the "Un" was pronounced, three holes almost touching each other in the cardboard head. M. Dreyfus' were more scattered and less rapid. I was unanimously declared the winner.

"Hé, Mademoiselle, I wouldn't like to fight a duel with you," said one of the journalists.

"No," I answered very clearly. "Women have as good sight and as good nerve as men. It is unjust that they are debarred from the protection of duelling. But if any man insulted me in any way detrimental to my work, I should take the insult as the challenge, and that," pointing to the cardboard figure, "would be my answer." And, followed by Dagda, I went out, hearing someone say:

"Mais elle est terrible, la belle Irlandaise." I never heard any more about the stolen papers.

At this time the vast majority of French people were bitterly opposed to any alliance with England. St. Helena had not yet been forgotten, and incidents of a more recent date, such as Fashoda, had kept this feeling alive. During all my stay in France, I found that the police on the whole shared this Anti-British feeling, and on several occasions I had reason to be grateful to them. Of course the French police as public servants had to behave, and, in fact, did behave, with great discretion. At this time Clemenceau's Pro-British party was not yet in the ascendant.

Once during the Boer War I got a verbal message from one of the high officials of the Prefecture, warning me to be extremely careful in answering letters I might receive from unknown correspondents and on no account to allow any parcels to be left at my flat when I was out, except those from big well-known shops like the Louvre or the Bon Marché. The message said my work in France was very displeasing to the British Embassy, who were looking for a chance of demanding my extradition.

A few days later I got a letter in French from a man who said he had been at some of my lectures and would like to help Ireland. He stated he was an inventor and had discovered something which would level matters a little for a small unarmed nation fighting against a great Empire. He asked me to appoint a time for him to bring enough to convince me of the possibilities of his invention. Had it not been for that warning, I certainly would have made an appointment. But as it was, my first impulse was to send the letter to the Prefecture; but, reflecting that possibly it might be from some half-crazy inventor or from some genuine revolutionist, instead I confided it to Millevoye to keep safe in case it might be useful as evidence.

Again, when a delegation, among whom were Arthur Griffith, Mary Quinn, Mrs. Wyse Power and some Irish Americans, were in Paris in answer to an invitation from the Municipal Council to visit the *Hôtel de Ville*, we were all shadowed by English detectives, one or two of whom appeared to be Frenchmen. At a public banquet organised in honour of the delegation by a Committee of French Friends of Ireland, whose President was Député Archdecon, and to which a number of the French Press had been invited, the shadowing by these detectives had got so much on the nerves of one lady of the party, that she mistook a reporter from the *Matin* searching for his place at the long table for a sleuth and, before anyone could stop her, she threw her glass of red wine over him, and spoilt his immaculate shirt front. I had to be summoned from the end of the table to try and soothe his ruffled feelings and explain the error. Duels were much the fashion at the time in

France, and the reporter was anxiously enquiring for the name of the gentleman responsible for the lady; it required some diplomacy before I could get him at last seated between myself and Député Archdecon and make him understand the error was due entirely to the English and the constant strain of for-ever being shadowed by their police. Shadowing does seem to get on some people's nerves though not on mine. I always try to turn it to good account and at least get amusement from it.

The day following the banquet Arthur Griffith and I were being closely followed, so we got into a *fiacre* and the detectives got into another. The Paris coachman entered into the spirit of the chase as well as the Irish Jarveys, but possibly thought that Arthur Griffith and I were an eloping couple escaping from detectives employed by some outraged husband. I told our coachman to drive to the Prefecture of police and both *fiacres* drew up outside. I ordered ours to drive into the big courtyard and sent my card to the Sub-Prefect whom I had once met at the races at Longchamps. In his office I immediately said I had come to enquire why I was being watched as I had certainly contravened no French law, and I had heard the detectives following me speak French. The Sub-Prefect looked amused.

"You, Mademoiselle Gonne, should know better than anyone that these are not French police. The French police have nothing against you. But what can I do? All the foreign embassies have their own agents; so long as they don't transgress our laws, we can do nothing," and he shrugged his shoulders.

"Then even in Paris I am to be worried?" And I told him of last night's incident at the banquet, at which he laughed heartily.

"Listen, Mademoiselle, we certainly can't allow our visitors to be annoyed. If anyone follows you too closely, call the first policeman you see and make a complaint and we will be able to act."

"Oh, what a great idea !" I exclaimed too joyfully. " 1 will do that. What fun to get an English policeman arrested!" And we all laughed.

But I had shown too much enthusiasm, and the Sub-Prefect, I fancy, did not want trouble and probably gave a hint to the International Police Headquarters. I never got the chance of invoking the help of a friendly *sergeant de ville*, as from that day the English sleuths became invisible to us in Paris.

CHAPTER XV

OCCULT EXPERIENCES

MADAME AVRIL DE SAINTE CROIX, whom I had met soon after I began work in France in the journalist world and with whom I had made a lasting friendship, sat on the end of my bed. She always edited my little paper, *l'Irlande Libre*, when I was away.

"Maud chérie," she said, "it is time you took over the paper. Do you realise you have been away more than three months and I am getting into trouble on the Irish side of the paper? I get articles and reports of meetings; I cut them down to a quarter for publication and then I get furious letters from the people whose articles I have cut and still more furious letters from other people who say they should never have been published in a Republican paper because they are not from the right party. I don't know anything about your Irish parties but the sentiments of the articles seemed all right to me. When I write, you never answer letters; it is very difficult."

I laughed. "Chérie, you are an angel; never mind what anyone says, our next number will be sensational. A Queen Victoria number that will please everybody at home and abroad. The old miser is having another Jubilee which will rake in money for her and she is threatening to celebrate it by coming to Ireland on a recruiting compaign to get Irishmen to join her army. She has given her gracious permisson for Irish Regiments to wear the shamrock on St. Patrick's day. A great concession to Ireland! We shall have to celebrate also. See, I have written our leading article—*Reine de la Disette*.

Arthur Griffith was so pleased with it that he made me put it into English. It will appear both in *l'Irlande Libre* and in the *United Irishman*."

It did and got the *United Irishman* seized. It figured also in a sensational libel action I brought some years later against Ramsay Colles, editor of a little rag called the *Dublin Figaro*, subsidised by Dublin Castle. The *Dublin Figaro* had a leading article entitled "Miss Gonne and her Government Pension" and had the country covered with posters with this heading. Taylor appeared for me and Mr. Campbell, afterwards Lord Glenavy, appeared for Ramsay Colles and the Police. I bought a new hat for the occasion. John O'Leary sat beside me in the court house which was crowded to overflowing. Mr. Campbell read out the Famine Queen article, to my great delight, to show the sort of woman I was. We won our case triumphantly. Meeting me later in London, Mr. Campbell apologised to me for defending the *Dublin Figaro*. "Believe me, Miss Gonne, I never liked a case less and I was glad you won." He owned that Dublin Castle had paid for Ramsey Colles' defence.

"I didn't mind; we had great fun over it and it helped the anti-recruiting campaign a lot," I answered. Arthur Griffith had gone to the office of the *Dublin Figaro* as soon as he had seen the posters and had horse-whipped Ramsey Colles, who was double his size, for doing which he got a month in Mountjoy and a Ceilidh-Reception from *Inghinidhe na hEireann* on his release.

I told Ghenia (Madame de Sainte Croix) that she must carry on with the paper, as I had promised Connolly I would return to Dublin to take part in our side of the Jubilee demonstrations which we meant to make lively. "Don't think I am lazy, though I look it, lying in bed reading novels."

"No one would call you lazy, only just a little inconsequent sometimes. You start a paper and then go away and forget it and trust to luck and your friends to bring it out; when you have one thing in your head you forget everything else."

"I suppose I am like that. It's the only way I get work done. I work night and day and don't sleep; then I forget how to sleep and have to take sleeping draughts."

"I wish you would see a doctor. Taking these drugs without a doctor will play a bad trick on you some day."

I knew it was doing queer things with me which I could not understand, not making me ill, but separating my conscious from my unconscious self; for instance that morning I had received a reproachful letter from my old friend Oldham, asking why I had returned to Dublin and not let any of my friends know. He wrote that he and Taylor had been together at a meeting at the Rotunda and had seen me come in and sit down; but when they tried to get near to speak to me I had disappeared in the crowd. I never succeeded in making those two old friends believe that at that time I was in bed in my little Paris flat, and had been there for the previous fortnight.

Ida and one of her maids had seen me in her home at Airfield and on the Donnybrook Road where we used to walk as children. But Ida, being used to such things, knew it was only an apparition. Another friend wrote that he had seen me in the Albert Hall; another,—on the boat crossing to France.

I was always unconscious of these things myself. I was not even thinking about the places or the people concerned, and it only happened, when, as at present, after some great nervous effort of will, I was resting and generally taking sleeping draughts.

Miss Barry O'Delany who did secretarial work in *l'Irlande Libre* arrived and told the maid I had sent for her. Her concierge had told her that Mademoiselle Miss Maud Gonne(!) had called and gone up to her room looking for her. I had not left my bed and had not even thought of sending for her.

Willie Yeats, always interested in psychic phenomena, had tried to make experiments and get me to visit him on the astral plane, as the theosophists call it, but never succeeded in seeing me. Willie and I had tried sending messages to each other. At a fixed hour he would try to send me a thought, or I to send him one, and we would both note down on paper any thought which came into our minds and compare them when we met. We were not very successful though once or twice I did get something vaguely resembling the thought he was trying to send.

Once, when I had got hold of some haschish, that strange Indian drug, I took the prescribed dose and nothing happened; it did not even send me to sleep, so I took a much larger dose and fell asleep; I woke a short time after and found my legs paralysed; I could not walk and my heart was beating queerly, but my brain was clear. For a moment I considered ringing for Maria and sending for a doctor; but then I thought that would be foolish and that, as I had taken it for an experiment, I had better see it through. I managed to scribble on a writing pad I had on the table beside my bed that I had taken haschish and that, if I did not wake, no one was to be blamed, and then I lay still and waited. I saw a tall shadow standing at the foot of my bed and it said, or more exactly, the thought drifted through my mind: "You can now go out of your body and go anywhere you like but you must always keep the thought of your body as a thread by which to return. If you lose that, you may not be able to return."

I wished to see my sister, Kathleen, and at once I was standing by her bed. She was asleep and her little son, Toby, was asleep beside her. I tried to make her know I was there by putting my hand on her, but she slept on. I looked round the room; it was not like her room; it was much smaller and the bed was not in the same position as I knew it. I thought I would go into the nursery, opposite, where the other children slept. Again the room was unfamiliar and, instead of the children, I saw my brother-in-law, Captain Pilcher, whom I disliked, sleeping in the bed.

Then I remembered the injunction never to lose the thought of my own body if I wished to return. So I thought of it. I had a vague, fleeting impression of sea and clouds and wind and was back in my room in Paris and saw my body asleep on the bed; then, with the sensation of falling from a height, I was really lying in my bed, conscious of my heart pounding queerly.

I wrote to Kathleen next day but I got no reply for several days. My letter, sent to her Dublin house in Ely Place, had been forwarded to her to Howth. Toby had been ill; she had taken him to convalesce at Howth in the little house in which we had lived as children,—near the Bailey lighthouse. He slept in her bed. Her husband slept in the room opposite. It was all exactly as I had seen.

It convinced me of the possibility of being able to leave the body and see people and things at a distance and to travel as quick as thought. If that could be developed, how interesting and how useful! But I wanted to do it by the power of will and not with haschish, which had made me feel very ill and shaky the next day. I made many experiments, some of them remarkably successful. It is an undeveloped faculty. Muscles never used get atrophied. The faculty of getting out of the body might be developed.

I used to concentrate my thoughts on the person I desired to visit. The effort of concentration generally sent me to sleep; but for a brief moment I would be able to see them and their surroundings as I had done under haschish and sometimes, not always, to remember when I woke. But I found these experiments very exhausting and they took me away from the work I had undertaken, so I resolutely put on blinkers as I had done about the acting and renounced the experiments after a time.

Though will is all powerful, I think each human being has only a limited amount to draw on and achieves little if he fritters it on many things, and I realised that was the danger against which I had always to guard.

Cipriani, the Italian revolutionist and companion of Garibaldi, was a friend of mine. He was a scoffer at the supernatural. He told me that while he was in prison his mother had appeared to him and he learnt later that it was at the exact hour of her death. Even this did not shake his unbelief. "It was a coincidence, nothing more," he said.

"Would you call it a coincidence if I, who do not even know where you live, were able to describe to you your room and what you will be doing in it to-night?" I asked. "Come and see me to-morrow and see if I cannot tell you."

It was at the time when I was making these experiments. Next day I described to him minutely the little room he lived in the *Rue Legendre*. It looked out on a small courtyard. I described the position of the furniture, the door, the window. "You were sitting writing at the table at twelve o'clock last night."

"That is correct," he said. "But it is only a coincidence; all these lodging rooms are much the same."

"There is something which puzzled me and which I did not tell you because I think it may be a reflection of my own thoughts about you and the red shirts of the army of Garibaldi; you seemed to me to have something like a big red scarf round your shoulders."

"Now you have said something which is really amazing," Cipriani exclaimed. "Last night, when I went home, I had a cold and a bad sore throat. My Landlady, who is a kind woman, brought me a large piece of red flannel and insisted on my putting it round my neck; she said there is great virtue in red flannel, and certainly my throat is better to-day. No, that you could not have imagined."

Another curious incident I will write down here, though it did not occur exactly at this time and is difficult to account for, but which is absolutely true.

I was engaged in fairly dangerous activities at the time; I was not the least afraid of death, but I was afraid of long imprisonment or of torture for information; I am not certain I would have the magnificent courage which so many soldiers of the I.R.A. have shown. I wanted to have a certain means of escape if ever I was taken, and swift certain poison is not easily obtained, though I knew several friendly chemists who supplied me with sleeping draughts and chloroform.

I was thinking about this a good deal one night as I was going to sleep. I woke when dawn was just coming, and, standing between my bed and the window, I saw a man. My first thought was, how had he been able to get into my room without rousing Dagda, my Dane dog whom I saw sleeping quietly in his accustomed corner. The man was young and dressed in a sort of uniform, like those worn by students in some of the German universities. I sat up in bed and we looked at each other intently; then I saw the pattern of the window curtains gradually appear through him and he faded out. Into my mind came the thought: "That is the man who will supply the poison."

I was in Paris and I looked eagerly among the many people I was meeting. But I never saw anyone who resembled him. Gradually I almost forgot the incident. Some months later, when I was in Dublin, Oldham wrote to me he wanted to bring a friend of his, a doctor, who had been studying in Germany and was anxious to meet people and hear how things were going in Ireland. There were a lot of people in my rooms that evening. In Oldham's friend I recognised the man who had appeared in my room in Paris. When my guests departed I asked him to remain and I told him of our first meeting; he was quite unconscious of it and rather aghast when I told him what

I wanted. However, a few days later, he brought me a tiny bottle for which I made a little silk bag and for many years wore it as a charm round my neck and felt much comfort from its possession.

There are so many strange unaccountable things in life which my blinkers prevented me fathoming.

The beautiful dark woman with the sorrowful eyes, whom as a child, I had seen bending over my cot, is another. I used to see her occasionally at night; her visits never seemed to relate to anything in my life, but I knew her quite well and could have painted her portrait. She was rather like me, but smaller and darker. A portrait of me, painted by Kreder, a young French artist, I thought resembled her more than it resembled me. I told Willie Yeats about her and he consulted a Scotch friend of his, McGregor Mathers, a magician and head of an occult society in London, the G.D. (Golden Dawn), about her. Together they evolved the theory that she was what, in old Egyptian magic, was called the Ka. As far as I could understand them, a part of my personality had survived death in a former incarnation. McGregor said that the priests in ancient Egypt used to preserve the mummies as a means to keep the Kas of the dead people, in order to use these to perform their magic. I think it was this that gave me the idea of trying to use my dark, beautiful friend. If she was really a part of myself, she should be able to become the expression of my will which I could send out to influence people and get them to do what I wanted. So, instead of merely watching her as I used to do when a child, I called her up and sent her to people I wanted to persuade. How far this was actual fact and how far imagination I do not know, but certainly I was able to influence people's minds and get them to do things in an extraordinary way. She seemed happy doing these things for me and looked less sad. As long as she was the expression of my will, I felt that it was well, but as she grew stronger through being invoked, she seemed to develop an independent personality. She liked some people, disliked others. I loved children; she disliked them.

Willie, McGregor and his pretty wife, who was the sister of Bergson the philosopher, had arranged a sort of séance with some members of the G.D. to find out about my grey lady, as we called her, for she was always dressed in grey veils. She appeared. Mrs. McGregor gave me an exact description of her. Willie couldn't see her. They said she had confessed to having killed a child and wrung her hands in sorrow and remorse. After this I began to think she must be evil and decided to get rid of her. It seemed to me I might not be able to control her. So, resolutely I put on the blinkers and denied her existence. It was not so easy, for, whenever I was with people who had mediumistic faculties, she could appear, in spite of me.

Princess Tola Dorian, a Russian married to a French deputy, was one of these. She said she was often quite unconscious of the verses she sometimes wrote and read them afterwards with astonishment. (They were not remarkable.) One day, sitting in the twilight at my piano, she was playing Russian folk melodies and improvising. I saw my dark woman standing by the piano and denied her existence. There was a little bell standing on the piano. Suddenly it rang; no one had touched it. Tola was so frightened she went away, saying the room was haunted.

My cousin May came to stay with me in Paris. She, like Ghenia, was worried at the use I was making of sleeping draughts and chloroform. Being a nurse she knew the danger. She had tried hiding the bottle, but it was quite useless,—I always found it without searching. One day she had hidden it under the ashes in the fireplace of the maid's room. As usual I could not sleep, so got up to get the bottle out of the dressing-room. "How stupid of you, May, hiding it again," and, like someone walking in their sleep, I quietly went out of the room and down the passage into the maid's room without waking her and took the bottle from under the ashes in the fireplace and returned triumphantly. I was so proud of this exhibition of uncanny knowledge that I boasted of it next day at lunch. Millevoye was lunching with us. "Yes," he said sarcastically, "it is just as wonderful as a drunkard who in a strange place can always find the pub." I was very angry, but the thought remained. After all, it was just the same force, some evil spirit perhaps guiding me.

I went into my room and took the bottle and broke it and after that fought insomnia without drugs. I refused to let any will, human or disincarnate, overpower my own. I was not quite certain I had won that battle till I got another bottle and was able to leave it untouched on the table by my bed.

The spirit world never seemed far from me. I never saw Tommy, but often I felt him near me; several times I heard his voice, sometimes comforting me when I was unhappy; once warning me of a danger which I did not heed, though I should have,—and yet I am as sure I heard him as that I exist.

While I was experimenting with the occult, always in the hope of gaining power to use for the great objective of my life, I joined the Theosophical Society and went with Willie Yeats to visit that strange old woman, Madam Blavatsky, its founder. There was a branch of the Theosophical Society in Dublin which used to meet in Ely Place. George Russell (A.E) was the only member of it who interested me. He was then an accountant at a large drapery Store. His lectures were always good. He told me he would not become an artist and preferred the dull drudgery of figures because it did not take him away from the spiritual life as Art might have done. Like me, he had put on blinkers. But he used to paint fairies and the Irish Gods on the dull walls of the rooms where the Theosophical Society met. Most of the members were Unionists and, though it was strictly philosophical and non-political,—which in Ireland means non-national,—some of its members raised objections to my political activities.

It was about this that Willie Yeats took me to see Madame Blavatsky in London. "My dear child," she said, "of course you can do what you like in politics. That has nothing to do with Theosophy. If a man, for instance, cuts off a cow's tail" (the English papers at the time were full of talk of Land-League actrocities) "it will injure his own Kharma, but it would not prevent him being a member of the Theosophical Society. They must be flapdoodles in that Dublin branch. I will tell them so."

She was a strange, interesting figure, with big pale luminous eyes in a large yellow face. She sat in a big chair at the end of a long room in Kensington; a table in front of her and a pack of cards with which she played continually and mechanically even while she talked. She made a place for me beside her. Round the room were seated the members of the Theosophical Society; I thought they looked a nondescript gathering, though Willie told me there were interesting people among them.

The room was lit by a gas chandelier and there was evidently water or air in the pipes for it flickered badly. "Spooks in the room," said Madam Blavatsky, and in a lower tone to me: "They are all looking for a miracle." The gas flickered and went out. "Spooks," she said louder. "Now they think they have seen one. They also are flapdoodles." It was a favourite word of hers.

By the time Willie Yeats had risen to be a member of the esoteric section of the Theosophists, he had discovered that there was another society where more practical magic might be learnt and he joined the G.D. of which McGregor Mathers, an extraordinary Scotchman, was high priest. He persuaded me also to seek initiation—I passed four initiations and learned a number of Hebrew words, but there also I was oppressed by the drab appearance and mediocrity of my fellow mystics. Mrs.

McGregor and Florence Farr, the actress, were exceptions. Algernoon Blackwood, the writer of occult novels (a friend of May's) and the Astronomer Royal of Scotland, Broodie Innes, whose witch stories were exciting, lent a certain literary distinction to the G.D. but, being only an occasional visitor on my short hurried passages through London and being only a neophyte, I never met them. The *fratre* and *sorore* who so kindly made me welcome among them seemed to me the very essence of British middle-class dullness. They looked so incongruous in their cloaks and badges at initiation ceremonies; their mysterious titles, "Guardians of the Gates of the East and of the West", "Commanders of the Temple", etc., fitted them even less well than the title of "Sword-Bearer" and "Mace-Bearer" fitted little James Egan and melancholy, lanky John Parnell. The Amnesty Association had secured the position of Sword-Bearer for Egan on his return from America. In the City Hall in Dublin, these titles often amused me, especially when Sword-Bearer Egan was ordered by some unionist Lord Mayor to eject me and a crowd of Dublin workers from the public gallery where we were demonstrating against some loyal address. With mock dignity, the Sword-Bearer would march from the Lord Mayor's side of the hall to the gate separating it from the public gallery, winking and smiling at me and whispering quite unnecessarily; "Stay where ye are, Miss Gonne." Nothing but a huge force of the D.M.P. with their batons could have dislodged us.

The English love of play-acting and grand-sounding titles always amused and interested me. They had imposed them on the Dublin Corporation, and here it was again spontaneous among this mixed group of British citizens! Usually the G.D. held their ceremonies in the drawing-room of some member of the Order, but on one occasion I was summoned to an initiation ceremony of the order in the Mark Masons' Hall in Euston Road. It set me thinking. If they met in a Free-Mason Hall, perhaps the G.D. was an esoteric side of Masonry. I put the question to Willie as we went there together, but he, who had by then passed all his initiations into the higher esoteric side of the organisation, assured me it was not. Possibly, he said, the G.D. were connected with the Rosicrucians, but certainly not with Masonry.

I was not convinced, for I noticed that McGregor Mathers made use of various emblems which evidently belonged to the Hall. I resolved to put the matter to the test. I had always kept up friendly relations with the Lanes. Claude Cane, I knew, was a Mason of high standing. One day, when I was alone with him in the library of St. Wolstons, I suddenly gave the pass-word I had learned at one of the ceremonies of the G.D. He gave the correct reply and, looking at me with great astonishment, said: "Is it possible you are a mason?" I did not answer. He gave another pass-word and I gave the correct reply.

"Answer me. Where did you learn that?" I told him: "In an occult society in London." He said: "I know there are no ladies with the masons in Ireland." He told me these pass-words belonged to the higher grades of Free Masonry.

That night I wrote resigning my membership of the G.D. Free Masonry as we Irish know it is a British institution and has always been used politically to support the British Empire. It was only when Edward the VIIth succeeded in unifying the Scotch Rite and the Grand Orient that the Entente Cordiale was brought about and it finally led to the Great War. I would have no connection with it, even to learn its secrets.

Willie Yeats was very disappointed when I told him I had resigned. He still held that the G.D. was not masonic, though admitted the possibility that McGregor might have been at one time a Mason and used its pass-words. He said he really believed it possessed occult knowledge and certainly McGregor was an interesting man. "As far as I am concerned," I said, "I have severed connection. They could use me. I could not use them. I have not time to try and learn their secrets."

Althea Gyles, a young Irish artist whom I knew in the Theosophical Society in Dublin, was trying to make a precarious living in London, having failed to do so in Dublin. She told me of a man she described as a magician and extraordinarily interesting, called Aleister Crowley. He belonged to the G.D., but I had never met him. It appears that Aleister Crowley and McGregor fell out—and the whole fabric of the organisation, material and spiritual, was shattered by the quarrel. The treasured secrets of the Order appeared in cold print in a magazine edited by Crowley. I bought a copy of it in Paris from which I extracted the ritual of the G.D., but burnt the rest when bringing my belongings to Ireland, for the remainder would not have passed the censor of the Irish Free State.

I met the McGregors again before the Great War in Paris. They had a studio at St. Cloud and Mrs. McGregor, pretty and charming as ever, was painting. She had real talent; but Art does not often enrich the artist. I am afraid they were having hard times, though both were too proud to admit it. I admired their courage. McGregor was ill; he believed he was bewitched. He had some nervous trouble which gave him twitches and he looked haunted.

One evening I met him going into a Catholic church. He was seeking refuge. I think he became a Catholic before his death; he died during the Great War.

The last authentic information I had about the Order was that they were holding ceremonies invoking peace.

CHAPTER XVI

VICTORIA'S JUBILEE

IN LONDON KEIR HARDIE wrote he wanted to see me and I called at the little office of his paper in the Strand.

He said he thought it necessary to organise anti-Jubilee demonstrations. I agreed cordially and said I was on my way to Dublin for that very purpose.

"But it is here, in the heart of the Empire, we want them. We want you to speak at a protest meeting and we want the Irish to organise it."

"I am only concerned," I answered, "in upholding the honour of Ireland, and our own Capital is the proper place to do that. I am crossing to Ireland to-morrow."

"At least, you will try to get the Irish here to do something and we will co-operate."

"Michael Davitt is the man you should go to for that. He believes in the Union of Hearts; I don't."

Keir Hardie looked pained. I liked his keen, handsome Scotch face; so I said: "You organise something and I am pretty sure the Irish in London will join in. But in this matter, which is certain to involve broken heads and men being sent to jail, if the English Socialists mean business, it is for them to take the initiative and do some of the fighting. Ireland will put up her own show in Dublin."

My thoughts went back to that great meeting in Trafalgar Square which I had seen melt away before about fifty policemen and I remembered the words of that foreign revolutionist: "The English are always like that." Keir Hardie must have had almost the same thought, for he said with a sigh:

"Your countrymen are much better fighters and we want their help."

I had learned to know that English Liberals and English Conservatives were exactly the same where Ireland is concerned, and I thought English Socialists, who had very little power and little chance of getting it, might be just the same. They would use Irishmen, sacrifice Irishmen for all they were worth and take the credit. I had no desire to get any of our people in London into trouble over Jubilee demonstrations when Ireland's protest from Dublin could be made with worldwide effect. The only real help I had ever got from English Socialists was in Newcastle in defeating John Morley, when he refused to release the Treason Felony Prisoners, and then it was unconscious help. The Irish there voted for the Socialist candidate who had no chance of winning, but a three-cornered election had secured Morley's defeat.

Years after, in 1930, when English Communist organisers came to Ireland and one young puppy had the cheek to tell me they had come to teach us how to fight, I made the same answer I had made, in less brutal terms, to Keir Hardie in 1897: "Begin first by teaching your own countrymen to do a little fighting in England."

Jubilee Day arrived. All the shops which relied on Unionist custom had decorations and electric lamps for night-display. James Connolly and other friends arranged our Jubilee display also. I had obtained a window in the National Club in Parnell Square from which, on a huge screen, Pat O'Brien's photos of the Eviction scenes could be shown and the photos of the men who, during Victoria's reign, had been executed or who had died in prison.

With the help of the Corporation workmen, we had arranged for the cutting of wires to prevent the display by the Unionist shops of their electric decorations and I had been busy making black flags with suitable inscriptions in white, showing the numbers who had died of famine during Victoria's reign, the number of houses destroyed and the number of men jailed, etc. It all had to be done secretly but the secrets were well kept. James Connolly had arranged for the making of a big coffin symbolic of the fate of the British Empire, and had obtained the services of a workers' band whose instruments were so old and battered that if they were broken by the police it would be no great loss. We had arranged for the Convention of the '98 Centenary Commemoration Committees to be held at the City Hall on Jubilee Day and delegates from all over the country attended. John O'Leary presided at the Convention which lasted all the afternoon. I sat beside Willie Yeats at the Executive table, listening anxiously for the harmonious sounds of Connolly's band, while Dagda lay at my feet. My black flags were hidden in the porter's lodge, wrapped in a huge paper parcel.

It was eight o'clock when I heard the first sounds of the band. I asked John O'Leary, as chairman, to suspend the meeting and to invite all the delegates present to come out on the steps of the City Hall to see our Jubilee procession.

It had crossed Capel Street bridge in safety, James Connolly leading. A rickety hand-cart had been draped in the semblance of a hearse and was pushed by members of the Socialist Party. When we came out on the steps of the City Hall it was being got into shape and the coffin of the British Empire disclosed and the distributors of the black flags were busy placing them advantageously. Willie Yeats and I and many of the '98 Centenary delegates joined the procession, which moved off down Dame Street to the strains of a Dead March played on the cracked instruments of the band.

The police were only beginning to realise the meaning of the procession and rushed for reinforcements from the Castle and other police stations. The crowd was so dense they could not attempt to break us up till they were in force. Then foot and horse police arrived and there were charges by mounted police and baton charges and people began to be carried off in ambulances. Connolly was not a man to be easily stopped and the procession arrived in fair order at O'Connell Bridge. Here the fighting was furious and, seeing the coffin in danger of being captured by the police, Connolly gave the order to throw it in the Liffey. The whole crowd shouted: "Here goes the coffin of the British Empire. To hell with the British Empire!" Connolly was arrested. People began to notice the city was in darkness; none of the Jubilee illuminations were visible. Everywhere could be seen excited crowds being dispersed by the police. Willie Yeats and I proceeded up O'Connell Street to see how my magic lantern show in honour of Victoria was faring. People coming from the square told me it had been very successful and had attracted crowds all the evening till the news of fighting in College Green had drawn the majority away.

When Willie and I got to the National Club there was only a small crowd looking at the pictures which had been shown over and over again. The doors of the club were locked but we were let in and they were carefully locked again by Lorcan Sherlock, the Secretary, who was feeling a little nervous about how his Committee would regard his having allowed me the use of a window for the magic lantern display. We were having tea when suddenly we heard a noise outside and cries of: "The police!" I rushed to the window. Some twenty policemen with batons drawn and a few people, mostly women and children, were running in all directions; a woman lay on the ground quite still; a girl was bending over her; someone called out: "The police have killed her." I rushed downstairs to the door; it was locked and the key in Sherlock's pocket. Willie was saying: "Don't let her out."

"I must get out," I called and was making for the back door when Lorcan Sherlock consented to unlock the front door and Willie followed me out. A crowd was gathering again and the police were in an ugly mood, but somewhat frightened at having killed a woman absolutely without provocation. I fancy that, taken by surprise at the demonstration in Dame Street and summoned from all quarters to cope with it, the police had never noticed the magic lantern show and now, patrolling the city, had suddenly discovered it and had made a wild baton charge on the few harmless women and children who were still looking at it.

On all sides I heard people saying: "They have killed an old woman, the cowards!" I pushed my way into the group round the prostrate figure. Someone said: "This is your work, Miss Gonne, I hope you are satisfied."

The girl kneeling beside the old woman said:

"Mother wanted to see the pictures so I brought her when the crowd had gone and they have killed her."

An ambulance arrived and the men lifted the dead woman, and her daughter followed. A man whispered to me: "We will avenge her, Miss Gonne," and rushed off after a group of men walking rapidly down the square.

The police had vanished with the ambulance. I had not thought of taking their numbers. I looked round for witnesses. One man said he had seen a few people, mostly women, standing looking at the screen,—maybe about fifty people. The baton charge was quite unprovoked. Slowly, Yeats and I walked down O'Connell Street. Suddenly we heard a crash of glass and a big plate glass window on the opposite side of the street was shattered. The news of the killing of the poor old woman had spread like wild fire and the people were avenging her death. £2,000 worth of plate glass in every shop with Jubilee decorations was smashed that night.

I was out early next morning at the Bridewell and sent Connolly his breakfast. He had never been arrested before and was hesitating about accepting the services of a lawyer who was hovering about the court. He did engage him, and afterwards regretted it, for he found that, when he wanted to speak, he was not allowed, as he was represented by Counsel.

"Let my wife know," he said to me, and I went off on a car to the room where they lived. Mrs. Connolly was bathing her baby, and little Norah, wide-eyed, was listening silently and breathlessly for news of her daddy.

"I was sure something like that had happened when he didn't come home," was all brave Mrs. Connolly said.

"Don't worry, he will be home again soon."

There had been a large number of men arrested later that evening when the glass-breaking began, and all were released on bail. I went back to the courts and arranged bail for everybody. Later, I got Tim Harrington to defend them. It was proved that the brutal murder of that poor old woman was the cause of all the broken glass and I think everyone got off.

The Dublin Jubilee demonstrations had head-lines in the press of all countries, but little was heard of disloyal demonstrations in London.

I was very tired and got a bad attack of rheumatism and was advised to take a three weeks' cure at Aix-les-Bains. I persuaded May to accompany me. Having nothing to do, we decided to try our luck at the gaming tables. We played timidly in five-franc pieces and were not very lucky. We were leaving Aix the following day. The maid of the hotel, when she brought in our breakfasts, told us of a wonderful fortune-teller who was in the hotel, telling the fortune of the lady next door. "Send her in to me when she has done," I said to the maid.

The fortune-teller was a commonplace-looking, middle-aged woman and told the cards on my bed. She began about a fair man and a dark man who were both thinking of me. I cut her short by telling her I wasn't a bit interested in either the fair man or the dark, but I was interested in gambling. So she cut the cards for that and told me to go to the casino and play boldly that afternoon and I would be sure to win; but at five o'clock I was to leave the tables and go back again later and play again boldly. "Boldly," she said.

I went and sat at the five-franc table and suddenly the croupier announced that the stakes were raised. The banker, who was a Russian prince, would allow nothing less than twenty francs to be staked. I had won about forty francs and hesitated, for I had very little money and had to keep enough to get home; but I remembered the words of the fortune-teller to play boldly, so I put the forty francs on the table and won,—and won, and won, again and again, till I had a big pile of counters. The banker again raised the stakes. "No stake less than a hundred francs." I had never played in such sums, but I went on and I soon had £200. I looked at my watch; it was five o'clock. The fortune-teller had said I was to stop at five. I got up and left the table in search of May who had left the table when the banker had raised the stakes. Not finding her, I went and had tea at Rumpelmeyer's with a little old French countess whom I knew in Paris. I told her about the fortune-teller and said I must go back and begin to play again in half-an-hour. "Come too and play with me as I am to win again."

"Ma chérie, I have no money, but I will come and watch you."

We went back. It was easy to get a chair now at the table, for the banker had been winning steadily, people told me, since I went away. I played again and won each time.

"I have put on a hundred francs for you," I told the countess.

"No, no, chérie, I have no money."

"You have now, for you have won. Leave the money on the table."

We won again. The little old countess was so excited she took the four-hundred-franc counters and wouldn't play any more. I knew she was desperately hard up and four hundred francs meant a lot to her. Money never meant anything to me, so I left the counters on till I had another £200.

Then, having a lot more than I needed for the defence of all the Jubilee prisoners and feeling sorry for the Russian prince who was losing a fortune, I got up and went to my hotel to pack. I felt uncomfortable because people round me at the table were all saying I was bringing luck,—and I knew that while I was playing I would go on winning. Unluckily for May she had met friends and had gone to the theatre with them. We left Aix next morning; I had to get back to Dublin for the trials.

A couple of years later I returned for another cure at Aix. Of course I sent for the fortune-teller. She again told me to go and play at certain hours, which I did,—and lost! But I was merely playing for myself that time and I never have luck when I try to do anything for myself.

CHAPTER XVII

IN AMERICA

THE AMNESTY ASSOCIATION had sent James Egan, the first of the prisoners released from Portland, to America to collect funds, for we were hard pressed for money to keep the prisoners' dependants from actual want. James Egan had only one thought,—to work for the comrades he had left in jail; but after some money, sent shortly after his arrival in New York, no more money arrived though American papers reported meetings and large subscriptions. Nasty things were being said which I was certain were unjust. Dr. Ryan asked me to undertake a lecture tour in America and made all arrangements. The tour was to be run by the section of the *Clan-na-Gael* Dr. Ryan supported. Half the proceeds were to go to the Amnesty Association and half to be retained by the organisation in America.

I started on a cold November day in 1894. The Cunard liner could not or would not come into Cork Harbour. Some said the two English shipping companies, the Cunard and the White Star, were refusing to enter Cork Harbour without cause because they wanted to divert American tourist traffic to Liverpool by making embarkation to and from Cork difficult and disagreeable. They certainly succeeded in this; and on the wretched little tender on which I and a large contingent of sad emigrants set out to join the liner, things were thoroughly uncomfortable.

Shivering and wet with spray, I retired at once to my cabin on the liner and miserably counted the days I would have to be at sea; eight or nine and no ports of call, as on my

voyage from Marseilles to Constantinople, to break the monotony. Only the rolling waves of the Atlantic to look forward to.
Ships being notably inhospitable to dogs, I had left Dagda
with friends; my tiny marmoset had succumbed to the rigours
of the Russian climate; so to fill my need of living comradeship,
of which I was a little ashamed, I had brought my tame
canary. Twee-Twee was a cheerful companion. He was rarely
in his cage and he used to fly in and out of the window and
come in when called. Fearing to be thought silly for bringing
a bird on serious expeditions, I had got a little round cage which
fitted into a black silk bag. I opened this and, much more
cheerful than myself, Twee-Twee flew round the cabin,
inspecting everything and finally perched on the ledge of the
port-hole, obscured by the dull green waves and sang the
beautiful little song he had learned in the Hartz mountains.
I told the stewardess I was going to lunch and dine on Chloral
and gave her my ticket so as not to be disturbed by the steward.
That night I was wakened by the wild flutterings and shrill
cries of Twee-Twee and, turning on the light, was only just
in time to save his little life. A huge rat had got on to the
open cage and was trying to drag him out; Twee-Twee lost all
his tail feathers. Ships are horrid places! After that I
had to sleep with Twee-Twee's cage on my pillow. Next
morning, when the stewardess brought my tea, I told her
my programme for the day as far as meals were concerned
was the same as the previous day. She came back after an
hour.

"Mr. Nansen says you are to come up on deck; he is calling
for you in half an hour."

"Whoever Mr. Nansen is, please tell him I am going to stay
where I am," I replied. I had never met the great Arctic
explorer; all the same I got up and struggled with my toilette.
In half an hour, a very good-looking man put his head in the
door.

"I have got chairs for us on deck, Miss Gonne, and have come to fetch you." And, feeling very shaky, I let Nansen help me up the stairs and settle me with rugs on a deck chair. "I saw you come on board yesterday. You looked as if this was your first voyage and I didn't want you to waste your time in a stuffy cabin." It was kind of him, and during the voyage I hardly spoke to anyone else. He was also going on a lecture tour; four lectures a week like myself.

Our tours crossed and I was able to go to one of his lectures which was illustrated with magic-lantern slides showing wonderful Arctic scenery and northern lights. I read in the papers that after a fortnight Nansen had broken his lecture contract and forfeited a lot of money; he told me after he had not been able to stick it; the banquets and receptions were worse than the lectures. "I want to keep my health and nerves for other work," he said.

I endured my tour, lectures, receptions, hand-shakings, banquets and all for a month; but I put a tariff on the banquets of a hundred dollars for prisoners for every banquet I attended. In a month I had £1,000 for the Amnesty Association and went home tired but content.

Nansen and I wanted to visit the emigrants' quarters on the ship; but a strict rule prevented any communication between the First Class and the emigrants and we couldn't persuade our wooden English Captain to relax it for us, and the big waves of the Atlantic had such a depressing effect on me that I hadn't the enterprise to devise a means of infringing it. My next voyage to America was on a French transatlantic liner and the French Captain took me over the emigrants' quarters. The emigrants were mostly Poles and Italians and uncomfortably crowded; but I think their conditions were better than on the English liners because the French Captain didn't mind showing them. He told me that the Shipping Companies make far more profit out of the emigrants than out of the First Class passengers who take too much space and eat more. English shipping has been largely built up on Irish emigrant traffic and I immediately began devising plans for diverting it to the French line. The French Captain and I got quite enthusiastic and later I got into communication with the *Compagnie Transatlantique* in Paris.

Emigration is the curse of Ireland, for every human being is a national asset; but till it can be stopped, at least the country whose robbery is the cause should not be allowed to reap a profit out of it. Later Sir Roger Casement and I spoke of this and he, being a man quick to translate thought into action, called a meeting in the Oak Room of the Mansion House where, to business men from Cork, Dublin and Belfast, he expounded the advantage to Irish Commerce of breaking through the stranglehold of England and using Ireland's unique position to make her a chief port of call for transatlantic shipping. He then went to Berlin and interviewed the directors of the *Nord Deutscher* Line and succeeded in getting them to open an office in Cork and there was great rejoicing and excitement when the date for the arrival of the first German liner was announced. But, as in the case of the *Compagnie Transatlantique*, English diplomacy succeeded in getting both the French and German Governments to interfere and prevent what England called an unfriendly act. Now emigration to America is stopped, but it has been diverted to England in even greater volume.

I was amazed at the amount of food first class passengers were expected to eat. Seven meals a day, counting the early morning tea and the dinners, reminded me of the long banquets of the rich Dubliners at which I had so often to sit in the old days with Tommy.

"Does anyone ever eat all this?" I asked the steward.

"Indeed they do, Miss. Many complain they have not enough. The sea gives great appetites."

On that first voyage of mine we came into a terrific fog over the Newfoundland banks. I can compare it only to being wrapped in wet cottonwool which muffled even sounds. The ship's syren was blowing her loudest all the time but it sounded strange and muffled; then, very faintly, like an echo, came another answering wail, a ghost's cry. I could hardly see Nansen sitting on the chair next mine; everything was wrapped in damp whiteness. "It is another ship," he said. For a long time the wail and its echo sounded continually. We got up and groped our way to the ship's rail; the ship seemed hardly moving; then very faintly we discerned a dim shadow in the whiteness. Another liner had passed dangerously near and soon the echoing wail ceased. No one ever knows how many fishing trawlers have been run down by liners over those Newfoundland Banks in the dread fogs. Those on the liners would notice nothing and if they did, could do nothing. The fishing boat would not come home when the fishing fleet returned to the Breton coast at the end of the season. Only the women, watching vainly for Jacques Marie or Jean Pierre would know the loss and the nameless tragedy. In those days the Bretons were most numerous on those dangerous fishing grounds, but since, to celebrate the Entente Cordiale, the French presented England with what was then known as the French shore on the Newfoundland coast, which was where the bait for fishing was procured, French fishing has been much curtailed and the Brittany and Normandy fishers have taken to raiding our Irish coasts, dragging the bottom out of the sea, as our fishers say, and unprotected Irish fishing has become a dying industry, quite inadequately replaced by a little daring smuggling of French wines and brandy. Foreign poachers can look amusedly at the *Murchiu*, the one boat of the Free State navy. In grateful return for "the French shore," the English statesmen of the Entente presented France with part of Morocco where German commercial enterprise was paramount and the incident of Agadir increased the tension between France and Germany which culminated in the Great War.

In spite of the interesting companionship of Nansen, I was overjoyed when land was sighted, for I never get over the "prison" feeling of a boat, or the nostalgic longing for green trees and the feel of earth under my feet. I could kneel and kiss the earth each time I get off a ship. Nansen and I were surrounded by a crowd who came on board with the pilot at the entrance to New York Harbour. One of them pointed out a boat bedecked with Irish and American flags from which the faint sounds of a band playing Irish airs could be heard.

"Your friends have been cruising for hours to meet you, but as your boat is so late, the captain refused to let them get you off. I guess they are just mad; another Irish grievance!" said the reporter of the New York Journal to me. I was quite ready to consider the English Captain disobliging, but secretly my longing for terra firma was so great that I was not altogether sorry not to be transferred to a small rocking steamer.

As I went on shore and one hand was grasped by a big heavy man who introduced himself as Mr. Lynam one of the chiefs of the *Clan-na-Gael* and the other by little red-haired Egan, Nansen called out: "Good-bye; you are in good hands now, Miss Gonne."

The Irish seemed to be all-powerful at the docks. Lynam introduced me to several imposing-looking officials, and custom-house officers assured me I need not worry about anything and, amid cheers and hand-shakes from a crowd of Irish people, Lynam and I drove off. I insisted on Egan coming too; he was the only one I knew and I did not want to lose him. At the Savoy Hotel the Reception Committee had engaged a magnificent suite of rooms for me.

Two reporters from New York papers were waiting. I was holding on to the little black silk bag containing Twee-Twee.

I slipped it under my chair and was giving an interview explaining how I had come to America to awaken indignation over the treatment of Irish political prisoners in Portland, and telling of my hope that the generous indignation of the American people would procure the immediate release of Dr. Gallagher, an American citizen. Suddenly, in a clear thrilling note, Twee-Twee joined his voice to mine. The reporters looked round. One said, "Sounds like a bird." Twee-Twee was ecstatically singing his unearthly little Hartz Mountain song. I said:

"What is that delicious music? Is it some wonderful new American invention of making invisible music?"

"It must be a musical box in the room below. Sounds mount," said one of the reporters and he continued the interview. Twee-Twee had finished his song and I could just hear the faint sound of cracking seeds, but as I was afraid he would give an unasked encore,—for he always liked joining in when there was conversation,—I told the reporters that I had a lot to talk of with Mr. Lynam, which indeed I had, and they departed. I then introduced Twee-Twee. James Egan was very much amused, but Lynam said: "Lucky these reporters didn't see him or there would have been head-lines in the papers."

I got through the whole tour without Twee-Twee being interviewed but it required some manœuvring.

I wanted to talk to Lynam about Ivory's trial and the discovery of the agent provocateur and what was going to be done about it. I knew he had received full reports of the whole case from Dr. Ryan. I found him embarrassed and evidently anxious to change the subject. He was trying to make out that Ivory's release was due to the impression made on the English Court by the American lawyer sent over by the *Clan-na-Gael* and minimised Mr. Taylor's work. I reflected that, as sending that lawyer must have cost the Clan a lot of money, he was trying to justify the expenditure.

After gratefully thanking Mr. Lynam for the great reception they had given me, I said that, having come to America to get money for the political prisoners, I wanted expenses cut down as much as possible, and that this beautiful suite of rooms at the Savoy must be very expensive. Mr. Lynam said the Reception Committee considered nothing too good for me. I again thanked him but said that, being a very simple person, I intended to move into one room in a cheaper hotel.

"Miss Gonne, you have got to leave all that to the Reception Committee; we know America. If you don't appear to have lots of money, you won't get money. You will be surprised to-morrow, after the meeting, to see a lot of big subscriptions,— five-hundred dollars, a thousand dollars, etc. That will be for publicity purposes in order to get more."

I became very grave: "Mr. Lynam, please remember this, and I mean it. Every subscription announced will have to be paid in full to the Amnesty Association, for if not, I shall write to the papers and say so. So please warn whoever is over publicity here. You may be right about the hotel, so to-night I will sleep in splendour and to-morrow you can send all the reporters to interview me here, but to-morrow morning I shall give notice to the hotel that I only need one room. The prisoners' families need the money and I am not going to allow it to be wasted on me."

Mr. Lynam sighed and said he had a lot to do but would return to take me to dinner before the meeting, and departed.

"Thank God you have come here and can see for yourself how things are," said Egan, who had been very silent while Lynam and I had been talking. "I am heart-broken. I can't get any money sent home for the prisoners. I have no means of knowing if the subscriptions published are genuine and I am always told that there is nothing left after expenses are paid. You will find it very hard to get the money for the Amnesty Association."

"I will get it all right. But I will keep my own accounts and keep expenses down. Egan, will you join me on this tour?"

"I would like to," he answered, "but Lynam, the big fellow we call him here,—won't allow it."

"Won't allow it," I laughed. "He will have to if I say that I need you as a first-hand witness to the horrors of Portland. You know the Clan here; you know who are the good men on both sides. I don't know anyone. Together we will be able to do more work than getting money for the Amnesty Association. We may be able to unite the Clan for their real purpose, the freeing of Ireland."

Being young, I never admitted difficulty in doing anything. Egan was less hopeful but he was very anxious to do real work for Ireland and for the prisoners. "There are such good men on both sides but somehow they are betrayed by the leaders and are being used for American politics instead of for Ireland," he told me. "That agent provocateur you mentioned to Lynam is back now, and though the reports from home have been received, he is still allowed to attend Clan meetings; I would not wonder if he is at your meeting to-night. I think Lynam is afraid of him and is preventing his being exposed."

"If he is at the meeting to-night show him to me and I will expose him before everybody," I said.

The Academy of Music was crowded. *Clan-na-Gael* guards in uniform formed a guard of honour; a captain who was decidedly too fat for his uniform read me an address. The chairman was speaking when James Egan came over and whispered: "Mr. X., the agent provocateur, is on the platform," and pointed to a man sitting in a prominent place in the row behind me. Mr. Lynam sat next to me.

I turned to him and said: "Mr. Lynam, the man who betrayed Ivory is on this platform. Will you order him to leave at once."

"Where is he," said Lynam.

"In the row behind us, on the right. Tell him to leave at once."

"That is impossible, Miss Gonne."

"I am not going to speak unless he leaves."

"But I can't—before all the people."

"Then, before I speak, I shall do so and moreover tell the whole story to the audience. I am sure it will interest them."

The chairman was just announcing me. I sat quite still. Mr. Lynam got up and went to Mr. X. I couldn't hear what he said; but the man got up and disappeared and I watched him, as did many others.

It was a magnificent meeting. The enthusiasm for Ireland was so sincere, so eager among all those exiles who, though they had found good homes and comfort in America, loved Ireland where they had suffered and hated England with bitter intensity.

Twenty million people of Irish blood. Surely enough to free Ireland.

Every meeting at which I spoke was crowded by Irish men and women eager to hear the latest news from a girl who had just come from Ireland, and eager to know how they could raise Ireland to a position of honour. In America they were working side by side with immigrants from many free nations. Ireland's subject status was a personal humiliation to them. Patrick Ford, editor of the *Irish World*, was waging a great campaign against the stage Irishman, the grotesque buffoon with his pig and shillelah whom England's centuries-old propaganda, too often unconsciously helped by the Irish themselves, had set up as an Irish prototype. I was the very antithesis of this and those Irish-American crowds loved me accordingly.

The halls in which I spoke were the largest that could be obtained, much larger than the halls in which I had spoken in Europe. There were no microphones in those days but my training and outdoor speaking on the hills of Donegal and Mayo helped me. If my sentences were not as flowery and perfect as the really remarkable oratory of some Irish-Americans such as Burke Cochran, who often spoke with me, they could hear me quite as distinctly.

What I had to say could not always have been pleasing, for I had to tell people to hope for nothing from the parliamentary party whose leaders they had hero-worshipped and generously financed. Before Parnell had been finally broken by the British intrigues of which Kitty O'Shea was the heroine and centre, his strength had gone from him when he broke with the Physical-force Party and repudiated the acts of violence of the Land League.

I told them that the men who had had the heroic courage to carry the war on to English soil and had tried to blow up the House of Commons, had done more for the cause of Irish freedom than the Irishmen who went into it; that some of those brave men had been shamefully abandoned in British jails where they were being treated as ordinary criminals under prison acts calculated to drive prisoners insane. I told them that Home Rule was the carrot dangled before the donkey's nose to keep the donkey quietly trotting along in the harness of the British Empire. Parnell was dead and Redmond and Dillon were quarrelling over who should hold the carrot. The freedom of Ireland would only be attained by the young men of Ireland in the only way the freedom of any nation and of America herself had been attained. I told them God in His justice had given those who had been driven out homeless from Ireland,—those to whom I was speaking,—the task of protecting America, the country of their adoption, from being ever lured into an alliance with the British Empire, the destroyer of nationalities, the enemy of human freedom.

By their numbers and organised strength they could do this for the honour of America and help Ireland by doing it.

I never appealed for funds and discouraged collections, for I had realised that half the proceeds of the lecture tour would more than supply the needs of the Amnesty Association, whose own increasing strength and number should soon make it self-supporting. When not necessary, Ireland should not appear as a mendicant. I was always out against the power of money, but I was businesslike, even hard with the organisers of the lecture tour, and Egan and I kept our accounts very strictly.

The *Clan-na-Gael* was split into two warring sections. I felt sure the British Secret Service had spies in both camps, as was proved by the Times Commission when it uncovered one of its agents, Le Caron, and put him in the witness box to discredit Parnell. From what I had learnt recently from the bogus Fenian-Nihilist plot against the Czar, I felt there must be such agents keeping up the division in the powerful Irish-American organisations; so I set my mind to uniting the Clan and I think I did something towards it.

All I knew about the split was that a Dr. Cronin, who was said to have been on his way to give evidence before the Times Commission, disappeared and his dead body was found some time later in a drain. John Devoy, one of the leaders of the Clan, accused another leader, Alexander Sullivan, of having instigated the murder of Cronin. O'Sullivan was exonerated in a sensational trial in Chicago. Some of the Clan took part with O'Sullivan, some with Devoy and the division grew. O'Sullivan died the year before I went to America. He must have been a remarkable man and a great organiser and had built up the power of the Clan. Patrick Egan, American Ambassador to Chile, who had been treasurer of the Land League, had been a great friend of his and often spoke to me of him in terms of warmest affection as a great man and a great leader. Patrick Egan, who called on me in New York, accompanied me to Washington and helped me greatly on the purely American side, in my Press campaign for the Treason Felony Prisoners, arranging interviews, and advising me how to get publicity in America, as I had done in France, from the Press of all shades of political opinion.

My lecture tour, being organised by the O'Sullivan section of the Clan, was severely boycotted by the Devoy section. I had a letter of introduction from John O'Leary to John Devoy, but determined not to use it till the end of my tour and unluckily Devoy was absent from New York on my return, so I did not meet him until my next visit to America.

I learnt from Patrick Egan and from James Egan that there were equally good sincere men on both sides and, at the risk of seeming the fool who rushes in where angels dare not tread, I made up my mind to see as many of them as I could and appeal to them to end the quarrel. James Egan knew many of them, so while I was kept busy before and after lectures, with Press interviewers and receptions and never-ending hand-shaking, he used to call on the leaders of the Devoy section and generally succeed in arranging for me to see them before we left the different towns.

I used to say: "I did not try to see you before my lecture, because I never seek help from the unwilling and my lectures are unimportant, but now that you can do nothing for me personally, I have sought to see you to ask you in the name of Ireland not to waste time on past regrets. Dr. Cronin is dead; you cannot bring him back to life. Alexander Sullivan is dead, more is the pity, for he seems to have been a great man, but he can do no more work for Ireland on earth. Why are you wasting the strength of this great organisation on dead men's quarrels? The British Empire is not dead yet and you are pledged to fight it. Get on with the work. Ireland is waiting in slavery."

We generally parted the best of friends. Luke Dillon, tall and resolute, was one of the Devoy section I met in Philadelphia.

Luke Dillon impressed me greatly, though when I met him then, I did not know what I learnt later, when he was dead,—that he and Hugh O'Neil were the heroic men who actually placed the dynamite in the House of Commons and caused the explosion which had shaken England to her foundations and converted so many English politicians to the necessity for Home Rule. As Luke Dillon intended doing even greater work he carefully guarded that secret, which might have made further work more difficult.

He said: "You are right, Miss Gonne, we will get on with it." And how he kept his word I heard later when, during the Boer War, not having succeeded in getting the whole Clan into action, he and a few went out in a heroic attempt to destroy the Welland Canal; and for fifteen years he was shut up in a British jail in Canada. Had he succeeded the food supply of the English army in South Africa would have been crippled.

In 1896, wanting money to keep Arthur Griffith's little paper the *United Irishman* afloat and money for organising the '98 Centenary demonstration, I again went to America on a lecture tour. It was organised by a man from the West known as "Rocky-Mountain-O'Brien" who, I believe, belonged to neither section of the Clan, but wanted to help Ireland. Again in 1901, needing more money for Griffith's paper, the *United Irishman*, and also for the anti-recruiting campaign, I undertook a third lecture tour, this time organised by the whole Clan, who had by then become united. The results financially, were exactly the same. In one month of four lectures a week, after paying expenses, I was able to bring home £1,000 each time.

The third lecture tour, which was during the Boer War, had another object than merely earning money. I had hoped to galvanise the Clan into putting into definite action the words I had so often heard its members use of "making

England's difficulty Ireland's opportunity" and in this I failed. The great Irish-American organisation, though re-united, let the occasion slip and did little but talk.

Some hitch having occurred, during the first lecture tour, about a hall in which Egan and I were to speak in Minneapolis, we found ourselves with a free day in Denver and were both delighted, as the constant travelling and lectures were very tiring and I was getting unbecomingly thin. As I was leaving the theatre, three boisterous lads pushed their way unceremoniously through the crowd who were seeing us into our carriage. "We have come to kidnap Miss Gonne; we are going to take her into the Rockies." They were miners from Victor and Cripple Creek; one of them had a strong Cork accent. There was no gainsaying them. "We were sent to get Miss Gonne; we are not going back without her; and we are all Irish up there."

It ended in Egan and myself getting into the carriage they had waiting and away into the moonlit night up the mountains, a wonderful journey through gorges and roads edging dark precipices. We arrived in the early morning at Cripple Creek where, in a wooden frame house, an Irishwoman from Co. Mayo welcomed us with tea and bacon and eggs and then put me to bed in a bare little room and told me to sleep till the men called for me at twelve o'clock to take me down a gold mine where I was to give the men from two shifts the latest news from Ireland. In the evening another lecture had been arranged in a hall at Victor. I spent the happiest days of my whole American tour in those mining villages. In their hard, exciting lives, these people never forgot Ireland, and Egan and I were both sad to leave the following day. It was a marvellous drive through the mountains in the clear blue air of the early morning; we had to catch the train for St. Louis to be in time for our next lecture. We were laden with all sorts and sizes of rocks, with little bits of shining gold glistening on them, given us as souvenirs, and three hundred dollars for the prisoners and messages innumerable for folk at home and promises that when the fight was on for Irish freedom the men would be back with us. These thirty-six hours stand out vivid in my recollection amid the confused memories of crowds and trains and hotels and reception committees, and kind, hospitable people whom I longed to have more time to know.

O'Donovan Rossa came to see me off at the boat. He was the great veteran Fenian whose indomitable courage England had not succeeded in breaking during all those years in her prison hells. In Dartmoor for weeks he had been kept in a dungeon, his hands chained behind his back and obliged to eat his food and lap his water like an animal from a bowl on the floor. He was an old man now, but his spirit unbroken and his faith in Ireland unshaken and anxious still to help every movement to free Ireland from the British Empire.

CHAPTER XVIII

FAMINE

ON LANDING AT Cobh after my second lecture tour in America in 1897 I turned the tables on the reporters trying to interview me by asking them for news. These eight days without news on the ship were always trying. "Not too good," said the reporter of the *Freeman's Journal*, "Potato blight in the West," and he handed me a copy of his paper which contained the insolent reply of Balfour to a question in the House of Commons in regard to deaths from starvation in County Mayo and the inadequate relief measures. Balfour had produced doctors' certificates of "death from heart-failure" and then said: "You can't expect us to supply your farmers with Champagne."

In Dublin I saw Arthur Griffith and James Connolly; I had money to clear the small debts of the *United Irishman* and wanted Griffith to accept at least £2 10s. a week as its editor, but Griffith, who was entirely unselfish and disinterested about money, refused. "Till the paper pays, I won't take a penny more than the Twenty-five shillings which I have to pay my mother for my board." I was often worried about Griffith's finances; I knew he had broken his engagement to a girl who was in the National movement because he saw no prospect of money to marry on; I also knew he had refused several good offers of work on other papers, for he was a brilliant writer, but though I insisted, I was never able to shake his proud resolve of living on a bare subsistence till the paper paid. It never did pay owing to its frequent seizures and difficulty of production under British coercion Acts.

Connolly was perturbed about the famine. He had terrible reports from Kerry. The people must be roused to save themselves and not die as in 1847. That evening we drafted a leaflet. "The Rights of Life and the Rights of Property." It ran as follows:

" 'The use of all things is to be common to all. It is an injustice to say this belongs to me, that to another. Hence the origin of contentions among men.'

His Holiness Pope Clement I.

'Let them know that the earth from which they sprang, and of which they are formed, belongs to all men in common and therefore the fruits which the earth brings forth must belong without distinction to all.'

His Holiness Pope Gregory the Great.

'In case of extreme need of food, all goods become common property.'

Cardinal Manning.

"Fellow Countrymen: At the present juncture when the shadow of famine is already blighting the lives of so many amongst us, when famine itself in all its grim horror has already begun to claim its victims . . . we desire to offer a few words of calm advice . . . to move you to action before it is too late and to point out to you your duty whether as fathers or sons, as husbands or as Irishmen.

"In 1847 our people died by thousands of starvation though every ship leaving an Irish port was laden with food in abundance. The Irish people might have seized that food, cattle, corn and all manner of provisions before it reached the seaports—have prevented famine and saved their country from ruin, but did not do so, believing such action to be sinful and dreading to peril their souls to save their bodies. In this belief, we know now they were entirely mistaken. The very highest authorities on the Doctrine of the Church agree that no *human* law can stand between starving people and their RIGHT TO FOOD including the right to take that food whenever they find it, openly or secretly, with or without the owner's permission. His Holiness Pope Leo XIII has lately recommended the writings of St. Thomas Aquinas as the best statement of Catholic Doctrine on Faith and Morals.

" Listen to what St. Thomas teaches on the rights of property when opposed to the right of life.

"In *Summa Theologica Quest.* 66 Art. 2.

"'Is it lawful to steal on the plea of necessity?

"'The institution of human law cannot abrogate from natural law or Divine law . . . therefore the division and appropriation of goods that proceed from human law cannot come in the way of man's needs relieved out of these goods . . . If however a need is so plain and pressing that clearly the urgent necessity has to be relieved . . . then the man may lawfully relieve his distress out of the property of another, taking it—either openly or secretly. . . .' "

Connolly said he would go to Kerry as soon as he had arranged for the printing of the leaflet and hurried off to the National Library to get the quotations from the Fathers of the Church. I gave him £25 from the money collected on the lecture tour to pay for printing and for the journey. I was starting next morning for Mayo on organising work for the '98 Centenary.

The approaching Centenary of Ireland's great fight for Independence in 1798 provided the opportunity for putting the Separatist idea before the people. Anna Johnson, Alice Milligan, Willie Rooney and myself prepared and delivered many lectures on the United Irishmen in many places and as early as 1896 Centenary Committees were being organised throughout Ireland with the object of erecting monuments in their honour. James Daly of Castlebar had asked me to go with him and inspect the graves of the French soldiers killed in the battle known as the "Races" of Castlebar where General Humbert and his thousand French soldiers, with the almost unarmed Irish, had routed the British army of General Lake who fled so fast that it gave the battle its name, "The races of Castlebar". They then proclaimed the Irish Republic which was maintained in Connaught for two months. Those graves had been piously guarded by the farmers on whose holdings they were situated. The plough had never been allowed to obliterate those little green mounds amid the furrows. We intended erecting crosses further to mark the spots before the arrival of the two French delegations which we had invited to be present at the laying of the foundation stone of the Ballina Memorial in honour of the men who died for Ireland in 1798.

James Daly presented me with an old French coin and a bullet that had been found in one of the graves; later I had these made into a brooch which I always wore. I learnt that, while there was great distress round Castlebar, the real famine area was in North Mayo. In Ballina I stayed with the Kellys. Thomas Kelly was the Secretary of the Ballina Memorial Committee. He was also an old friend of mine in Land League campaigns and his wife and big family gave me a warm welcome. Thomas Kelly was a commercial traveller; he told me how, returning from Ballycastle, he had seen ten new un-finished graves in the little cemetery between Ballycastle and Belderrig; the people were too weak to do the work of burying properly. The priest, Father Timony of Ballycastle, was down with the fever which always accompanies famine. I took the Mail car for Ballycastle the following morning in spite of the hospitable remonstrance of Mrs. Kelly.

Miss May, the proprietress of the hotel in Ballycastle, told me a man had died of hunger in the town the day before I arrived and that the doctor had signed the usual certificate of "death from heart failure".

"Why is he such a coward as not to say from starvation?" I asked indignantly.

She shrugged her shoulders: "If he did he would be prosecuted for manslaughter for not having ordered relief. If he ordered relief sufficient to prevent deaths, he would bankrupt the Union and lose his job. The Belmullet Union has already been declared bankrupt."

In the evening, people hearing of my arrival surrounded the hotel and I addressed a big meeting and distributed the leaflets of which I had received a large supply from James Connolly and arranged for a group of young men to distribute them in outlying townlands. Next day I got on to the Mail car for Belderrig; I got the driver to halt a moment to let me inspect the barely covered graves in the little wind-blown cemetery of which Mr. Kelly had spoken.

The pretty young wife of the man who kept the general store in Belderrig looked doubtful when I told her I wanted to stay.

"You had better go back to Ballycastle," she said. "We have no accommodation for a lady like you. Things are so bad I find it hard even to get a drop of milk for my own children."

I told her I didn't mind; all I wanted was a room.

She said: "We haven't a room fit for you." But when she found me determined to stay, she added she would do her best, which she certainly did.

That evening, in her kitchen, round the turf fire on an open hearth, I heard pitiful tales from a few famine-stricken women with shawls over their heads, come to fetch little bags of meal or sugar for which they had no money to pay. "But for Mrs. Kelly we would all be dead," was the refrain.

One woman whose father and brother lay in the little grave-yard I had visited told me her remaining brother was down with famine fever but was on the mend. "If only I could get food to keep the life in him! Father worked on the Relief Works till he came home to die. He was old; the Relief Works are so far away. No, he didn't die of the fever; he just came home one night tired out and went to bed and next morning he couldn't rise and he died,—without a priest," she said with a sigh.

"Father Timony, God bless him, is down with the fever." She told me she was going to work on the Relief now her brother was no longer raving and she could leave him.

A Coast Guard from a station along the coast came into the shop. He had heard there was a stranger in Balderrig and had come to see. He looked curiously into the kitchen and said good evening politely. We made a place at the fire for him. "We give the poor people all the scraps at the Station and indeed a good share of our own food, more than we can afford," he told me. "They come round every day and when some don't appear we know they are down with the fever. They would do far better to go to the workhouse, though I hear the fever is there too. Yet at least they would get food, but they won't go. You see, if they go into the workhouse they lose their title to the land and they prefer to starve."

I asked him about the relief works.

"They are all right of course," he said, "but they can't take on any except the heads of families and the 6d. a day they earn can't keep big families. The Government is doing its best; there are four Relief Works started in Erris; but the people are starving and I wish I was out of this part of the country. Where are you going, young lady? It's not much of a place for you."

"Oh, I'm going to stay here, or around here, for some time I expect. I am going to write about this famine and try to get help."

"Well, I wish you luck and that you get something done for the poor people." And he got up and went into the shop.

I turned to the woman who had said she was going to try to get onto the Relief Works; she was gazing at me with clear grey eyes, her shawl had fallen back from her fair hair, bleached by sun and sea and I noticed she was beautiful. "If you can leave your brother, will you come and show me round the country instead of going to the Relief Works? I want to visit some of the sick people."

"Of course I will. But aren't you afraid of the fever?"

I laughed. "I am afraid of nothing and you are not either."

"Indeed she is not," said another woman. "Peggy Hegarty goes to all the houses where people are ill and does what she can for them and puts them in their coffins when they're dead."

"How old are you, Peggy?" I asked.

"Thirty," she replied.

"Two years younger than I am." She looked ten years older. "Well, Peggy, we will do some work together and stop the famine. People who are not afraid can stop it."

They all looked at me and one old woman crossed herself. The women, except Peggy, got up and went out into the wet night. Mrs. Kelly came in from the shop and said:

"They all go together: they are feared to walk alone these times."

"What are they afraid of?" I asked.

Mrs. Kelly laughed: "They say the good people are angry because they have nothing to leave in plates outside for them."

I met a lot of people who had seen the fairies in Mayo but it was seldom they would talk about them. Mrs. Kelly said my room was ready and I followed her upstairs to a bare room. She was very apologetic about the bed and said she was afraid I would not be comfortable though she had put a hot jar in it. I looked at the little bit of guttering candle and asked for more candles. I did not think it necessary to tell her but I had so much writing to do I had no use for the bed. Wrapped up in

my big seal-skin cloak with its immense bear-fur collar that
Uncle Charlie had given me when I came of age and which
had protected me from many storms, I sat by a rickety little
table and wrote all night. I was unutterably lonely and sad and
frightened, for the task seemed too big for me. I thought of
Tommy's words, "You must never be afraid of anything, even
of death." Peggy was afraid of nothing because she had lost all
and was not afraid of walking alone in the fairy-haunted night
with her little bags of meal and sugar. The people must be
taught to be afraid of nothing, neither death nor war, if the
famine was to be stopped.

I wrote to James Connolly, chiefly because he was the bravest
man I knew, and to Ellen Ford, reminding her how I had asked
for no subscriptions in America and had refused to allow collections to be made at my meetings, but telling her that now I
was up against it and must appeal for help for the famine-
stricken areas. I told her I wanted money to feed the children
in the schools and money to nurse the fever patients. Ellen
Ford did not fail me. She opened a subscription list in the
Irish World and I got money for both these things; and I put
Peggy, who had no fear, in charge of the nursing,—such as it
was. I wrote an article describing just what I had seen for
the *Freeman's Journal*. I did not know if it would publish it
because I was already looked on as an enemy of the Parliamentary Party.

It was day-light when I had finished writing. I tossed the
bed clothes, for I did not want Mrs. Kelly to be worried by
thinking the bed was too uncomfortable for me to sleep in and
I did my best with my toilette and went downstairs for breakfast.

"Up so early!" exclaimed Mrs. Kelly. She was in the kitchen
struggling with the curly tangled hair of her youngest girl. "I
sent Jimmy out an hour ago to get a sup of milk for the tea. We
have only opened this shop recently and have no cows of our

own yet and the bailiffs seized all the people's cows for arrears of rent when they saw the famine coming. It's true the people wouldn't have had feeding for them through the winter; but milk in these parts you cannot get. Jimmy is not back and I will have to give you condensed milk in your tea and you won't like that."

"Don't bother about me, Mrs. Kelly. But we want a lot of condensed milk for the sick people," and I arranged with her to order in a good supply. Peggy was waiting outside the shop. I made her come in and share my breakfast which she did with some shyness and reluctance, for Peggy was proud. Then we went out together.

Peggy was well known to all. She was used to going into the houses where there was sickness and helping the women to tidy up their places. Many of the sick lay on rushes and rags on the floor. I reflected that it was perhaps better than beds for the rushes could always be burnt afterwards and end the infection. Some of the hovels beggared description, but there were fewer down with actual fever than I had feared. There was a listless misery over everyone that was indescribable. Food was the most pressing need. I told them all that the worst was over, that help was coming and they would soon be well. I pretended to knowledge I did not possess and said that Peggy would bring them something that would make them well; that "something" was only oatmeal gruel and condensed milk but it worked wonders; we cooked it over Peggy's little turf fire; we collected three or four women from homes like Peggy's where someone had already died of the fever, so that they had no fear of going into infected houses, and we organised a rough and ready scheme of nursing. All the credit for the nursing scheme was due to Peggy who was far more knowledgeable and helpful than myself, but my cheerful confidence was more infectious than the fever. I told the men I wanted to hold a meeting on the quay, where the fishing boats came in, that evening and to gather the people there so we could decide on the necessary measures to end the famine.

A large crowd attended and I told them a fish-curing station was needed so that when they got a big catch of herrings they should not go to waste and each house should have some for preserving as the people in France had when the weather was too bad for the Curraghs to go out, and I told them that if they demanded this as a right, I would see they got it and the building of it would be better paid than work on the Relief. I distributed the leaflet. I could see that Mr. Kelly the owner of the store did not altogether approve of the leaflet and one man said to me:

"But what is there for us to take? There is nothing except at Mr. Kelly's store and it is Mrs. Kelly who is keeping us all alive."

"Are there not sheep upon the mountains that belong to the landlords?" I replied.

There was silence. Someone said: "We are not sheep-stealers." Another: "We don't eat meat."

"You are worse then sheep-stealers if you allow one of your children to die of hunger when there is food to be taken. Sheep can be killed and made into soup which will keep your wives and children alive and if you go to jail for it, you will go as honourable men, for a decent cause, but if you are clever, no one will go to jail. Who is to stop you on these lonely mountains! Be men. Go out hunting!"

The men shuffled uncomfortably; I saw that the fish-curing station was a more popular idea, but it was of no immediate value and it was immediate results for which I was looking to stop the famine. I told them about the '98 Centenary and about the Frenchmen who were again coming to Ireland and that the Irish people were determined to be free. This roused a little enthusiasm but they were too hungry. However, they raised a small cheer as Peggy and I walked off.

"Will they take the sheep?" I asked her. She shook her head. Later I learned that a few had taken my advice, but not to the extent I would have wished.

Next day the doctor from Ballycastle arrived; it was weeks since he had visited the district.

Mrs. Kelly said: "I suppose he has heard of you being here and thinks he must show up."

I had a long talk with him. He seemed a kindly well-meaning man; he was very apologetic. "Sure, what good can I do, Miss Gonne? It is food the people need, not medicine."

"Order food supplies," I answered.

"And if I do, the Killala Union goes bankrupt. What good has it done them in Bellmullet? They have Dublin Castle vice-Guardians now, but that won't prevent deaths from starvation."

"Order this food all the same, doctor," I said.

"If I get the sack my wife and children will starve then."

He went round and visited all the sick people and ordered some food and medicine to be supplied. "You certainly have put great heart into the people," he said; "they are all talking of you." He also told me that two of the boys who were distributing my leaflets round Ballycastle had been arrested. I sent a wire by the Mail car ordering more leaflets with my name printed on them this time so that if the distributors were arrested I would have to be prosecuted also.

The *Freeman's Journal* published the first of my famine articles; I received a cheque for two guineas from the editor and a request for more articles, especially on the Relief works, and a few cheques from people who had read the article, which were very useful for immediate relief. Leaving Peggy Hegarty in charge of the nursing I proceeded by Mail car to Belmullet.

Monsignor Hewson, the Parish Priest of Belmullet, received me kindly when I called, for which I was surprised and thankful, for the Bishop had denounced me and the '98 Centenary Committee in Mayo for stirring up old hatreds which should be forgotten and for encouraging revolutionary spirit. All the young priests who had joined our committees had been ordered to leave them.

"What is this I hear," said Monsignor Hewson; "you are teaching my people it is no sin to steal." But there was a twinkle in his eyes and he smiled.

"I have the backing of Popes and of Saints for that," I replied, handing him a leaflet.

"I don't blame you," he said; "the condition of the people is desperate and the M.P.s are doing nothing. I read your article in the *Freeman's Journal*. You have understated things. You have not said the worst, which is that they have been forced to eat every seed potato and it is time for spring-sowing and there is nothing being put into the ground, so famine next year is inevitable." He was evidently seriously alarmed.

I told him the *Freeman's Journal* had asked me to write an article on the relief works.

"Say they are only organising famine. Sixpence a day for useless work, making roads leading nowhere, or moving hillocks from one side of the road to the other. Sixpence a day to feed a family often of twelve or thirteen people!" He was particularly enraged over the rule which allowed only the head of the family to be taken on. If it happened to be a woman she had to go while her grown-up sons remained idle. "Only yesterday," he said, "I was called to see a little child who is nearly burnt to death from falling into the fire while his mother was on the Relief road. My curate shall drive you round and show you the four Relief Works to-morrow and then you can write."

Next day, driving to the Relief Works, Father Munelly told me a man had died on the works a few days previously. The overseers and gangers were respectful to Father Munelly and the people crowded up to see a stranger. The overseer knew nothing about a man having died at the works; he said, when pressed by Father Munelly: "Oh, I suppose you mean the poor fellow who had fits. He got one on his way home, I heard. He was taken to a friend's house and died."

I saw the people stir and look at each other uneasily. Many had no English; those who had were telling the others.

Father Munelly, speaking in Irish, asked: "Is that what you all say?"

Some shook their heads, but no one spoke. They seemed terrorised.

"Here, Tom Mulherne, speak out and tell this lady how Patrick Duane died."

"Right here, your Reverence, on the road we are making yonder. We carried him all the way to Moran's but he was dead."

"Get back to your work, all of you," said the overseer angrily.

"Stay," I called, climbing back on the car and standing up. "Before you go, I have something to say and Father Munelly will translate for those who don't understand me. This famine must be stopped. We know the way to stop it. Come to Belmullet to-morrow at eleven o'clock, all of you, and bring every grown man from your districts who can walk. You will find it worth your while."

The overseer came forward: "Very sorry, Miss, but none of these people can come; they have to be at work."

"Work will have to stop to-morrow," I answered loudly, "the people have something more important to do. Will you come?"

Some shouted: "We will."

The overseer looked angry and called out: "Any man or woman absent from the works to-morrow will be sacked and get no pay on Saturday."

"Any man or woman who is sacked will be taken on at my employ at double wage. Please, Father Munelly, will you translate."

We drove off. "How will you keep that promise, Miss Gonne, if they are sacked?"

"I don't know. But I must have them all in Belmullet for the Board meeting if we are to stop the famine. I wonder, will Monsignor Hewson take the chair for me."

"Monsignor doesn't like public meetings; but he is so upset about the famine he might," said his curate.

At each of the four Relief Works I told the people the same thing and ordered them all to be in Belmullet at eleven o'clock and asked them to collect the people of their districts.

We drove back to Monsignor Hewson's and I asked him if he would take the chair at the meeting I had called.

"You don't expect me to preach to them that they are to steal? But I will take the chair for you. I have just heard of your work in Belderrig. Good work. You have put new life into the people there; they say there have been no more deaths since you got the nursing going."

I drew up a list of minimum demands.

(1) The sixpence a day paid on Relief work to be raised to one shilling.

(2) No woman who could get a man to replace her to work on the roads.

(3) 1s. 6d. a week extra as lodging money to any who had to walk over a mile to the Relief works.

(4) Immediate free distribution of seed potatoes to prevent recurrence of famine.

(5) The work of preparing the ground and planting the seeds on the holdings to be paid a shilling a day as relief work.

The two curates saw me back to the hotel. As we passed, a woman snatched up her child and drew it into the house as though afraid; another woman shrank back into her house and crossed herself; a girl caught the end of my cloak and kissed it and a woman pulled her back.

I said to Father Munelly: "Why do some of the people seem afraid of me?"

The curates laughed. "You haven't heard?" said Father Munelly.

The other curate said: "Don't tell her."

"But I want to know."

And Father Munelly said: "Did you ever hear of Brian Ruadh and his prophecies?"

I shook my head.

"Brian Ruadh was an old man, reputed to be very wise and a great scholar. He went to a fair and was late returning and couldn't cross the ford in the dark and went to sleep in the fairy wood where none should ever linger. People found him there in the morning and helped him home. He said he knew he was going to die and asked them to send for the priest and he then wrote down the things revealed to him in the haunted wood. First, that his own death was near and to prepare for it. Second, that news would be carried into Belmullet on the top of sticks and that carriages without horses would drive through the mountains. That there would be a great war, multitudes would be killed and soldiers would land in Blacksod Bay. That there would be a famine and that a woman dressed in green would come and preach the revolt. After that, men would rise and there would be fighting and many killed but that the English would in the end be driven out. All the people know the prophecy of Brian Ruadh. He died the day after he wrote it down.

"Telegraph posts have brought news to Belmullet on the top of sticks; the light railway has come as far as Killala and there are plans to bring it as far as Belmullet. That is the carriages driving without horses through the mountains. Soldiers were landed from a warship in Blacksod Bay during the evictions. And now there is a famine and you have come and are wearing a green dress; so you are the woman of the prophecy,—the woman who is to bring war and victory. Do you wonder that some of the women are afraid of you and that the men are ready to follow you anywhere?"

"Of course, Miss Gonne," said Father Byrne, "that is all nonsense and superstition, but the people are all saying it."

In Donegal, being the woman of the Sidhe had helped me to put evicted families back in their homes and release prisoners. I hoped that being the woman of the prophecies in Mayo would help me to stop the famine. I went to my hotel and wrote an article on the Relief Works for the *Freeman's Journal*.

Next day the people from the whole countryside crowded into Belmullet. The biggest meeting, people told me, Belmullet had ever seen. The Relief Works were entirely deserted in spite of threats of dismissal from the overseers. Some twenty constabulary men looked on helplessly. It was a quiet, anxious crowd of ragged barefooted men and women.

Monsignor Hewson blessed the people and spoke about the famine and told them to trust in God and to stand together and said a few bitter words about the British Government. The people raised a shrill cheer when they saw him, then he introduced me.

I told them that those who had no fear could stop the famine; that God, having given us life, it was our duty to protect it; that men were cowards if they allowed their children to die of hunger; that, after consultations with many, I had drawn up the minimum demands of this great meeting of the people of Erris which they were to endorse and that I was going to present them to the Vice-Guardians at the Board meeting in progress in the Court House and would bring them the answer immediately. Above all, no one was to leave this meeting till I returned with the answer.

Monsignor Hewson called on them to endorse the demands by acclamation and the people responded by another shrill cheer, more like a cry than a cheer. He told his senior curate to accompany me as a witness to the Court House. An old man, helping me from the wagonette, said: "They'll never give all that, but God bless you."

At the Court House, Father Byrne and myself were at once admitted. There were the two Vice-Guardians from Dublin Castle, a representative from the Congested Districts Board, two representatives from the Government Relief Works who were in charge of the famine roads, and the Town Clerk, seated round a table in the Board Room. The chairman was one of the Vice-Guardians.

He said, in a hectoring tone: "Miss Gonne, what do you mean by bringing all these people into the town? What good will it do? You know it will mean many being turned off the Relief Works."

"They have come to formulate their demands because the Relief Works are not stopping the famine or famine deaths. They have elected me as their spokesman to present their demands. Here they are." And I read them slowly and distinctly.

I saw sneering smiles on the faces of the officials, especially at the clause that the people were to be paid for work on their own holdings.

"Of course these demands are ridiculous and impossible," said the chairman.

"I am sorry you should say that," I answered very gently, "because I hate violence and bloodshed and if that is the answer of the board, this is what it means. You are quite right in saying I brought all these people here. I did so because I cannot watch any more deaths from starvation. If people are

to die, they shall die fighting. You know they are desperate
and that they will do whatever I tell them to do." I looked
at the overseers of the famine roads. "Your overseers told
them not to come; I told them to come; they obeyed me.
They will do whatever I tell them. And if that is the answer
you are going to give I shall have to take it to them and tell
them what to do next."

"What are you going to tell them to do?"

"To take food; to begin here, at once, in this town and
take everything there is in it and neither you nor your policemen can prevent it. It will mean bloodshed, perhaps death
for some, as your twenty policemen are armed. But ten thous-
and people will soon take the guns from twenty policemen
and it will be at least two, perhaps three days before you can
get reinforcements of either police or military. There is no
railway, remember. By that time the people will be scattered
over the hills. You may make some arrests, but in jail the
prisoners will be fed. You may arrest me and much good it
will do England in America and France to arrest a woman
trying to save life."

The gentlemen were looking uncomfortable and whispering
to each other. The chairman said:

"Miss Gonne, you talk very unreasonably. Let me see these
demands again and please withdraw while we consider them."

I handed him the paper. "There is nothing unreasonable
in these demands and please remember they are the minimum
and I hope you won't be too long in giving me the answer,
for the people are waiting."

Outside, through the open window, we could hear the
confused murmur of that great throng and the strange soft
sound of thousands of bare feet beating on the hard earth.
The curate and I withdrew to the outer office. I felt horribly
anxious, for though I had spoken with quiet confidence of
what we intended doing, I realised that starving people are

not the best material for a fight; that the prejudice against stealing was inbred and hard to overcome; that, if it came to violence, I doubted of the moral support of Monsignor Hewson and his curates; the one with me was looking out of the window rather dismally. The prophecy of Brian Ruadh was my best hope. Some of the men, I knew, would obey me and people would certainly get killed. It was a great relief when the door opened and the Town Clerk summoned us, after about ten minutes, to the Board room.

The chairman had the paper of the demands in his hand. He spoke in a different tone to the one he had previously used.

"Miss Gonne," he said, "I want you to understand we have the welfare of these poor people as much at heart as you have. If you had spoken differently we would have told you so at once and considered these requests. We have done so now and have come to the conclusion that there is nothing unreasonable in them; and if you will send those people back to their homes quietly and at once, you can tell them that their requests will be granted."

"All of them," I said, refraining from noticing the change of the word 'demand' and trying hard to conceal my joy and to speak quietly.

"Yes."

"To-morrow, Saturday, they will all receive six shillings instead of three."

"Yes, but in the matter of free distribution of seed they will have to wait, for there are no seed potatoes to be had in the district. They will have to come from Scotland."

I knew it to be true that there was no seed to be got in the whole of Mayo.

"How long will it take to get it?" I asked. "It is high time it was in the ground if there is not to be a worse famine next year."

The chairman and the Town Clerk were speaking together about the sailing of a boat from Glasgow. "About a fortnight. We are telegraphing to Dublin to-day. The order will be given at once. It is of course necessary to avert another famine."

"The people are to be paid a shilling a day for planting them on their holdings?"

"Yes."

I got up and bowed politely. "Father Byrne and I will convey your answer."

"You will send that crowd home at once?" said one of the officials, as I passed.

"Certainly. That is our side of the undertaking."

The Town Clerk, as he showed me down the stairs, patted me on the back: "You are a wonderful lady. No one else could have done it," he whispered excitedly.

"Will they keep their promises?" I said.

"I think so; you scared them stiff."

"The crowd did," I laughed.

Father Byrne went off to report to Monsignor Hewson who had retired into the presbytery. Father Munelly joined me on the edge of the crowd. We got into the wagonette and Monsignor Hewson came out and resumed the chair. He told them to be very grateful to the young lady who had come to their help and said a lot of kind things about me. I then read out each of the minimum demands which had been accorded and Father Munelly translated them into Irish.

"Now," I said, "you all understand and you can return to your homes; but remember you have won these small things by your numbers and by your united strength. By your strength and courage you must win the freedom of Ireland."

It was an indescribable scene. People crying and laughing at once; crowding into the wagonette, kissing my hands and my dress. "You must stay with us. If you go, they won't keep their promises."

"You will see that to-morrow, pay-day, at the relief works. No one is to accept less than six shillings. I have other work to do; I must leave to-night. But have no fear. It is you yourselves, by refusing to be frightened of the overseers and coming here in spite of them, that won the victory. Trust in your own strength. Good luck and God's blessing on you all."

Monsignor Hewson and the curates had to use all their authority to get me out of that excited crowd into the presbytery till they gradually dispersed.

The promises were all kept, so I had no need to return and I wanted to get back to Dublin to see about a fish-curing plant for Belderrig. I secured this through the kind-hearted support of an old official of the Congested Districts Board, Sir Joseph Robinson. But I returned to Mayo and spent nearly two months there wandering from place to place, arranging school-feeding and rough-and-ready nursing and working up enthusiasm for the local '98 Centenary monument. Before leaving, I presented Peggy with two lambs so that next year she would have wool to spin herself the making of a dress.

I was worn out when I got back to my little flat in Paris where I stayed lazily in bed for a fortnight, reading novels and answering no letters, but I had stopped the famine in Mayo and, I think, saved many lives.

Talking in the British House of Commons would never have done it.

CHAPTER XIX

THE '98 CENTENARY

THE CENTENARY COMMEMORATION, for which such great preparations had been made, seemed to me a little disappointing, as public ceremonies so often are. The preparations for it had been the really important part, for it had given an opportunity to bring the hope of complete independence and of the means of its attainment,—Wolfe Tone's means,—slumbering in the hearts of the whole Irish race, to the surface consciousness of the people.

Vast crowds attended all the ceremonies, especially those in the country, and people, even the old, walked miles, sometimes all through the night, not to miss them. Perhaps they did not feel the same sense of disappointment of which I was conscious, for they had not been mixed up with the bickerings and intrigues continually going on in the Central Committee sitting in the City Hall, presided over by John O'Leary.

He was a noble figure-head but too old to grasp and make use of a situation, and Connolly, the only man who would have known how to, was not on that Central Committee. Indeed I think he must have been away organising for his party in Belfast, for I cannot remember him at any of the Commemoration Ceremonies.

The bishops, more swiftly aware than the British of the stirring of the deep-rooted desire for complete independence, to which they are always consistently hostile (perhaps because they put interests of the Church first and judge that a Catholic Ireland within the British Empire is of greater missionary value than a small separate Catholic nation would be) had, some of them openly, all of them tacitly, opposed the Commemoration

Committees and had withdrawn the priests from them in the early stages of preparation. But in spite of their influence they had not been able to keep the people away. Archbishop Walsh of Dublin, however, subscribed £20 to the Wolfe Tone Memorial Fund. I shocked a meeting in Kerry by saying I was delighted that the bishops had withdrawn the priests, for I did not think either a priest or a publican should be chairman of any National committee or hold key positions in the National movement, because they were not free agents. The priests had a higher spiritual allegiance and the publicans depended on the police for their licences and so for their daily bread. When their hearts were with us we were thankful and they could help quietly; but it was unfair to put men in positions where their duties might clash. Freedom could be won only by free men with one allegiance,—Ireland. I did not know it, but the chairman of this meeting was a publican, a good and sincere man. He shook hands with me after and said I was right but that he personally was ready to sacrifice his daily bread for Ireland, if the choice came.

The Parliamentary Party, both Parnellites and anti-Parnellites still dangling the wilted carrot of Home Rule before the donkey's nose, could not afford to remain outside such a popular national movement and their adherents on the central and local Committees were constantly wangling to get them elected as orators at the public meetings. Undoubtedly, being more practised, they were better orators than most of the young men of the Revolutionary movement and many of them shared sincerely in the National love for dead heroes. In the Revolutionary movement itself the split in the *Clan-na-Gael* in America was faithfully mirrored in Ireland. John O'Leary personally favoured Devoy and had a large following in the I.R.B.; Dr. Mark Ryan, who had an equally large following, supported the O'Sullivan side; Fred Allen was chief lieutenant of the Devoy section.

I was always opposed to him and suspected him of helping intrigues to let the Parliamentary Party control the movement.

What worried me the most was that, while there were many good, sincere unselfish men, I did not see one on the Central Committee who, I felt, had the capacity for revolutionary leadership.

There were always contentions over the Memorial. Most of the Central Committee wanted all moneys concentrated in raising a great Memorial to Wolfe Tone in Dublin, but the Country Committees very naturally wanted their own memorials to local heroes. I supported the local Committees in this because of the greater opportunities it gave for preaching Wolfe Tone doctrines throughout the country.

Willie Yeats accused me of responsibility for encouraging much bad art. His faith in the capacity of local committees to select artists to execute the monuments was weak. Their taste was certainly influenced by the cheap Italian plaster statues decorating the churches and reproduced in marble or stone in the cemeteries. (How could it be otherwise, with a School of Art which deprecated nude models for students?) I was equally doubtful of the selection of the Central Committee, though I know Willie Yeats would have put up a gallant fight for good art.

Personally I would have rejoiced if all the monuments could have taken the form of great rocks with names inscribed on them or of well-copied Celtic crosses, but I knew it would have been waste of time to try to have this done. To me it was primarily the thought of Wolfe Tone, and securing the achievement of his work, that counted. I often blessed the forethought of Robert Emmett in forbidding a monument to be raised to him till Ireland was free.

Certainly the local committees showed more grit and determination than did the Central Committee, for all the local monuments were up, paid for and unveiled within the year, while the Central Committee never got beyond laying a foundation stone for the monument of Wolfe Tone at the top of Grafton Street, which stone the Cosgrave Government, after the Treaty of 1921, had dug up and thrown on the Corporation rubbish yard, where it lies alongside the statue of King Billie blown up by the I.R.A.; and in this year of 1937 not a trace of even the humblest Memorial exists in the Capital city of Ireland to the name of Wolfe Tone or the Rebellion of 1798,—although thousands of pounds were subscribed for this purpose.

I had the honour of laying the foundation stone of a very creditable monument in Tralee which was later destroyed by the Black and Tans and saw a good Celtic Cross unveiled in Mount Mellick; and if the monument in Ballina is unsatisfying as a work of art, the laying of its foundation stone and its unveiling formed the occasion for two French delegations to Ireland and a return invitation for an Irish delegation to visit France.

I remember how, at the unveiling of that Ballina monument, where a lot of people had walked in from Belmullet and Belderrig, one old man came to me after the ceremony and whispered: "But where are the French?" I pointed to Professor Meuis, Commandant du Château, George d'Esparbes and Madame de Ste Croix, still on the platform. "No, no. I mean the French army." So I think some of the people were vaguely disappointed like myself.

The great shipload of Irish-Americans, so loudly announced, did not arrive; the war in the Philippines was given as an excuse and the American delegates came in dribs and drabs and too late for many of the principal events, such as the banquet at the Mansion House and the laying of the foundation stone of Wolfe Tone's Memorial in Dublin. They were always wandering off to look for the homes of their ancestors or to see relations and were very hard to keep together. The Reception Committee spent a lot of time hunting for the delegates. Mr.

Bulfin and his Argentine group were always ready; I had no difficulty with the French delegation and Mr. Gillingham from South Africa and Cipriani were always in time.

The Country committees naturally wanted some foreign delegates at their celebrations, while the French delegates, speaking no English, refused to be separated, and we had a busy time trying to satisfy everybody.

On the 15th of August contingents from every county and every town in Ireland gathered for the laying of the Foundation Stone of the Wolfe Tone Memorial in Dublin. Unanimously John O'Leary, the veteran Fenian who had never compromised Wolfe Tone's claim for the Sovereign Independence of Ireland, was selected for laying the Stone. Sharp divisions occurred in the Central Centenary Committee over inviting members of the discredited Parliamentary Party, who had whittled down Ireland's claim to Home Rule under an English king, to speak on the occasion. In the end the desire for a united National demonstration, in honour of the man England had murdered, prevailed and John Redmond, representing the Parnellite section, and John Dillon representing the anti-Parnellite section, received invitations. As compromise never stands still, the Lord Mayor of Dublin, who had refused the use of the Mansion House to the Wolfe Tone Memorial Fund Committee, was also invited. To offset him, after much discussion, Willie Yeats, as an I.R.B. man, was also asked to speak. In the end so many people crowded onto that Platform that it was a wonder it stood the strain.

Standing in the crowd, for I did not care to be on the platform while Parliamentarians were eulogising Wolfe Tone and trying to keep the people from following his teaching, my hand was grasped by Mr. Birmingham, an old Fenian workingman member of the Dublin Amnesty Association.

"Why are you not up there on the platform?" he said.

"Because I don't like the company."

"There are enough of us here to put you up and insist on hearing you."

I shook my head: "That would not be wise. There must be no clashes that the enemy Press would make use of. Besides we all love John O'Leary, and there are the foreign delegates."

"Come with us then and see the stone," said Mr. Lambert, president of the Amnesty Association and, pushing their way through the crowd, the two old Fenians led me to the back of the platform and we climbed down a little ladder into the foundations of the monument. The workmen who had built them were standing around; they had been manœuvring the pulleys which had lowered the stone into place when John O'Leary had performed the ceremony.

"We have seen to it that it is well and rightly laid and the parchment and pieces of money and flowers are under it. While those blatherskites are talking on the top, you make the oration down here."

And in a low voice I promised for the Irish people that we would achieve Wolfe Tone's work,—an Independent Irish Republic.

One of the stewards of the Centenary Committee, wearing a green sash, looked down the hole. The crowd, who had recognised me, seeing me go to the back of the platform, were ready to give me a cheer when I appeared and, when I did not, were pressing round to the back to see what was happening; their movement had been noticed by those on the platform. The stewards were watching out to prevent any counter-demonstration.

"What are you doing down there?" he called.

"None of your business. Go back and listen to Mr. Redmond and Mr. Dillon!" Mr. Birmingham answered.

"You can't disturb the meeting, Miss Gonne. Your place is on the platform."

"No," I answered. "The followers of Wolfe Tone are speaking to him. You need not pay any attention. We are not going to disturb the meeting. We have done and I am going home"; and, helped by the workmen, I climbed up the ladder and walked down Grafton Street.

I felt depressed.

The Commemoration ceremonies were a little dispiriting and disappointing, in spite of those huge crowds.

CHAPTER XX

"ENGLAND'S DIFFICULTY . . ."

THE BOER WAR was on. "England's difficulty is Ireland's opportunity." How often I had heard these words! I was determined to put them into acts.

Though Cecil Rhodes was distributing fortunes in the lobbies of the House of Commons chiefly in the form of Stock Exchange advice, the Irish parliamentary party were pro-Boer.

The *United Irishman* started a vigorous campaign. Griffith had worked with John MacBride in the Langlaarte mine in the Transvaal until home-sickness brought him back to Ireland. He wrote well-informed articles under different pseudonyms and in different styles. Few knew that they came from the same pen.

It was in this year that I at last succeeded in founding *Inghinidhe na hEireann* (the Daughters of Ireland).

I called a meeting of all the girls who, like myself resented being excluded, as women, from National Organisations. Our object was to work for the complete independence of Ireland.

Willie Rooney and Arthur Griffith helped us; the sisters of both and Willie Rooney's fiancée, Maire Kileen, were on the Committee. Among others were Mary, Bridget and Julia Maher, Marcella Cosgrave, Maggie Quinn, Mary Macken, while Mary Quinn became our very active and efficient secretary.

Besides organising free classes in history, the Irish language, music and dancing for children, we started an intense campaign against enlistment in the British Army. To make recruiting easier, the Army Authorities altered their rule of obliging the men to sleep in barracks, and O'Connell Street at night used to be full of Red coats walking with their girls. We got out leaflets on the shame of Irish girls consorting with the soldiers of the enemy of their country and used to distribute them to the couples in the streets, with the result that almost every night there were fights in O'Connell Street, for the brothers and the sweet-hearts of *Inghinidhe na hEireann* used to come out also to prevent us being insulted by the English soldiers and the ordinary passers-by often took our side. The Dublin Police were slow to interfere, for we managed to get some Clergymen to denounce the danger to the morals of young innocent working girls consorting with the military, and persuaded the Dublin Guardians to raise the question of illegitimate babies in the Workhouses,—for which there was enough justification to make it unwise for Dublin Castle to allow cases where such issues would get publicity in the police Courts; fighting soldiers became quite a popular evening entertainment with young men,—in which Arthur Griffith and Mary Quinn's brother used to take part, though Griffith I think hated it. Our girls used bravely to follow the recruiting sergeants even into the public houses, distributing thousands of leaflets written by a courageous priest, the Rev. Father Cavanagh of Limerick, setting forth Catholic teaching to the effect that anyone taking part in a war, knowing it to be unjust, and killing anybody, was guilty of murder.

Father Cavanagh was a Franciscan engaged in writing a history of '98 and, like Father Anderson, an Augustinian monk, honoured me with his friendship. I greatly reverenced both these men; the sane atmosphere of quiet holiness surrounded them both, though they were very different types,—Father Cavanagh, tall, ascetic, looking as if the spirit had burnt the flesh away,—Father Anderson stout and jovial. They both loved me because they knew I was sincerely working to free Ireland from the British Empire and helped me whenever they could. I think they were often in hot water with their superiors because of their passionate devotion to Ireland, for which they would have sacrificed every earthly thing, but of this they said little to one who was not of their Church; yet I often saw the same wistful, almost rebellious look in their eyes when they were unable to take part in actions of which they approved. They seldom spoke of religion to me, though both told me they were praying that I would one day join the Church. Father Cavanagh said: "I am certain you will."

He also made another prophecy which is almost fulfilled. I had heard that both these monks had helped the Fenians, and one day, when I was speaking enthusiastically of the I.R.B. and inveighing against the Church's denunciation of Secret Societies, Father Cavanagh said: "My child, even if as a priest I was not bound to disapprove of secret oath-bound societies because no one should surrender his free will, I would still oppose them. I believe they are worse than useless for the freeing of Ireland; the British Secret Service will always get inside and use them. If you live to be as old as I am you will realise this too; I make that prophecy."

I have come round to Father Cavanagh's point of view as I believe Ireland's cause was never on such a secure foundation as since the establishment of the I.R.A., an open military organisation which does not offer the same facilities to informers who, if they take the risk, are almost certain to get a bullet for their crime with the approval of the Irish People.

Inghinidhe na hEireann was one of the first societies for open Revolutionary work, and we almost stopped enlistment for the British Army in Dublin and considerably reduced it throughout the country.

This evidently so disturbed the authorities that they arranged that Queen Victoria should visit Ireland to stimulate recruiting.

She arrived in Dublin and was received and duly presented with the keys of the City of Dublin by a grovelling Unionist fishmonger who had succeeded in getting elected as Lord Mayor of Dublin with the assistance of one of the foremost members of the I.R.B., Fred Allan. This pure-souled revolutionist had come to the '98 Centenary Committee with cheques of £10 from Alderman Pile, the fishmonger, and £5 from Councillor Jones, his henchman. I had moved that the cheques be returned, as neither of the donors stood for Irish independence, and I had been outvoted on Fred Allan declaring he had converted them both to the National Cause. There was so much joy over the sinner that repenteth that these cheques led to the election of Alderman Pile to the mayoralty and the pure-souled revolutionist became his secretary and sat in the gilded Mayoral coach which, escorted by foot and horse police, drove through streets lined with military to present the Keys of the City to Victoria. The Dublin crowd had no chance of getting near the ceremony, but on its way back, when returning from the Royal procession, the gilded coach was sorely battered and its glass broken by the infuriated crowd on the quays and, white and trembling, the Lord Mayor and his revolutionary secretary were barely saved by the police from a dip in the Liffey.

At the Vice-Regal Lodge in Phoenix Park, Victoria the Famine Queen gave a treat to 15,000 school-children. Convent schools vied with the Protestant ascendancy in sending the largest contingents of children, shepherded by holy nuns. Obviously we could not interfere with nuns and children, and the Unionist papers revelled in picture and print descriptions of this spontaneous display of loyalty.

Inghinidhe na hEireann got out posters announcing a Patriotic children's treat to all children who had not participated in Queen Victoria's treat; and some twenty-thousand responded. We opened a subscription list to defray expenses and all our time, for two days and nights before it, was spent in cutting up hams and making sandwiches in a big store we had secured in Talbot Street. Headed by beflagged lorries piled with casks of ginger beer and twenty-thousand paper bags containing sandwiches, buns and sweets, that wonderful procession of children carrying green branches moved off from Beresford Place, marshalled by the young men of the Celtic Literary Society and the Gaelic Athletic Association on the march to Clonturk Park. Mary Quin and I, on an outside car, drove up and down the line, for the safety of such a huge concourse of children was a fearful responsibility; but there was no hitch. When the last child had left the Park I drove round to all the city hospitals. "We have never had a Sunday so free from child accidents," was the reply everywhere, and one enthusiastic young doctor said: "You should organise a children's treat every week."

The Patriotic Childrens' treat became legendary in Dublin and, even now, middle-aged men and women come up to me in the streets and say: "I was one of the patriotic children at your party when Queen Victoria was over."

Queen Victoria's children's Treat had been eclipsed. We knew that many unemployed Irishmen were being recruited in England, so we decided to carry our campaign there also. The courageous vicar of Plumpton, the Rev. Mr. Kennedy, who had helped in the Amnesty meetings, and I addressed a series of great meetings in Lancashire.

These meetings were so successful that the English, who pride themselves on always allowing free speech, banned them. I think they were the first meetings banned in England in our generation. We held them all the same and there were some dangerous rough-and-tumbles; the police joined the jingo mob in breaking them up. Irish crowds are not easily intimidated and there was some pretty hard fighting. Once I was rescued from the police by Jim Larkin and a band of Liverpool dockers;

once I was rescued from the mob by some Canadian volunteers on their way to South Africa to fight for the British. When they got me safely in a hotel and barred the doors I thanked them for their chivalrous conduct and I hope our conversation damped their ardour for the British Empire. They offered to stay and form a bodyguard for me if I was going to hold another meeting. But I was on my way to Paris where I had to make arrangements for French passports for Irishmen going to join the Irish Brigade.

Lieutenant Duboc of the French navy, author of a book which had created a sensation, *Le Point Faible de l'Angleterre*, showing England's vulnerability in regard to food, was a friend of mine. He put me in touch with a Captain Robert,—I think that was only his Christian name. He was quietly influential in army circles and ready to help us to help ourselves and the Boers. To him I spoke of an offer made a short time previously which I had been instructed to transmit. The I.R.B., owing to its scattered membership, was in a position to supply valuable information. Captain Robert and I shook hands on a bargain. I gave a letter of introduction to a friend of Captain Robert, a French colonel, who was to go to London.

Things were moving in the way I hoped. I deposited part of the funds of the Transvaal Committee, which we feared might be seized in Dublin, in the Crédit Lyonnais, and I arranged with the brother of Colonel de Villebons Mareuil (who was afterwards killed fighting for the Boers outside Ladysmith) and with a French ambulance going out under the Red Cross, that our doctors and a limited number of stretcher-bearers should travel with them. I then returned to Dublin, where I was billed to speak at a pro-Boer meeting arranged by the Transvaal Committee in Beresford Place.

I was in bed asleep when a knock came to my door. I sleepily said "Come in," and was surprised to see my landlord in his dressing gown.

"The police are downstairs; the Inspector says he wants to see you."

It was one o'clock. "Tell the police this is no hour to call and I will see them in the morning after breakfast."

"I have already said that," replied my landlord. "But the Inspector says he must see you to-night."

"He will have to come up then, for I am certainly not getting up to see him."

My landlord disappeared and presently I heard heavy trampling in the passage and he again knocked at the door. With him stood a big D.M.P. Inspector and behind them several constables. I sat up in bed.

"This is a strange time to disturb a lady. What is the meaning of it?" I asked.

The Inspector looked embarrassed. "Very sorry, Miss Gonne, but I had to deliver this into your own hand to have the proof that you received it," he said, holding out a large roll of paper.

I was curious to see what it was, but I replied: "Well, you can put it down on the table and I will read it to-morrow,"— and I yawned ostentatiously.

The sergeant unrolled the paper, a poster, and proceeded to read it to me. It was the ban on the pro-Boer meeting in Beresford Place.

"And you really think it worth while to disturb me at this hour for that?"

"You will be arrested, Miss Gonne, if you try to speak. I hope you will not: we wouldn't like that."

"Thank you, Inspector; good-night. You needn't have wakened me for that," and I lay down in the bed and the police and my landlord retired.

John O'Leary was to preside at the meeting. Michael Davitt, Willie Redmond, Griffith, Connolly and myself were the speakers. Great posters banning the meeting were posted up in the streets. The brake which was to serve as platform was standing at the door of our office in Abbey Street when I arrived. I nodded to the driver and went upstairs, wondering if all the speakers would turn up.

Arthur Griffith was writing out the resolution at the table. John O'Leary was beside him. James Connolly smiled at me.

"Our M.P.s are conspicuous by their absence," he remarked.

I knew Davitt was no shirker. He was resigning his seat in the British Parliament as a protest against the iniquity of this war. A few months later he went to the Transvaal and wrote the best book ever published on it. This extract from his preface to it gave Ireland's views on the subject and was much like what was said at many of our pro-Boer and anti-recruiting meetings, though I always insisted that, apart from rights and wrongs, it was the duty of Irishmen, till Ireland was free, to fight England whenever and wherever they could and use whatever means came to hand. The following is the extract:

"England has killed 14,000 Christian children, has imprisoned 45,000 Christian women in barbed-wire enclosures, has devastated two Christian countries where there was less poverty and less vice than in any other Christian community in the world and has armed savages to help her in a war which has its origin in motives as base and as odious as ever prompted a Sultan of Turkey to burn an Armenian village or to massacre his rebellious subjects. And yet Cardinal Vaughan, in the name of the Catholic Church of England, the Archbishop of Canterbury, on behalf of the Protestants, Mr. Hugh Price Hughes of the Nonconformists of the same enlightened Christian nation, piously call down God's blessing upon the arms which are killing and exterminating little Christian nations in South Africa."

I wondered why Davitt was not with us.

Willie Redmond's absence also surprised me. He was actually vice-President of our Transvaal Committee and I knew he was in Ireland. There was no excuse for him.

He was killed fighting in the English Army in 1915. It is the inconsequence of some Irishmen which leaves Ireland still unfree!

"Well, we had better be going," said John O'Leary and we all got into the brake. I noticed James Connolly climbed on the box seat by the driver though there was plenty of room for him with us. Just as we were starting Pat O'Brien came up.

"Have you a place for me? I'm coming. It's not Davitt's fault he's not here, but his wife is expecting a baby and if he got arrested it would upset her badly. Have me instead." I made a place for him beside me.

Beresford Place is a big space to hold. There was only a single cordon of police and big crowds standing outside. As we turned out of Abbey Street, a group of police came forward and stopped the car. "Go back. You can't pass, the meeting is banned."

I heard Connolly say: "Drive on," but the driver hesitated. "Go back, I say," called the sergeant, and because he didn't and the horses moved a step forward, the police made a dash and pulled him off the driver's seat and arrested him. I understood then why Connolly had taken the box seat. While the driver was being hauled off he seized the reins, whipped up the horses, and at a furious gallop, scattering people and police, he drove right through the police cordon, the brake swaying dangerously over the rough ground, the crowd cheering wildly and rushing in through the broken cordon and breaking it on the opposite side.

In a moment Beresford Place was a seething mass of people all shouting: "Up the Boers! Up the Republic!"

"Quick," Connolly said to me. "Get O'Leary to put the resolution. We are not likely to have much time."

O'Leary, looking very happy, rose, his grey beard blowing in the wind, a frail venerable figure the people honoured. When he could get silence, he said:

"There is no need for speeches. We are here to pledge all the help in our power to the Boers whose enemy is ours," and he called on me to read the resolutions. I had hardly finished reading them and getting them passed with acclamation when the mounted police arrived and, employing our tactics, succeeded, with the foot police, in forcing a way through the crowds and surrounding the brake. This time the police held the horses' heads and led them and, surrounded by a huge guard of police, we were all slowly driven to Store Street police station. The gates of the yard were opened and the brake driven in. We were all prisoners.

Out from the office came the station sergeant, more policemen and another Inspector; there were consultations between them and the Inspector who was in charge of us and some plainclothes men. The mounted police formed up outside and we heard them trot away, probably to patrol Beresford Place. I heard the station sergeant say: "We can't keep them here." All the police kept looking at the people in the brake, and there was consternation on their faces.

"John O'Leary, Maud Gonne, a Member of Parliament, they have more than they bargained for," said Connolly, an amused smile on his face.

The two Inspectors went inside and the station sergeant advanced. "You can't stay here," he said abruptly.

"We don't want to," said Connolly, resuming the reins.

The gates were opened; Connolly turned the horses. As we drove out I saw the rueful face of the driver of the brake, looking out from the barred window of the lock-up, an illustration of the truth of the saying: "He who hesitates is lost."

"If you go back to Beresford Place you will be arrested," the sergeant called after us; but Connolly was heading the horses up Abbey Street. I climbed up over the rail to the box seat beside him.

"I didn't know you were such a great driver," I said.

He laughed. "We might resume the meeting in College Green," he said. "All your speeches were cut rather short," and he drove over O'Connell Bridge and up Westmoreland Street.

Trinity College was conferring Honorary Degrees on Joseph Chamberlain to show Ireland's loyalty to the British Empire; I believe this was the official reason for banning our meeting. A dozen or so policemen were trotting along the side-walk trying to keep up with the brake which Connolly drove at a quick pace. The streets were crowded with people, all talking about the banned meeting. A rumour that we had been arrested had gone round and groups cheered delightedly as they recognised us. We drew up in College Green and a big crowd gathered around. I stood up amid wild cheers and told the people we thought they would like to hear the resolutions which had been passed in Beresford Place.

Connolly was arguing with a policeman who was saying we could not hold a meeting there. Pat O'Brien called for cheers for the Boers, which was responded to wildly by the crowd. The noise and the cheering must have considerably marred the dignified proceedings within the College and made Chamberlain doubt about the love and loyalty of the Irish nation of which he was being assured. Then police reinforcements arrived and there were baton charges and charges of mounted police which are really much less dangerous. The horses never want to trample on people, and the Dublin crowd, being used to them, had developed the excellent tactics of opening before them and closing up again, so that generally the crowds had the satisfaction of seeing one or two police unhorsed as their horses slipped on the greasy pavements. Baton charges are much nastier.

However, gradually our brake was forced out of College Green and strong cordons of police established round Trinity College; but as Connolly drove slowly down Dame Street one or other of us made speeches to the crowds which followed us.

"There are only two sentries at the gates of Dublin Castle," whispered Connolly to me. "Shall I drive in and seize the Castle?"

"There are soldiers inside. It will mean shooting and the people are unarmed," I said, hesitatingly, and Connolly turned down Parliament Street and over Capel Street Bridge.

I sometimes wonder if I was wrong to hesitate. It would certainly have caused a great sensation, but I doubt if that unarmed crowd could have taken the Castle. John MacBride, to whom I told the incident later, said I was wrong not to have tried. But I don't think James Connolly thought so. If he had, he would not have asked me but would have done it. Though at that time Connolly was little known outside the labour movement, I had absolute confidence in him, but the people with whom I was working hardly knew him and distrusted all Socialists.

I knew very few people were armed and I had plans for arming which I hoped would materialise. We drove O'Leary back to his lodgings. He was tired but satisfied; we had held the banned meeting; we had considerably disturbed loyal addresses and no one could say Dublin was loyal to the British Empire.

Connolly drove the brake back to its stables; Griffith went off to look after newspaper reports and publicity. Pat O'Brien asked me to have tea and on the way I said I must look after our only casualty, our imprisoned driver.

We found he had been released. It would have been too absurd to have arrested the only one of the party who had not been at the banned meeting.

CHAPTER XXI

END OF THE ALLIANCE

Kᴀᴛʜʟᴇᴇɴ ᴀɴᴅ ʜᴇʀ children had been wintering in Italy and were staying in Switzerland on their way home. I joined them at Vévey after the Irish delegation had left Paris, for I was tired and wanted a rest and I had not seen Kathleen for a long time.

Millevoye wrote to me from Lyons that he needed a rest too and asked me to meet him at Chamonix. We had not seen much of each other in Paris except at the public demonstrations; and one night at the opera; Mr. Boyer, its Secretary, thinking the Irish Delegation was still in Paris, had sent me a box for the performance of *La Valkyrie*, my favourite opera, in which Bréval, an ideal Valkyrie, was singing. I regretted the delegation had left. Arthur Griffith and Mary Quinn would have enjoyed it so much. I invited Ghenia de Ste Croix and Millevoye who loved music and had a lovely, though untrained, voice, somewhat injured by much public speaking. I had quite succeeded in making him get over his patriotic prejudice against German music and he was nearly as enthusiastic a lover of Wagner as myself. We had often planned going to Bayreuth together but never found time.

That night he told me and Ghenia de Ste Croix that he knew a woman who sang some of the Valkyrie music better than Bréval but that her talent was never rewarded. "She should be in the opera, but she has no chance because she will not give herself to Ministers."

"They don't take singers from café-chantants generally at the Opéra," said Ghenia rather acidly.

Millevoye looked annoyed and turning to me said: "I will bring her to see you. She is very anxious to meet you and said she would sing at any of your parties."

"I am not giving any parties and have not time to meet anyone before going to Switzerland."

And then the curtain went up. On the way home Ghenia said: "You are away from Paris too much, Maud chérie."

It was in a flowery meadow, surrounded by snow-capped mountains at the foot of Mont Blanc, that the alliance against the British Empire, which had meant so much in my life, ended.

I held a copy of *La Patrie*, the French evening paper of which Millevoye was editor and which I always received.

It was I who had made him take up the editorship of that paper, owned by Jules Jaluzot, the Director of the *Printemps* shop. It had been at a time when Millevoye was so utterly discouraged, after the death of General Boulanger and his own political eclipse, following the cleverly engineered plot of the Norton forgery which had separated him from his friend Henri de Rochefort, that he was inclined to leave political life. He said he was too old to begin again. I had put my whole will into making him regain confidence in himself and realise that, with his wonderful power of literary expression, he would be able to make that little-read paper an instrument with which to rebuild the shattered fortunes of his party and regain his old influence.

Luck, the will of the gods and Millevoye's own hard work had made *La Patrie* one of the most influential of the Paris papers.

I said now: "How could you have written this article which is so bad and which contradicts all we have been working for?"

It was a sentimental, exaggerated appeal for Alsace-Lorraine, based on the sufferings of its people, not in accord with material facts, and pointing to Germany as the one and only enemy of France.

"It is so unlike your style," I said.

Millevoye answered: "I did not write it. I only signed it. It was written by a woman who loves Alsace-Lorraine as you love Ireland."

For a long while I did not speak. I gazed at those cruel snow mountains which were turning my heart into stone in spite of the scent of the flowers and the hum of the wild bees around us, whispering of life.

Millevoye was talking a great deal; I hardly heard what he said. I think it was about the change which he said had come over me since I had taken up with those absurd Irish revolutionists who would never do anything and would let me down.

"I have seen them and judged them. Go back and work with the Home Rule party. Outside parliament you won't be able to do anything for Ireland. Take my advice."

My voice sounded strange and toneless to myself as I replied to these last words: "I would be foolish to do that, now our alliance is at an end. It has lasted for thirteen years, a long time in human life."

"Don't talk nonsense. You know I will always help you."

"You can't now, for we have different friends, different enemies and our roads lead different ways. You need not tell me the name of the writer of that article. It is the singer you wanted to bring to see me in Paris, a friend of Clemenceau. He has triumphed at last through her and broken our alliance. Good-bye, old friend, I go on my way alone and carry on the fight."

Though casually we met again several times we neither ever alluded either to the singer whose musical talents were unrequited or to our old alliance, because Millevoye became a supporter of the "Entente Cordiale", the pact between

France and England which eventually brought the World War and the restoration of Alsace-Lorraine to France at the price of ten million dead, and to England vast colonial territories, to defend which she is preparing a still greater war.

Millevoye died when I, with Constance Markiewicz and Tom Clarke's widow, was a prisoner in Holloway Prison, accused of taking part in a German plot and grieving that the charge was false.

CHAPTER XXII

BETRAYAL

I WAS TO GO to Brussels to see Dr. Leydes, the Transvaal representative in Europe, in order to make arrangements for the reception of the Irish Ambulance and I wanted to explain to him verbally that we had a waiting list of thousands of men all anxious to go to fight for the Boers if travelling arrangements could be made for them. It took £40 to equip a man in Dublin and get him out to the Transvaal; and the funds at our disposition were very limited. Before setting out I saw a member of the I.R.B., for I had a still more interesting plan of war to suggest.

England was finding it very hard to get recruits for what was now acknowledged would prove a long campaign. If even one British Transport could be sent to the bottom it would considerably increase recruiting difficulties. Through my French friends the means of doing this were available,— bombs disguised as lumps of coal. Had the I.R.B. the means of getting these into the coal on the ships? The idea was accepted and I was authorised to make concrete proposals to Dr. Leydes.

Dr. Leydes was a polished diplomat. He received me cordially and formally sent the thanks of his Government to the Irish people for their proof of sympathy in giving an ambulance. He had heard of my anti-recruiting campaign and was very interested in it. I spoke to him of the number of Irish volunteers only waiting for the means of transit to join Colonel Blake's Brigade; but to this Dr. Leydes replied that untrained men who did not know the language or the country would be of little use. Stopping recruits for the English was far more valuable assistance, he said.

I then told him of our revolutionary organisation.

"This is Ireland's war as well as yours. Ireland and the Transvaal Republic are both fighting for their independence. A British Transport sunk would mean more to you than winning a battle, for it would make recruiting almost impossible, and it can be done." Dr. Leydes looked startled.

"But that is not a recognised means of warfare," he said.

"I do not know," I replied, "whether you kill your enemies on land or at sea, it does not seem to me to make any difference. And are evictions and concentration camps, which mean killing women and children, recognised forms of warfare? They are being used by the British Empire against both our countries."

"Can you really do it?"

"I think so. I am authorised to make the offer. Remember it is our war too. Ireland is always at war with England till she is free. We would need your help in the matter of finance, but only sufficient to ensure that the men who do the work shall have the means of getting away at once to America. £500 should cover that. We could raise the money ourselves, but it would take time and, what is more important, it might involve telling more people, which is inadvisable. So far only three people know of this offer. It might be worth your while afterwards to pay on results and give us, for our own side of the war, whatever you consider a British Transport sent down is worth to you. The English are fighting to get your gold mines; if you could strike at their trade through their shipping, they might find the gold mines too expensive. You have no men in a position to carry out this form of warfare; we have. Our organisation is strong in many countries, in England and particularly in America."

Dr. Leydes did not speak for a long time; he sat at his desk.

His face was impassive; he was thinking deeply; the silence was oppressive. At last he said:

"Miss Gonne, I can't accept your offer. If it were ever to become known, it would put the whole of the Liberal Party in England against us and they are trying to stop the war."

I got up and held out my hand. "I am very sorry, we will say no more. The English Liberals will not be offended, I hope, at the ambulance, which is what I came here to ask you to accept."

We shook hands limply, but as he was seeing me to the door, I said:

"Dr. Leydes, when you know the English Liberals as well as we do, I think you will be sorry that you have worried about them. Good-bye." And I took the next train to Paris.

I was not up next morning when Marguerite my maid brought me a card from a gentleman who wanted to see me urgently. I dressed hurriedly and found a soldierly-looking Dutchman waiting in the drawing-room. He was Dr. Leydes' secretary.

"Mademoiselle, I have just arrived from Brussels. Dr. Leydes told me to see you before you left for Ireland and to tell you he had thought over your conversation and if you can delay your departure till to-morrow, he is arranging for me to bring you £2,000,—he said you know what it is for. I am going to catch the train for Brussels now, but will be here again to-morrow afternoon."

"Yes, I will wait for you," I answered. "Give my kindest regards to Dr. Leydes."

Next day he was back at the appointed time, but without the money.

"Mademoiselle, yesterday, while I was in Paris, a gentleman from your party called on Dr. Leydes. He said you were so valuable to the Irish Movement that it was undesirable to allow you to run such risks as are involved in negotiations with us while we are at war with England, and that he had been sent over to get Dr. Leydes' answer. He took the £2,000 and is to see you in London."

"Who is the man?" I asked.

"Dr. Leydes did not, I think, say his name, but he told me you know him and that he was an Irish Member of Parliament at one time."

"Tell Dr. Leydes from me that he has most assuredly handed £2,000 over to a British agent and that my 'party', as you call it, could not have sent anyone with such a message, and that, while I am quite ready at any time to take risks, I am not ready to walk into traps. I don't think it likely that mysterious ex-M.P. will try to see me and certainly he will not bring the money. But if he does, I shall say I don't know what he is talking about and that he must be a raving lunatic."

"But Mademoiselle, your Party sent him."

"I am sure my Party did not send him. My visit to Dr. Leydes was quite open. I went to arrange about the ambulance we are sending to the Transvaal; there is no risk in that. Tell Dr. Leydes he has been swindled out of £2,000 by a British agent and I can have nothing more to do with the matter."

It seemed an eternity to me till I got off the train at Victoria and was able to make contact with my friend in the I.R.B.

He was not as perturbed as I expected. He declared he had sent no one, but the English must have watched me and tried to find out how Dr. Leydes and I had got on together.

This didn't satisfy me.

"Only you and I and Arthur Griffith knew of my particular mission to Dr. Leydes. It was only four days ago that you decided it could be done and authorised me to make the offer and insisted that I should get the money to carry it out. Are you quite certain you have spoken of it to no one?"

"Of course I am," he answered, and went on talking of Dr. Leydes' folly in letting himself be swindled.

I took the night train to Dublin and next morning, in the little office of the *United Irishman* in Fownes Street, I discussed the whole matter with Arthur Griffith. He was as perturbed as I was and quite as dissatisfied with the almost casual way our friend seemed to have taken such a serious affair.

"Leydes' secretary told you the messenger was an ex-M.P.? Well, an ex-M.P. was sent to me with an I.R.B. introduction and a suggestion he should write articles for the *United Irishman*: I think he called on you too."

I remembered (when Griffith reminded me) a tall, thin, goodlooking elderly man with rather an affected manner who talked in a brilliant, but bitter, sarcastic way. I had taken one of those unaccountable instinctive dislikes to him, which I have always found one should never ignore; I had told myself that it was because of his eye-glass and affected, slightly supercilious manner, but though he had been very friendly and was quite amusing, I had avoided asking him to any of my rather free-and-easy evenings to which so many people used to drop in. He had been at some of the '98 Commemoration meetings in the West. Griffith said:

"His articles are good; but I must look up his past history: He is clever and may have won confidence by his denunciations of the Parliamentary party."

That evening Griffith told me he had been reading up about the ex-M.P. and found out that he had been turned out of the Parliamentary party by Parnell for having taken an independent libel action against the London *Times* for a series of articles entitled "Parnellism and Crime", which Parnell had decided to ignore, not wishing to put himself in the position of having to break with the physical-force party in America from whom he was getting much financial support.

The action must have cost a lot of money and it was thought had been taken in collusion with the *Times* for the sake of forcing Parnell's hand, which it did and resulted in the setting up of the Times Commission. This Commission, which committed Parnell to repudiating all acts of violence, compromised his relations with the physical-force party.

After this, little had been heard of the politician until he turned up as a writer, loud in denunciations of Parliamentarism.

"He is probably a British agent; he has certainly swindled the Boers; he will write no more in the *United Irishman*," said Arthur Griffith, "and I think you should have no more to do with this affair."

I was surprised to get a note from Millevoye asking me to come at once to Paris on a matter of urgent importance. We had not met since the day we parted in that flowery meadow under the snowy whiteness of Mont Blanc, and I did not want to meet him, though consciously I had never tried to avoid doing so; as in everything concerned with my personal life, I let chance, or the Will of the Gods, rule.

I never indulged in self-analysis and often used to get impatient with Willie Yeats, who, like all writers, was terribly introspective and tried to make me so. "I have no time to think of myself," I told him which was literally true, for, unconsciously perhaps, I had redoubled work to avoid thought.

People wondered at the scope of my activities and at the intensity of work I would put into each of them. These activities were all connected with the main objective,—breaking the power of England in Ireland. The lack of personal thought may have made me at times lose sense of proportion. Dimly, I think I always realised I had not the qualities of generalship. I would get so absorbed in a small corner of the battlefield that I would lose sight of the important spot; so I trusted blindly to the spiritual force of Ireland to supply the need and remained passively impulsive to do the work to hand. I would take as much trouble preparing a history lecture for the children of the Dublin slums whom *Inghinidhe na hEireann* gathered in the evenings in our three halls in Dublin, as I would in preparing a speech for a big political meeting; in trying to bring to justice some ruffianly land-agent who had burnt the thatched roofs of the unfortunate tenants he was evicting as in stopping recruiting for the British Army. Probably I would have been better employed in working in Paris to prevent Clemenceau pushing through the Entente Cordiale than in stopping a famine in Mayo; but I was incapable of working any other way, and while working thought of nothing else.

I wrote a brief note to Millevoye, saying I was too busy organising pro-Boer meetings in Ireland to come to Paris at the moment, but, as I was closing it, changed my mind and sent a telegram saying that I would be in Paris next evening. He would hardly have written like that without cause.

My unexpected return caused great excitement and joy to my household, which was now quite large and presided over by an old French widow, Madame de Bourbonne, who took care of a charming child I had adopted called Iseult. Daphne, now a bright girl of sixteen, also was there. My old nurse had died suddenly and I had brought her to Paris for her to learn French till her mother, still in Russia, decided on her future.

I was eating a hastily prepared dinner when Marguerite, the maid, announced that M. Millevoye and another gentleman were waiting to see me in the drawing-room; so Madame de Bourbonne and Daphne carried off the protesting Iseult to bed.

Millevoye looked very grave. "I wrote you at Captain Robert's request. There are some questions he wants to ask and I thought it urgent for you to be able to clear yourself."

"Ah non," interrupted Captain Robert, "no one suspects Mademoiselle Gonne."

"Suspects of what?" I said, looking from one to the other.

"You gave a letter of introduction to some compatriots of yours in London to Colonel L. of our Military Intelligence Service."

I nodded.

"Well, they betrayed him and he is being sent back to France in disgrace, under arrest."

My heart stopped beating; I could hardly breathe. Before my own experience with Dr. Leydes I would have indignantly retorted that it was impossible. But how could I now? I turned to Captain Robert.

"Please, tell me," I said in a low voice, "are you certain he was betrayed? Couldn't the English have been just suspicious of his movements?"

"I am afraid there is no doubt he was betrayed. He is a very clever agent and has been on similar missions before. He was an invalid travelling with his daughter. There was nothing to make him a suspect. Tell me who, outside the man to whom you gave him an introduction, would he have been in contact with?"

"I do not know. All I know is that the I.R.B. has wide ramifications and some are in positions to get the information he wanted. I do not know any of these personally or their names. but I was told all was going well and that the colonel had asked our friend to find him an Irish secretary to help him with his work and to make travelling arrangements, the Colonel's English not being very fluent."

"Do you know the secretary?"

I shook my head.

"Perhaps now you will believe me when I say your Irish revolutionists are only a set of *farceurs*. Your Parliamentarians are no better than our own, a lot of job-hunters and careerists; but at least they are less dangerous than would-be revolutionists playing at revolution. See what your blind confidence in them has done. You have broken all your work in France; our Military Party will never trust the Irish again and it has broken the career of a distinguished officer," said Millevoye.

"Oh no, it is not as bad as that," said Robert. "Colonel L. was, after all, doing the work of his department, the work that officers of every country are doing, obtaining information that may possibly be useful to their own countries. Our pro-English government can't do anything to him for that, except rub it in that he was a fool to trust the Irish. The matter won't be heard of at all by the public, for the English and our own Government who are trying to arrange an *Entente* will be both equally anxious to keep this incident secret. Colonel L. was not arrested by the English. With great tact they informed our Ambassador and asked him to take action. Colonel L. travelled back to France with a man from the French Embassy. You need not worry about that side of it, Mademoiselle, they can't do anything to him. But perhaps Millevoye is right; you are trusting the wrong people, and though I will always try to help you personally in any of your undertakings, I am afraid it will be quite impossible for me to obtain the facilities we spoke of. It is most unfortunate; I am very sorry." And he got up and held out his hand.

I sat with my head in my hands, seeing the whole of what I had worked for and counted on to make "England's difficulty Ireland's opportunity" crumble to dust. I felt utterly broken.

"Stay for a moment," I said, without looking up. "I have more to tell you. I see that you cannot possibly trust me after what has occurred. You are probably right and Colonel L. has been betrayed by an Irishman. Millevoye is perhaps right in saying a secret revolutionary organisation cannot keep out spies and traitors when the English Secret Service is so powerful; it seems the I.R.B. has not been able to. When I have exposed this matter and know exactly who the traitor is, I shall leave the I.R.B. I think it right to tell you of another betrayal, because it is evidently the same British agent who worked both."

Very interested, Robert sat down again and I told him and Millevoye about the way Leydes had been swindled out of £2,000.

Next day I took Iseult and Daphne to the Zoo where we ate "*gauffres*" and rode the elephant and afterwards I took the night train to London.

My friend Mr. X. sat in his study, drumming on the table with his fingers. He was very embarrassed. He now admitted that he might have told the ex-M.P. of my journey to Brussels to see Dr. Leydes but never dreamt he would follow on and get the money, and he said he would make him disgorge it. Now he admitted having consulted him about getting a suitable secretary for the Colonel.

I stood by the table and asked;

"What are you going to do about the traitor?"

He fidgeted with his fingers and did not reply. At last he said:

"I don't know that he is a traitor. He is a queer cranky man full of vanity. You must have snubbed him badly some time, for he hates you. I think he has done both these things to spite you."

I would listen to no more nonsense of that sort. I barely knew the man; I had met him once in the office of the *United Irishman*; he had called on me once. I am invariably polite to visitors and had complimented him on an article of his which had appeared in the *United Irishman*.

I said: "I am leaving the I.R.B. and I shall tell my reasons to everyone it may concern. It is not fair to allow young enthusiastic men, willing to risk their lives for Ireland, to remain unknowingly in an organisation where such things can occur and you, after a spy has wrecked our chance of a lifetime, seek excuses for him."

I kept my word. Before leaving London I told all the members of the I.R.B. whom I could get together that I had resigned and gave them a full account of the two incidents. In Dublin I did the same thing; I said I would waste no time on an organisation which had successfully prevented Ireland making England's difficulty our opportunity.

I had come to realise there was much truth in Father Cavanagh's words.

The only logical way to deal with spies and traitors, when you have no prison in which to shut them, is to shoot them as an example. The shooting of Carey, the informer, was approved of by the nation generally; the only regret was that it cost the life of a brave man. But Carey's betrayal of the Invincibles was public and it is often impossible to make public the treachery for which death is the penalty. The killing of Dr. Cronin in America led to more mischief than any treason (if there was treason) he might have committed because it split and paralysed the *Clan-na-Gael* for over a quarter of a century. The condemnation of Dreyfus to Devil's Island,—justified or unjustified,—did more to weaken the French Army than any secrets he could ever have divulged.

Undoubtedly the traitor deserved a bullet, but in face of the fact that three governments were interested in keeping his treachery secret, would it have been possible to make his execution appear justifiable in Ireland?

There was another reason which weighed with me. I had made it a rule of life never to ask any man to do a thing I was not ready to do myself or to take a risk I was not ready to share. I was not ready to shoot this man. I always carried my little revolver with me and on two other occasions it had protected me since the evening on the Greek sea where it had enabled me to catch my boat to Constantinople; but I had never fired it at any human being and I would have disliked doing so extremely.

This was an old ruin of a man, shunned by the Parliamentarians since Parnell had expelled him from his party and now thoroughly discredited among the revolutionists,—Griffith and I had seen to that,—he could do no more mischief and I thought he could be left to die miserably in disgrace and the isolation of old age, a far worse punishment than death. I think he had to disgorge some of the £2,000, for a few months after, Griffith told me, he had been offered money for the *United Irishman* and Boer propaganda, which, suspicious of its source, he had refused. The rest the traitor used in trying fruitlessly to get elected by an English constituency to Parliament. No one would have him, not even the English whom he had served so well.

My admission into the I.R.B. had had a comic side as many things in life have. It was at a time when I was much impressed by the romance of secret societies though a little sceptical about the importance of the invisible revolutionary work of some of their literary members and of their capacity for keeping secrets.

I had learnt that one of John O'Leary's chief lieutenants,— rightly esteemed as a poet, less rightly as a revolutionist,—had suddenly left the movement after giving a mysterious but solemn warning that he knew many arrests were threatened. The warning was taken seriously but bravely and caused suppressed excitement while the defection of so shining a light was a source of great gloom. I thought it was extremely unlikely that there would be arrests at that particular time, as there was little activity to justify them, so I set out to trace the origin of the scare and was intensely amused when I discovered it had all come from the prophetic dream of a young poetess. I was in London shortly after and could not resist chaffingly telling Dr. Ryan that I knew more of his organisation than he did himself. "For instance," I said, "I know it has sustained a recent and great loss and is threatened by a great danger; and if its distrust of women was not so inveterate I would offer to take the place of the resigned member, and you would find that women are better realists than men and quite as capable of guarding secrets. I call now to tell you something you don't know and to prove my extreme courage in offering to join up at such a moment of danger,"—and then I gave him a detailed account of the origin of the scare.

Dr. Ryan, who had a sense of humour, was so delighted that there and then he swore me into the I.R.B.,—a comic entry, a tragic exit to and from that body whose Fenian tradition was noble and beautiful and who in 1914, reorganised and rejuvenated by men like Padraig Pearse, Sean Mac Dermott and Tomas Mc Donagh and the young, and the steady determination of Tom Clark, brought the Republic into being, but whose inherent faults caused its overthrow in 1921 when the I.R.B. by secret influence forced the Free State Treaty on a reluctant Republican Dail.

CHAPTER XXIII

DAYS OF GLOOM

ONE DAY IN Dublin I got a note from Oldham asking me and Dagda to the Contemporary Club; he wanted a good debate on the Home Rule position since Parnell's death, as Henry Nevinson, an English journalist, would be present. I knew I was as useless as Dagda in debate but I liked listening to brilliant talk and I liked Nevinson who was friendly and sincere and had been helpful about prisoners. He was usually well informed and he might be able to tell us if anything was likely to be done in the British Parliament about the evicted tenants and about the new Land Purchase Acts then being discussed in Westminster.

That afternoon James Tully, of Woodford, in Co. Galway, had called on me. I had never met him before but heard he had been ruthless in shooting landlords and I had even heard him called "the mild-eyed assassin". As I listened to his soft Western voice and looked at his white hair and extraordinary clear yet dreamy grey eyes, I doubted the ruthlessness and I remembered regretfully that Lord Clanricarde, the great Galway evictor, was still alive, a very rich old miser, living under police protection in London Clubland. A bullet would surely not have been wasted on him.

James Tully, like Michael Davitt, had been a Fenian and had joined Davitt's land League. John O'Leary and many Fenians disapproved of linking the agrarian to the National issue, as likely to distract the people's mind from the direct objective, the freeing of Ireland, and disapproved of its methods as likely to alienate the landed aristocracy and the people of the towns and provoke class war. It is easy to say that the agrarian struggle appealed to personal greed and the National cause to higher idealism and point to Lord Edward Fitzgerald and Robert Emmett and many young Ireland leaders graduated from Trinity. The landlords were the British garrison and Trinity a British institution. I believed, with Davitt, that the agrarian and National struggle were inherently one; the land and the people, from whose union the national soul is born. That soul may incarnate itself temporarily in individuals from any class, for the spirit bloweth where it listeth. Centuries of oppression had left the mass of the people unduly dependent on leaders, as I knew from my own small experience. Tully said he was a ruined man; that did not worry him, he could always emigrate and join his brother who was doing well in Australia, but he was concerned about the fate of friends and neighbours he had induced to join the movement and who were now living in miserable Land League huts, eating their hearts in idleness, watching their derelict farms and starving children. Now the movement had broken down, politicians avoided them,—public opinion was no longer interested, the rigid boycott of land grabbers no longer enforced and the evicted farms were being given to landlords' men who had stood apart from the struggle and would profit by Land Purchase Acts from sacrifices they had refused to share. A defeated constitutional movement entails as much suffering for people as defeat in battle; the reprisals, if less spectacular, are quite as cruel. The Parliamentary Party had deteriorated. O'Leary blamed the Land League, I blamed Westminster. I would hear a lot about this at the debate at the Contemporary Club.

Tully startled me by saying he had been sent to Dublin to ask me, because I stood apart from all political parties, to lead the evicted tenants' movement. If I consented, he and other equally determined men were ready to back it. As I listened I had longed to consent and devote my whole energy to organising these victims into a formidable body which it would be hard to crush; but I was pledged to force open the gates of Portland Prison where twenty-seven still more unselfish men were being driven mad; the Amnesty movement, in Ireland, England and Scotland, was becoming a great and growing force and the Irish cause in France, which depended entirely on my work and from which I hoped so much, absorbed all my time and thought. Reluctantly, I told Tully the evicted tenants must find some other leader but that I would speak about them at every meeting I addressed. He looked very disappointed; he knew as well as I did that speaking of them at meetings, as most of the Parliamentarians were doing, would be of little use. It would take one man's or one woman's whole time, force and energy, regardless of risks and consequences, to galvanise the remnants of the defeated Land League movement into active life again. I believed then it could be done. Now I doubt if it would have been possible, because it is harder to resuscitate life than to create it; and movements, like individuals, suffer the universal law of age and decay out of which new life will arise.

I always realised I was not a leader because I could work effectively only by intense concentration of my whole being on some particular point to the exclusion of all others; and the release of the Treason Felony Prisoners was that point just then, but I felt angry with myself for refusing.

The interview with Tully spoilt my usual enjoyment of the debate at the Contemporary Club where the importance of uniting the leadership of the Parliamentary Party loomed large with most. Nevinson thought the fate of the evicted tenants depended on it. I listened to oft-heard criticisms of John Dillon and William O'Brien and slightly less scathing criticisms of John Redmond, who at least had not deserted Parnell when ordered to do so by Gladstone. I didn't much like these criticisms before an Englishman, especially the old gibes about O'Brien and his breeches, for he had put up a great fight for the political status of prisoners by refusing to wear prison clothes and had been left for weeks without his nether garments and I thought it an equally dignified and perhaps a more practical attitude than that of the Fenians who refused to complain, whatever the enemy inflicted on them. The argument of taking one's medicine never appealed to me. Perhaps it didn't matter, as Nevinson was a friend of Ireland, but I felt that gibes made us a little cheap and I grew so depressed that I was relieved when Dagda, who had been lying at my feet, got up and gently put his two front paws in quite a friendly way on the shoulders of the harmless and rather ineffectual little civil servant who was acting as chairman, and, the chair being unsteady, chair and chairman toppled over.

Nevinson saw me home, but his cheery friendliness didn't dissipate my depression, and the strange clear eyes of Tully with their reproachful look came between me and sleep.

In the morning I told Dagda I felt we both needed to get away from Dublin and that the West was nice, and the dog agreed.

At Broadstone Station I took tickets for Loughrea and thought we would drive about on Mail cars and see the country. Vaguely I thought I would like to see Tully again. An old gentleman with a red face who might have been some sort of land agent glared disapprovingly at me as I pushed past him and sat down at the far side of the carriage, Gruffly he said:

"That dog must travel in the dog box."

"We always travel together," I answered.

Muttering something about Company by-laws he called a porter, a young inexperienced lad, and told him to take the dog out.

"May I take him, Miss?"

"If you like to try, but I don't advise it, as I think he doesn't want to go."

"Take him out," repeated the old gentleman.

Dagda, his great head resting on my knees, opened his one blue and one brown eye and smiled. The porter advanced a timid hand. "Come on, old fellow." Dagda gave a very low growl.

"He says he doesn't want to go," I translated.

"Take him out," blustered the red-faced man.

"That, Sir, is hardly fair on the porter. If you are so anxious for the dog to go, why don't you ask him yourself?" I said politely.

This was too much for the irate gentleman who, saying he would report him, jostled past the porter onto the platform in search of the guard.

"Miss Gonne, the dog can't travel in the carriage if any of the passengers object," said that official.

"But the dog-box is too small," I objected, "and I have his ticket."

"I will take him in the van with me."

"You will have to take me too, as we always travel together, but have you accommodation?"

"Afraid not, though I'd like to have your company," said the guard smiling.

"Well, why not?"

It was time for the train to start. The guard suddenly seized the luggage of the old gentleman. "Come on, Sir, I have a nice corner for you in another carriage," and, spluttering with rage, the old gentleman followed the luggage, and Dagda and I were left alone. I felt cheered. "That's the way to treat them," I said.

There were many constabulary in the village of Woodford as I got off the mail car a day later and also in the hotel. The landlord's wife ushered me into a little private room for lunch.

"What are the police here for?"

"To stop the proclaimed meeting."

I enquired for Mr. Tully.

"He's still in Dublin and lucky he is, for they are looking for him," she answered.

A tall countryman in a frieze coat came in. "It was good of you coming, Miss Gonne," he said, "but it isn't fair to ask you to speak at a proclaimed meeting."

"I am here by chance," I said, "but I'll speak at the meeting if you want me to."

"I thought Mr. Tully had sent you."

"No, I came to see Mr. Tully but I hear he is away."

I arranged to meet my new friend and a car at the cross-roads outside the village. As we drove he told me the meeting was called to protest against some land-grabbing and call a boycott on the grabbers; the police held Woodford, so word had been sent out to meet elsewhere. Dagda in great spirits trotted beside the car. Near a little wood we found a couple of hundred men gathered and great cheers were raised when they recognised me.

The chairman was speaking and when he got down I climbed on his car and spoke, first on the National question, that the people would only get their rights when Ireland's freedom was won and then of the immediate duty for them all to stand together and to boycott any land-grabbers. I had not got far before I saw a body of some hundred Royal Irish Constabulary marching along the road towards the meeting. I bent down and asked the chairman, who looked nervous, if we were to go on.

"Just do as you think best, my lady."

I continued speaking. The constabulary formed up in ranks on three sides of the meeting. The crowd gathered closer round the car. "Go on, Miss," they shouted to me and, being excited, I repeated myself; it didn't matter, for everyone was too excited to notice what I said. The officer in charge of the Constabulary and a superintendent of police pushed their way towards the platform. The superintendent said:

"Miss Gonne, if you continue, I shall arrest you."

"That's your affair and much good it will do you," I laughed and continued my speech.

"If you go on I shall give the order to fire," said the officer.

"Go on, go on," cheered the crowd.

I heard an order given. I saw the constabulary get their rifles at the ready and heard the click of the triggers. Most of the men now had their backs to the platform and were facing the police; they had nothing but ash plants in their hands but were ready to fight; some still shouted to me to go on.

"No," I said. "Men, you know your duty; the proclaimed meeting is now over," and I got off the car.

There was disappointment; one man said: "You should have gone on." I heard another man say: "You couldn't expect a woman to fight." I said:

"If you had guns I would have gone on; the rifles were pointed at you, not at me; I couldn't see unarmed men shot down."

Again a wave of depression overwhelmed me. I thought of France; some day help might come from that quarter if the British alliance could be prevented. Perhaps I had been wrong in not letting the Woodford evicted tenants fight and be shot down. Dead men might have aroused the country as living men could not and at least made the evicted tenants a live issue. I had not dared take the responsibility; I had refused leadership and the situation was not of my making.

The morning papers spoke of fresh evictions on Lord De Freyne's estate in Roscommon. I would at least see they got all the publicity I could give them.

John Fitzgibbon met me in Castlereagh. He told me that a number of tenants on the De Freyne estate had been served with ejectment orders. Some had obeyed them, some had crept back to their homes and refused to lease. One night the agent and his man had poured paraffin on the roofs of the houses and fired the thatches. A little child had been badly burnt. I hired a car and drove to the village. The mother of the burnt child, surrounded by a large family of children, was sitting with the moaning baby on her knees in the back kitchen of the village shop.

She told me she and some of the other evicted tenants had gone back to their houses after the bailiff had put them out, because they had nowhere else to go but the workhouse, and there they would be separated from their children. One night, the land agent and some of Lord de Freyne's men, protected by police, had come and set fire to the roof.

No, she had not seen him pour the paraffin, but people outside the houses had. "Inside," she said, "we knew nothing till we heard the roar of the fire and the place became thick with smoke. We got the children out of bed and all rushed out."

When she got out she couldn't find her second youngest child, so she put her baby in a neighbour's arms and rushed back into the burning house and found the child in the bed which had already caught fire. She seized it up and ran out nearly stifled by the smoke. "Look," she said, pointing to her head, "half my hair is burnt. But God is good, only my hair and my clothes caught fire and the child's legs are only scorched," and she pulled up the baby's dress and showed small blisters on one leg and red marks on both legs. I insisted on getting a doctor and having the legs properly dressed.

The people had lost all their belongings. There was great indignation and that evening I spoke at a meeting and called for the arrest of the criminal incendiaries, and a collection for the homeless people was made. I telegraphed to Harrington and also wrote to him and to William Field and to the papers of all parties. Harrington replied that John Redmond would come down and address a meeting and the people begged me to stay for it. Harrington, who was a barrister, also wrote that we should be able to get the man

responsible punished, for there was a severe law against setting
fire to dwelling houses. It was a law made to protect the landlords from reprisals and the agent could be caught under it.

John Redmond arrived, looking impressive in his top hat,
and we drove together to the meeting in the Parochial Hall.
As usual Dagda accompanied me onto the platform and lay
down.

"Miss Gonne," whispered Mr. Redmond, "would you mind
letting our driver hold the dog in the body of the hall?"

"Why? Dagda is nearly as popular with the people as you
and myself," I said politely, because Mr. Redmond was *not*
very popular, being looked on as rather a landlord's man for
allowing several years too many annuities in the Land Purchase
Acts.

"It doesn't look well to have a dog on the platform, I don't
like it," he said; he was evidently living up to the top hat and
I wondered whether he slept in it. Not wanting to make
difficulties however, I called the driver who was standing in
the hall and told Dagda that, as Mr. Redmond objected, he
was to go with him into the body of the hall and obediently
he went.

The Reverend Chairman spoke and a town councillor and
then Mr. Redmond got up to speak and the newspaper correspondents got busy at their table. "Ladies and gentlemen, men
and women of Roscommon . . ." Suddenly Dagda spoke
from the end of the hall. Mr. Redmond looked annoyed and
began again: "Ladies and gentlemen——" and Dagda spoke
again; he insisted on punctuating every sentence Mr. Redmond
uttered. "But this is intolerable," and he turned to me.

"He is protesting because he knows it was you who ordered
him off the platform and he thinks he has a right to be there.
He won't be quiet till he has his rights."

"Let him come up, he is a grand dog," said the Reverend
chairman, who had a sense of humour and liked Dagda.

I whistled and with a bound Dagda sprang on the platform amid the cheers of the crowd and lay down right in front of the stage, while Mr. Redmond, very ruffled, continued his dignified speech and there were no more interruptions.

I spoke of getting the agent ten years in jail; I was much applauded but I should have known that British law in Ireland follows British policy and British policy was supporting land-lords and their agents.

After interminable delays had allowed the horror of the deed to be forgotten, we got the case into court and the agent was acquitted and got costs, though all the facts were proved and were not disputed by his learned counsel who proved, to the satisfaction of the judges, that houses which had no locks on the doors were not really dwelling houses under the act, and therefore not protected by the law. Half the cabins in Ireland at that time were only fastened by strong bolts and had no locks, so land agents could with impunity have set fire to any of them according to British law.

During Victoria's reign alone, one million two hundred and twenty-five thousand people died of famine in Ireland; four million one hundred and eighty-six thousand emigrated; three million six hundred and sixty-three thousand were evicted from houses they or their fathers had built.

More and more I realised that Ireland could rely only on force, in some form or other, and that it was absurd to say that any Irishman, whatever he did, had committed a crime against England or against civilisation.

CHAPTER XXIV

THE NEW CENTURY

THE TREASON FELONY Prisoners were now all released. Out of seven driven insane in Portland hell, four recovered but Dr. Gallagher and Whitehead died in asylums in America and John Dunne in Grangegorman. I saved young Jimmy Cunningham, one of the first released, by taking full responsibility for him and then confiding him to my old nurse in her peaceful little home. She justified her Howth reputation as a healer, for in a month he was able to travel to America.

The three worst prisoners, according to the published official prison records of punishments, were the three who came through that awful ordeal best both physically and mentally, though they had suffered more days on bread and water in unspeakable punishment-cells than the rest; but their constant defiance had kept all their faculties alert.

John Daly, elected Mayor of his native city Limerick on release, filled that office with such ability that he was re-elected Mayor three times in succession. James Egan was elected Sword-Bearer to the Dublin Corporation and retained the office till his death and Tom Clark was the first President of the Republic in 1916.

One of the first acts of John Daly's as Mayor was to confer the Freedom of the City of Limerick on his tried and trusted comrade Tom Clark and on me for my work for their release. It was when staying with the Dalys for the ceremony that Tom fell in love with John's pretty niece Cathleen and carried her off as his wife to America where he worked unselfishly for years organising for the Republic, for which in the end he gave his life. None of these men ever envisaged less than an independent Republic.

Arthur Griffith and I worked much together. I was a link between him and James Connolly on one side, and between him and Yeats on the other; and I helped a great deal with the *United Irishman*, getting subscriptions for its publishing fund and articles from various writers. Without money it is hard to get good articles and it was not rich enough to pay for them. Sometimes Griffith had to write almost the whole paper himself under different pseudonyms, and while he never complained, and was an indefatigable worker, I felt the *United Irishman* would gain by a widening of interest.

It was in my little house in Coulson Avenue that together we drew up the programme of *Cumann na nGaedheal*. It was our purpose to link up all existing National societies into an open Separatist movement. As a nucleus we had the Celtic Literary Society, with strong branches in Dublin and Cork, and *Inghinidhe na hEireann*, with branches in Dublin, Ballina, Cork and Limerick. Terence MacSweeney had helped in the formation of the Cork branch and Miss Margaret Goulding,—now Mrs. Buckley, to-day president of Sinn Fein, was its president. In almost every county there were Young Ireland Societies and Literary Clubs in rather dormant condition, because unconnected with a central movement. There were also many '98 Centenary Clubs, who, once the Centenary was over, found themselves without work. There were Athletic Clubs and Hurling Clubs, with strong national membership; these had greatly helped our Transvaal Committee and anti-recruiting campaign, and I was particularly anxious they should be included to give the movement a physical as well as an intellectual side. I thought that this had been lacking in the Young Ireland movement of 1848.

Willie Yeats, who had left the I.R.B. when I did, was greatly interested and, I think, helped in the drafting of our programme; I know it was he who suggested the names of Samhain and Beltaine for our bi-annual festivals, to perpetuate the autumn and spring festivals of ancient Ireland.

We adopted Griffith's Sinn Fein policy; it taught self-reliance and called for the withdrawal of the Irish members from Westminster and the setting up of an Irish Council responsible only to the Irish Nation. Griffith and I went on an organising and lecturing tour in the South. He was not an orator and was at first very shy and inaudible when addressing meetings, but every word he said was clearly expressed and worth listening to and he often helped me to prepare my lectures.

George Russell lived in the house next to mine in Coulson Avenue and used to drop in and bless the work; he was himself so absorbed in Horace Plunket Co-operative schemes and Creameries and in his own painting and Hindu mysticism that he had no time or energy for anything else.

Cumann na nGaedheal offered prizes for poems and plays and stories on national subjects. Padraig Pearse was on the judging Committee. The prize poems and stories were often published in the *United Irishman* and the plays acted at the Beltaine and Samhain festivals. John Rogan, a good musician, had trained excellent choirs composed of men and women members of the various National Societies, and used to help at our festivals. At first these were held in the ancient Concert Rooms, but as the movement grew rapidly, we soon had to secure the Rotunda or the Mansion House.

If the secret Revolutionary Movement represented by the I.R.B. had failed us, we were determined to have a big open Revolutionary Movement to create an atmosphere out of which something vital might develop.

At the end of 1900 Griffith got a letter from John MacBride announcing his return from the Transvaal; the war was not over and we were astonished, though Arthur Lynch had returned some months earlier. Griffith and I decided to go and meet him in Paris, as of course he could not come to Ireland. Griffith could leave Dublin only for a few days because of the paper and I invited him to stay at my flat.

Stephen McKenna and some of the Paris Young Ireland Society went with us to the Gare de Lyon to meet MacBride, whom I had never met, though I had corresponded with him about sending men to his brigade. Griffith and he were old friends, so there was no difficulty about recognising him as he stepped off the train. He was a wiry, soldierly-looking man, with red hair and skin burnt brick-red by the South African sun. Griffith called him Rooinek, at which he laughed. It was the name by which the Afrikanders called the English because, while other races burn brown, they burn red; the natives apparently give nick-names to everybody. Griffith's nickname had been Cuguan, the Dove; at first he had thought it was a compliment and that it meant they thought he was gentle, but he discovered it was on account of his peculiar walk which resembled a dove's strut. MacBride said the only nickname he ever objected to was one his school mates gave him,—Foxy Jack. He was in great spirits and delighted to meet so many friends. He and Griffith and McKenna went off together to the room McKenna had secured for him in the Quartier Latin. He was to come back later and dine with me.

We sat up all night talking. MacBride said he had come back hoping there would be something doing in Ireland. The war in Africa was not over and England had still De Wet to deal with, but most of the foreign volunteers had been sent back and the Irish Brigade had been disbanded because the war was entering on another phase. There would be no more regular battles; and in guerilla warfare only those who knew the country and spoke the language would be of use. Blake was staying on, but MacBride wanted to get back to take a hand in things in Ireland. Griffith had already told him how the I.R.B. had spiked our guns. MacBride had been in the

I.R.B. since he was a boy and was very disappointed. "America is our only chance now," I said. "You may be able to get the *Clan-na-Gael* moving." Griffith said he thought it was quite useless for him to take the risk of going to Ireland as things were and MacBride decided to go to America.

"Have you notes on the work of the Brigade?" Griffith asked. "I want them for the *United Irishman* and you had better prepare a lecture, for you will have to lecture in America."

"You will have to write the lecture for me, then," he answered.

It was so late that it was not worth while for MacBride to go to his lodgings, so he shared Griffith's bed. Next morning, seated at my writing table, Griffith wrote the lecture, supplementing the sparse notes from MacBride's memory. I sat in an armchair, smoking cigarettes and listening. It was great to hear of Irishmen actually fighting England. The capture of General Buller's guns near the Tugeela was thrilling; the capture of English officers delighted me; the English have imprisoned so many Irishmen that it was good at last to have it the other way round.

"I hope you treated your prisoners decently to give them a good example and show how much more civilised we are than they?"

"Yes," said MacBride. "We took possession of their arms, but we fed them well, same as ourselves, and they thanked us and said it was the fortune of war when we handed them over to the Boers, who treat their prisoners quite well in the prison camps near Pretoria. They had quite a lot of English prisoners, a tremendous lot of Irishmen among them. I wanted Kruger to let me pick some of these to join the Brigade. A lot of these Irish lads would have gladly joined; some of them told me they had let themselves get captured in the hope of joining us, but old Kruger wouldn't allow it,—said it was not done. The Boers are queer people; they may not have trusted them, though I said I would be answerable for them."

I told him of the scenes I had witnessed in Limerick when the police were rounding up militia men for the war and putting them on the boats in handcuffs; and I showed him our leaflet with Father Cavanagh's words on Catholic teaching and the sin in taking part in an unjust war. "We got these well circulated among the Irish regiments."

John laughed: "Well, a good many deserted and if Kruger had only consented we would have had the Brigade up to full strength."

I felt that little band of Irishmen in the Brigade had done more for Ireland's honour than all of us at home, for it is action that counts. MacBride said the flag sent out by *Inghinidhe na hEireann* had been greatly appreciated.

"We had it up at our camp and at night I often saw one or other of our lads go up and kiss its folds. When the fighting got livelier we had to send it back with the rest of our belongings to a man in Johannesburg to keep it safe for us."

Years after, when the fighting was on for the Republic in Ireland, I got a letter from a man called Burke in the Transvaal, asking if he should send me the flag of the Brigade, but as all the Republican houses were then being constantly raided by the Free State soldiers, I felt it would not be safe and wrote asking him to keep it a little longer. When things were quieter, I wrote to him to send it to me, but never received an answer.

After a reception by the Paris Young Ireland Society and talks with a few friends from Dublin MacBride went to America. In a few weeks he wrote me, urging me to accept an invitation to come on another lecture tour arranged by the now united *Clan-na-Gael*. He added that he could not get things going unless I came.

He was with a crowd of friends belonging to both sections of the united Clan who met me when I came off the French Trans-Atlantic liner at the docks in New York; and there was a great meeting in the Academy of Music the night after my arrival. MacBride gave his lecture on the work of the Brigade and I spoke of Ireland. We had a splendid press.

John Devoy called on me the following day. It was the first and only time I met him; he came with MacBride, a short, elderly man and very short-sighted. He tripped over a footstool and landed on his knees at my feet. MacBride and I helped him to rise quickly and got him comfortably seated in an armchair, but that incident was most unpropitious. MacBride told me afterwards that Mr. Devoy was extremely tempera-mental and self-conscious and could not stand anything which upset his dignity. I don't know if it was owing to this, or to the fact that, the first time I went to America, it had been under the auspices of the O'Sullivan section of the Clan, and that I had considerably helped the rank and file to insist on unity, and that the second time I had been in America I had gone quite independently of either section and had a remarkably successful tour,—but I felt he disliked me. I could not get him talking on any vital matter and he very soon took his leave,— a most unsatisfactory interview. MacBride treated him with great deference and I hoped he would succeed in getting him to do what he wanted, that is, to galvanise the Clan into action while the war was on; for undoubtedly Devoy had great influence.

MacBride was in charge of this lecture tour. While I was kept busy with reporters and reception committees, he visited the camps of the *Clan-na-Gael* and in the trains we discussed plans. I could see he was not satisfied. The men in high places, distinguished lawyers and politicians, were not revolutionists and they had much control. It was inevitable that they should look on the organisation from an American point of view,—the great voting power of the Irish. Many of these successful men were sons of parents who had been driven from Ireland on emigration ships; their fathers and mothers had transmitted their hatred of the oppressor; they all had a sentimental love for the old country, kept vivid by their Catholic faith, but their American education, their successful business careers, made most of them adverse to revolutionary schemes. They made wonderful chairmen at our meetings and delivered grand speeches on Ireland's right to freedom; they could be counted on to exert their influence against an Anglo-American alliance, which England was always trying for. That in itself was a great thing, for to make the holding of Ireland injurious to England is one of the means towards securing freedom. No doubt they would back up the fight in Ireland when it started, but they were happier supporting constitutional leaders like Parnell and were hard to convince that there was nothing to hope from men like Redmond or John Dillon. They would go on supporting constitutional politicians, even when these were trying to stop the violence which had brought any of the successes they had attained. They were full of sympathy with the Boer Republic, but not to the extent of involving America or of revolutionary action such as MacBride and I hoped for. Among the rank and file of the organisation there were men ready for anything.

In Boston, I got a cable from Griffith, telling of Willie Rooney's death. It was a great blow. Rooney was a fine National thinker and a convinced Separatist; his influence on the young people of his day was comparable with that of Thomas Davis in his. He was Griffith's greatest friend and helper in the paper. His loss was irreparable; I wondered if Griffith would be able to carry on without him. I wrote, saying the only consolation I had ever found for sorrow was in redoubled work. In Philadelphia I got a short, broken-hearted letter from Griffith. Rooney had literally killed himself from over-work; obliged to earn his daily bread as a clerk, he spent his nights working for Ireland. He had a cold and should have stayed in bed, but he had meetings in the West for the week-end and insisted on going. He came back very ill and never recovered. He was engaged to be married to Marie Killeen, one of the executive of *Inghinidhe na hEireann*, a dark girl who, in our *tableaux vivants*, looked very beautiful as the Dark Rosaleen. He had done a lot to help our women's organisation. If he had lived his influence might have prevented Griffith accepting the disastrous Treaty of 1922.

In St. Louis, where we had a huge meeting and the backing of a number of Irish priests, I got another letter from Griffith, begging me not to stay too long in America as I was badly needed in Dublin where another Royal visit was threatened. So in the afternoon, when MacBride and I were visiting the stockyards, where most of the mules for transport for the British Army were bought, and wondering if a way could be found to stop the shipments, I told him I had decided to return to Ireland and would leave him to finish the lecture tour to the Pacific coast alone. I said I was not really needed as it was the lecture on the Irish Brigade people wanted to hear and it was his work (going round the camps of the Clan) which was useful.

He tried hard to keep me but I was resolute, and after a big meeting at Chicago we separated, he to go on to San Francisco and I to return to Europe. Except for the money our tour had ensured for the *United Irishman*, I didn't feel I had accomplished much, but I still hoped MacBride might succeed in setting the match to the inflammable fighting forces of the *Clan-na-Gael*, in spite of the politicians.

CHAPTER XXV

THE BATTLE OF THE ROTUNDA

KIND AUNT LIZZIE and Uncle Charlie were both dead, and Chotie and May lived rather aimless lives together in a charming house in South Kensington, which had filled their lives while they were adorning it and making it rather perfect; but, that work accomplished, they had nothing to do. As Aunt Lizzie had predicted, May had lost interest in nursing once she was independent of the family and had replaced that interest with Bridge, which seemed to me unsatisfying. I could never take interest in games, even though luck, replacing skill, generally made me fairly successful at them.

Kathleen had married an English officer I disliked and I had done my utmost to prevent the marriage; it turned out as badly as I had feared, and she was very unhappy. She was too beautiful and too sensitive for the rough-and-tumble of life and needed someone to take care of her, but instead, she had all the brunt of commonplace worries thrust on her without the compensating love and affection which make such things endurable. She and her four lovely children lived a great deal with the cousins. I loved the children, who looked on Auntie Maud as attractive and mysterious; and especially the little girl Thora was very fond of me.

On my return from America I found a letter from May telling me she was engaged to be married to an English Civil Servant stationed in India and home on leave. She wanted me to meet him and stay with them for the wedding. I was glad for May. With her red hair and Celtic spirit she was more adventurous than the rest of the family. In spite of their beautiful house, each time I stayed with them I felt that all their lives were drifting in a dull monotony. Youth was passing and they were not living. Chotie, I think, was the happiest; she was always so absorbed in the small joys and sorrows of the family, or of the cats and dogs, that she had no time to feel the stagnation of their lives. I hoped marriage would prove a great adventure for May.

Kathleen, looking more than ever like a tall lily, with her pale gold hair and white evening dress, had been watching for my arrival with Chotie and met me in the wide hall furnished as a smoking-room in which so few smoked. They said May and her young man had gone to the station to meet me but had missed me or gone to the wrong station. "Are they as badly in love as that?" I laughed.

"I hope so," answered Chotie, "but I don't know." And she looked a little anxious.

From upstairs the voices of the children were clamouring for Auntie Maud. "You will have to go up to them or they won't go to sleep," said Kathleen, and we went, Chotie carrying a milky dachshund puppy I had brought for May. He was the son of my famous pair of Irish dachshunds which at the French dog shows on the terrace of the gardens of the Tuileries had won so many prizes that they had been declared *hors concours*.

The three little boys were in three white beds in one room and Thora slept in a cot in Kathleen's room across the passage, from which, under the disapproving eyes of Kathleen and their nurse, I carried her into the boys' room, for of course she wanted to see the dachshund and help to unpack my handbag full of smuggled French scents and bonbons.

"Why didn't you bring Iseult for the wedding?" asked Toby.

"Because I am going on to Ireland for meetings. Iseult and Daphne are still in the convent of Iseult's godmother where

they stayed while I was in America. I went to see them
there to bring Iseult a tiny alligator I brought from
America."

"An alligator?" screamed the children. "But isn't it
wicked?"

"No, it's very sweet, with pale blue eyes and eats tiny bits
of raw meat and drinks milk."

"Oh, Auntie Maud, why didn't you bring Iseult and the
alligator to May's wedding?" insisted Toby. "I am to be a
page and wear a satin coat and carry May's train; Iseult
would have loved to come."

"Iseult is very happy in the convent. All the nuns love her.
Sister Marie de l'Incarnation and Sister Beatrice des Anges
play great games with her. There is a big garden with big
trees and a pond with fishes in it and Iseult and Sister Beatrice
are going to tie a ribbon round the alligator's neck and let
him swim in it. There are little altars and statues and grottos
everywhere in the gardens; you would love to play cubby
houses in them, but the nuns wouldn't have you because
you are only a boy."

"They would let me come. Do take me when you go back,"
said Thora. A convent sounded to them a very mysterious
place and full of adventure.

"Auntie Maud must be starving. You must let her come
down to dinner," said Chotie, extracting the dachshund pup
from Pat's bed where it had snuggled down under the bed
clothes, while Kathleen carried Thora back to her bed and
nurse switched off the light.

May and her young man had returned. I never discovered
how they had missed me. He looked presentable enough and
made some quite polite remarks about wanting to know May's
greatest friend and added that, being a broad-minded Englishman, he hoped politics would never be a bar to our
friendship.

While we were still at dinner Willie Yeats arrived to see me and we all went into the drawing-room for coffee. Kathleen and I sat together on a big sofa amid piles of soft cushions. I was still in my dark clothes with the black veil I always wore when travelling instead of a hat, and we must have made a strange contrast. I saw Willie Yeats looking critically at me and he told Kathleen he liked her dress and that she was looking younger than ever. It was on that occasion Kathleen remarked that it was hard work being beautiful, which Willie turned into his poem *Adam's Curse*.

Adam's Curse

We sat together at one summer's end
That beautiful mild woman, your close friend,
And you and I, and talked of poetry.

I said, 'A line will take us hours maybe;
Yet if it does not seem a moment's thought,
Our stitching and unstitching has been naught.
Better go down upon your marrow-bones
And scrub a kitchen pavement, or break stones
Like an old pauper, in all kinds of weather;
For to articulate sweet sounds together
Is to work harder than all these and yet
Be thought an idler by the noisy set
Of bankers, schoolmasters and clergymen
The martyr's call the world.
                              And there upon
That beautiful mild woman for whose sake
There's many a one shall find out all heartache
On finding that her voice is sweet and low
Replied, 'To be born woman is to know—
Although they do not talk of it at school—
That we must labour to be beautiful.'
I said, 'It's certain there is no fine thing

Since Adam's fall but needs much labouring,
There have been lovers who thought love should be
So much compounded of high courtesy
That they would sigh and quote with learned looks
Precedents out of beautiful old books;
Yet now it seems an idle trade enough.'

We sat, grown quiet at the name of love
We saw the last embers of daylight die,
And in the trembling blue green of the sky
A moon, worn as if it had been a shell,
Washed by time's waters as they rose and fell
About the stars and broke in days and years.

I had a thought for no one's but your ears
That you were beautiful, and that I strove
To love you in the old high way of love
That it had all seemed happy, and yet we'd grown
As weary hearted as that hollow moon.

Next day when he called to take me out to pay my customary
visit to the Lia Fail, he said:
"You don't take care of yourself as Kathleen does, so she
looks younger than you; your face is worn and thin; but you
will always be beautiful, more beautiful than anyone I have
known. You can't help that. Oh Maud, why don't you marry
me and give up this tragic struggle and live a peaceful life?
I could make such a beautiful life for you among artists and
writers who would understand you."
"Willie, are you not tired of asking that question? How
often have I told you to thank the gods that I will not marry
you. You would not be happy with me."
"I am not happy without you."
"Oh yes, you are, because you make beautiful poetry out

of what you call your unhappiness and you are happy in that. Marriage would be such a dull affair. Poets should never marry. The world should thank me for not marrying you. I will tell you one thing, our friendship has meant a great deal to me; it has helped me often when I needed help, needed it perhaps more than you or anyone ever knew, for I never talk or even think of these things."

"Are you happy or unhappy?" he asked.

"I have been happier and unhappier than most, but I don't think about it. You and I are so different in this. It is a great thing to know one can never suffer again as much as one has suffered; it gives one great calm and great strength and makes one afraid of nothing. I am interested in the work I have undertaken; that is my life and I live,—while so many people only exist. Those are the people to be pitied, those who lead dull, uneventful lives ; they might as well be dead in the ground. And now, Willie, let us talk of the Lia Fail. You know I hate talking of myself; I am not going to let you make me."

We stood in the great grey Abbey in front of the great grey stone, the stone that belongs to Ireland, that must be brought back to Ireland, the Stone of Destiny, the stone on which the kings of Ireland used to be crowned. We spoke of the four great jewels the Tuatha De Danaans brought to Ireland in the dim past ages; the stone, the cauldron, the spear and the sword, and of the ancient gods which old writings connect with them. And Willie said they had their counterparts in the legends of the Graal which originated in Ireland and are a part of universal symbolism and of Catholic symbolism. The stone,— the altar, which even if it is made of wood must have a stone embedded in it. The cauldron,—the chalice. The spear of Lugh,—the spear which pierced the side of Christ. And the sword of the Virgin Brigid of the Judgments,—the sword which Christ said He brought, the sword of the Crusaders whose handle is the cross. They are on the Egyptian Taro cards and in a debased form they are on our playing cards.

"It is very heavy," I said, looking at the iron clamps which hold the stolen stone under the British Coronation Chair. You and I could not lift it. It would require several men."

"Could we get the spirit of the stone to Ireland and only leave its cold, dead weight under the chair in cold, dead London till we could bring it to Ireland, as it must be brought one day in triumph and ceremony, and rejoicing? Have you magic that can do that? It should be possible." And we spoke of the "Golden Dawn" in which Willie was now one of the high initiates and which I had left because of its connection with Freemasonry.

We had tea in Willie's rooms in Woburn Buildings in the little room over the cobbler's shop with dark blue hangings and prints of Blake's drawings on the walls. What strange talks that room had listened to! Men of the I.R.B. had met there. William Sharpe had told us of his spirit love, Fiona McLeod. Mac Gregor had talked of his Rosicrucian mysteries. Sarojini Naidu, the beautiful Hindu Nationalist, "the little Indian princess", as Willie called her, had read her poems there. The American poetess, Agness Tobin, had spoken of her determination to save Arthur Symons and had by her strong magnetism brought him back to life from an asylum, only to find the walls of another asylum close on herself. Lionel Johnson had recited his poems and talked of Ireland there and Mrs. Emery had chanted her strange chants to a musical instrument invented by Dr. Elgar.

"Willie, I like this room better than Chotie's house," I said. "Without money you have made life interesting."

He made me sit in a big leather armchair, a new expensive addition to his furniture; he told me it was a present from Lady

Gregory. "She is very kind to me," he said. I was glad he had found a good friend, but I feared she would take him away from the fight for Irish freedom.

She had called on me in Dublin,—a queer little old lady, rather like Queen Victoria. She told me she was learning typewriting to be able to type Willie's poems and plays. She was also translating from French translations of Irish literature appearing in Gaidoz' *Revue Celtique*. Then she had asked me if I would marry Willie Yeats. It did not seem exactly her business, and I had answered rather shortly that we were neither of the marrying sort, having other things which interested us more; and I had thought she seemed rather relieved. I had felt astonished and not very pleased when she deserted the Hibernian Hotel, where she used to stay when in Dublin, and took rooms in the house where I lived in Nassau Street. Through Willie she had got to know all John O'Leary's literary group and invited many of them to stay with her in her Galway home; I wondered if it was because of her newly-found interest in Gaelic literature and the Irish theatre or of a desire to draw them away from too vehement expression of Irish Independence. Her interest and appreciation of the old Irish legends was very real and I loved her books,—*Cuchulan of Muirthemhe* of the Finn periods, *Gods and Fighting Men*, and of the early Irish saints, *Saints and Scholars*. They were a real joy to people who, like myself, were unable to read the old Irish texts and records. But when these writers came back from Coole, they seemed to me less passionately interested in the National struggle and more worried about their own lack of money. George and Violet Russell, who had stayed a month at Coole, on their return told me that they hated being patronised and would not go again.

Lady Gregory and I were gracious to each other but never friends and in the later struggle in the theatre group,—Art for Art's Sake or Art for Propaganda,—we were on different sides. I had been much amused in Dublin watching the rivalry between Lady Gregory and a rich English woman, Miss Horniman; both were interested in Willie and both were interested in the Irish theatre. Miss Horniman had the money and was willing to spend it, but Lady Gregory had the brains. They should have been allies for both stood for art for art's sake and deprecated the intrusion of politics, which meant Irish Freedom; instead they were rivals; they both liked Willie too well. Lady Gregory won the battle; Miss Horniman's money converted the old city morgue into the Abbey Theatre, but it was Lady Gregory's plays that were acted there. Miss Horniman brought back Italian plaques to decorate it but Lady Gregory carried off Willie to visit the Italian towns where they were made and Willie's national outlook underwent a complete change. There would be no more poems against English kings' visits.

May's wedding was a picturesque affair. I helped to dress her and tie in the little blue bow to her garter, as a white bride must always wear a scrap of blue for luck, and fasten on the white satin train which Toby as page was proud of holding up. The display of wedding presents was gorgeous and there were enough ice creams to satisfy even the desire of the babies. But for some reason I cannot explain, both Chotie and I felt sad and anxious; and, sitting on my bed that night, Chotie reminded me of a story her mother, who was always fond of delving into old family records, told about a curse put by a priest on a Gonne in the past, who had acquired land which belonged to the Church. It was to the effect that no daughter of the Gonnes should ever find happiness in marriage. Our grandfather's only daughter had married a man who became insane; Kathleen couldn't be said to have found happiness in marriage and now May was taking the risk.

"But the curse should not affect any of us now," I said.

Our great-grandfather had been disinherited by his father and we had now no land in Ireland or money coming from it. All we have comes from the business in Spanish wine which our disinherited ancestor set up.

"May's husband seems devoted to her; they are both well off; May is so easy to get on with, why shouldn't they be happy?"

But twelve months later they were separated; so I suppose the old curse is still in working order, though it seems vindictive and unreasonable.

Victoria was dead. There were the usual demonstrations of loyalty for Edward's coronation in Dublin. The counter demonstrations by the people, who repudiated the claim of English kings to rule and rob Ireland, had not been vigorous enough to get much publicity.

Willie Yeats saw me off at Euston Station the night following May's wedding.

"I suppose you should go back," he said doubtfully, "you have been away nearly three months from Dublin and things are apt to get dull when you are not there. Willie Rooney's death has had a depressing effect on the movement. The Unionists, some of whom I met in London, are in great spirits and say Edward VII is sure of getting a royal welcome when he visits Ireland. They are busy creating a king's legend. His many love affairs make him rather popular in England; people are getting tired of the virtuous dulness of Victoria's Court. Edward is to be a Royal king and the people's king. To placate Ireland it is being industriously whispered that he is secretly a convert to the Catholic religion and has a deep affection for his Catholic subjects. I hear he is to be received at Maynooth by the bishops."

"The coronation oath should dispel that legend. I will get it printed and circulated," I said. "We will prevent the keys of the City being presented to him as they were to Victoria.

Tim Harrington and not Pile is Lord Mayor now. I don't see him going on his knees to an English king."

"The keys will be presented all right and you won't be able to prevent it," said Willie, "but if the story printed in Griffith's paper is true, Tim Harrington will not have to present them but only go away on a holiday." And he took out a copy of the *United Irishman* he had just received.

In it Griffith published information he had got of a Unionist conspiracy to arrange that the Lord Mayor should be away from Dublin on holiday during the Royal visit and that his locum tenens, Alderman Cotton, a Unionist, should receive the king.

"I wonder," said Yeats, "where Griffith got the information. He doesn't publish that, so it won't carry much weight; none of the daily press will take it up. But it sounds likely enough. Harrington is dreadfully in debt and they can bring pressure to bear on him. You won't be able to stop it."

"Yes, I will," I said, as the train moved off. But I had no plan.

I had given up my rooms in Nassau Street and had taken a tiny house in Coulson Avenue next to the Russells. As my slow four-wheeled cab drove past the hoardings near Harcourt Street station I saw a big poster announcing a meeting of the Parliamentary Party in the Rotunda to be held the following evening. Tim Harrington was to take the chair and John Redmond was to speak. This gave me an idea and a plan. Tim Harrington must be asked publicly to repudiate the statement published in the *United Irishman*. That would ensure publicity.

I stopped my cab at the Rathmines post office and sent a sheaf of telegrams to Griffith, to Edward Martyn, to Father Anderson, to Seumas Mac Manus, to George Moore and to Mary Quinn, secretary of *Inghinidhe na hEireann*, telling them of my arrival, and asking them all to come to tea with me that afternoon.

They all responded, for they were all glad to welcome me home. I asked Griffith how he had got the information about the Unionist plot. He said it was from a man who had been engaged as a waiter at a Unionist dinner presided over by Alderman Cotton, but he couldn't give the name of his inform-ant as it would have cost him his job, but he was certain of the facts. Harrington was not at the dinner and perhaps had as yet no knowledge of the plot; but Griffith knew that he was up against it financially and might not be able to resist pressure, which only involved his taking a holiday at a particular time. "Unfortunately," added Griffith, "the *United Irishman* has not the right circulation to affect him."

"Well," I said, "we are all here citizens of Dublin, and it is our duty to prevent the capital of Ireland being disgraced. I propose we take the name of the Citizens' Watch Committee and go as a delegation from our committee to the Rotunda meeting to-morrow and put the question to Tim Harrington. That will get plenty of publicity."

They all looked at me, astonished. The idea was so simple, Mary Quinn was enthusiastic, so was old Father Anderson, but he said that, to his regret, the rules of his Order would prevent him being one of the delegation. George Moore got up and said that, though he was an Irishman, he was not disloyal to the English king and could not be associated,— and withdrew.

"Five are quite enough for any delegation," I said. "It is going to be great fun."

We named Edward Martyn spokesman for the delegation and he and Arthur Griffith set about writing a short speech and the question he was to put. Mary Quinn, giving me a great hug, went off to summon as many members of *Inghinidh na hEireann* as she could get to be present at the meeting at the Rotunda.

"Tell them to bring their friends and sweethearts to take care of them, for there may be a rough house. And, Mary, if you can, come back and sleep here to-night. I have been away so long you must have lots of news I am longing to hear."

"All right," said Mary, "I will tell the girls to take up strategic positions in the Rotunda as we do when we upset British propaganda plays," and she went off.

Next night the delegation from the Citizens' Watch Committee arrived at the Rotunda. The stewards at the door were delighted to see me and thought we were coming to support the Parliamentary Party's appeal for election funds and offered us places on the platform. I told them we were only there to put a question we wanted answered.

The hall was packed as we went on the platform and great cheers were raised for Maud Gonne. I think I was the only one that most of the people knew by sight. Tim Harrington rose and shook hands with me, and I introduced the others. The meeting was about to begin. I told him why we were there.

"We want you to kill a British plot by at once reassuring the people of Dublin that our ancient city will never again be disgraced by the recognition of an English king."

Harrington looked worried. "You should know me well enough to know that I, as Lord Mayor, will not receive him."

"We do, Tim," I answered, "but have you read the *United Irishman*?"

He was getting angry. "Miss Gonne, you can't interrupt the meeting. No question can be asked till the end." And he proceeded to open the meeting.

I knew Harrington was an old parliamentarian, up to all the tricks, and would arrange that there would be no time left for awkward questions. He was already announcing Mr. Redmond when I stood up and said in a clear voice, which rang through the building:

"Mr. Martyn will now put a question about the king of England's visit and we will go when it is answered."

Mr. Redmond was on his feet and had begun: "Gentlemen, and ladies, people of Dublin——" But no one was listening to him.

"Sit down, Miss Gonne," thundered Harrington, above the din which was beginning to arise in the hall.

"When our delegation from the Citizens' Watch Committee has been answered," I replied, equally loud; and I have often found that a woman's voice carries better than a man's in a stormy meeting. "Put the question, Mr. Martyn," I said, "now."

Edward Martyn was standing near me, the paper on which it was written in his hand.

"I can't," he said helplessly, "I have never spoken in public, my voice would not be heard."

"Go on, you must; quick," I urged.

"I can't. You must put it," said Martyn, thrusting the paper into my hand, and I began reading it amid cheers for Miss Gonne and cries of "Silence, we want to hear" and counter shouts of "Sit down!" Then one of the stewards near the platform shouted: "Throw her off!" and a steward climbed on the platform dangerously near me and another rushed from the back and caught hold of my arm. "Don't you dare touch her!" and "We want no king!" were the last articulate words I heard in the general hubbub which ensued, and the steward who held my arm was roughly thrown to the ground by a young man who had climbed onto the platform. In every part of the hall people were now fighting and sounds of breaking wood could be heard as chairs were taken as weapons. Bits of wood were being hurled at the platform. I saw Mick

Quinn, Mary's brother, fighting desperately; he had a cut on his head which was bleeding; he was always a great fighter. Then someone, very tall and strong, seized me and lifted me off my feet and carried me off the platform. "You will get hurt." I struggled to get free, thinking it was one of the stewards; but it was Seumas Mac Manus. I was angry. In the comparative calm behind the stage, Griffith said: "Mac Manus is right; you would get hurt. No one could prevent you getting struck with the chairs they are throwing. We have, I think, accomplished all we came for."

And we certainly had. Most of the crowd left after the delegation, some to avoid arrest by the police when they arrived, not wishing to be held responsible for the broken chairs, of which very few remained intact.

Mr. Redmond spoke to a wrecked and almost empty hall, and Irish and English papers issued columns of abuse of the disgraceful rowdies who had disturbed a peaceful meeting, and contradicted the alleged information in the *United Irishman*.

It was the last big meeting the Parliamentary Party was able to stage in Dublin. I was sorry for Lord Mayor Harrington, for he was a good Lord Mayor and a good Irishman, but after all this really got him out of some of his difficulties. No one could now even suggest asking him to leave Dublin. We had beaten even the secret money power which is covertly and unscrupulously used by the English and which is behind so much that is incomprehensible and inconsistent in Irish affairs.

I got a letter from Yeats: "You certainly have succeeded." Luck and the will of the gods had not deserted me in public affairs, though I had begun to doubt them, and as for my private affairs, why should the gods look after them? I had long ago chosen to devote my life to the one objective of freeing Ireland, and since then I had invariably found that anything

I undertook for myself personally never succeeded, and so had given up trying. So long as I was working for Ireland I felt safe and protected. So protected that I never raised a finger or spoke a word against any enemies I made, who tried to injure me. I was sometimes almost frightened to see how misfortune always fell on them. Queer misfortunes, loss of health, or money, or children.

CHAPTER XXVI

THE INEVITABILITY OF THE CHURCH

It was at Royat in that beautiful rugged Auvergne I loved so much, a Celtic country, that I met the Catholic priest who led me into the Church. Some six years after my first visit to Royat, I was again staying there, but this time, not in any of the fashionable hotels, but in the charming little inn of '*La Belle Meunière*'. I was combining a rest, after a strenuous lecture tour, with meeting a few of '*La Boulange*'; among them was a young priest, l'Abbé Dissard, a fervent Nationalist whose hero was Napoleon.

Many a talk we had, sitting beside the mountain stream, which used to turn the old mill wheels, and watching the little black trout jump.

"Why are you not a Catholic like your Nation?" he asked one day.

"Because I believe in reincarnation; I believe I have lived in this beautiful world before. Some of the people I meet are people I have already known so well that I know the things they are going to say. Some I like, some I don't, and if I try to get over these instinctive dislikes I always regret it, for such people prove generally hostile and dangerous to the things I love, while those I remember with love usually help my work. Our friend, Millevoye, for instance,—I was so certain we had met before that I told him so when we were introduced."

"The soul comes from God and returns to God when purified, when all things will become clear; and who can tell the stages of its purification? It may be possible some souls may work out their purification on this earth. On the other hand, the memories you speak of may be ancestral memories transmitted in the blood. My own name Dissard comes from two words: Dis,—the God Auvergne worshipped, and Ard,—high, and was the name of the Chief Druid who died fighting against the Roman legionaries. Local tradition has it that my family are his descendants; it is certain they have lived on the land for numberless generations and there is a little hill on it which we guard piously and which is said to be the Druid's burial place. From a tiny child I and my mother knew I would be a priest of God. It is not re-incarnation, but ancestral influence. I had to be a priest."

Years later, the Abbé Dissard had become a Canon and was Chaplain to a Carmelite Convent in Laval. Some archaeological society connected with the Museum of St. Germain-en-Laye, of which Solomon Reinach was curator, succeeded in getting authority to excavate the Druid hill. Canon Dissard was furious at the desecration, so were most of the people living on the land. If he could have left his work in Laval I have no doubt there would have been serious trouble in the district, but, as it was, the excavators tore open the burial mound and discovered, first the bones of many horses, then the bones of men and many valuable arms and ornaments which were transferred to the St. Germain Museum. Canon Dissard went there and had a stormy altercation with the curator, which actually ended in blows, when the enraged Auvergnat priest knocked out the curator, and archaeological reviews barely succeeded in covering the scandal by learned controversies on the Druidical origin of the treasure. When at last Canon Dissard got his holiday and was able to visit the desecrated tomb of his ancestor, the excavators had departed, leaving great scars on the hill. Canon Dissard stood on the hill in no happy frame of mind; his foot struck some metal object; he stooped down and picked it up, a small semi-circle-shaped instrument, which, when polished, proved to be made of gold. It was the sickle of the Chief Druid, used for cutting the sacred mistletoe from the oak. It was certainly a miracle that it had escaped the searchers. Canon Dissard said his ancester had protected it and kept it for him. He put it in a glass case where it became his dearest possession.

The Abbé Dissard had the tenacity for which the Auvergnats are famous. Like Father Cavanagh, he predicted that I would join the Church and he helped his prediction with constant insistence.

"It is unthinkable that Maud Gonne should belong to the Church of England," he said another day. "You won't recognise old Victoria politically and yet you recognise her as head of your religion."

"No, I don't," I laughed, "I was baptised into her religion because unfortunate babies are not consulted on such matters, but it never meant anything to me except horrible boredom as a child when I was made to learn catechism and collects and listen to long sermons and, as I never suffer boredom willingly, I never went to these services when I was a free agent. Besides, it is the Church of the evictors, of the pious people who destroy houses and leave children to die; but I very often go to Mass."

"I know you do; I watched you praying in the Cathedral of Clermont Ferrand and you were so absorbed I didn't venture to speak to you. You will become a Catholic one day."

"I belong to no church because I want to remain free. You and I are good friends and like talking together because we have many thoughts and many dreams in common but I would not like to have to confess to you or to any man my weaknesses and sins."

"In the confessional you don't confess to man but to God, who has chosen to work through man and so has delegated

His power to remit sins to His consecrated priests. You would be freer than you are, if you were in the Church. We all make mistakes, sin, do things we regret. Through confession we can rid ourselves of the burden of vain regrets and are freer because of that."

I shook my head: "The Pope is doubtless a more dignified head of a church than old Vic and divinely appointed according to tradition and when I saw him carried like a white light through St. Peter's I knelt in reverence, almost in ecstasy, as before the highest expression of humanity; but when I learnt later that he had listened to that English envoy, Errington, and had sent a letter to Ireland, condemning the Plan of Campaign, the people's only protection from the evicting landlords, I doubted his infallibility."

"But, of course the Pope is not infallible on political matters; only Protestants think that claim is made for him. Your Ireland is still saturated with Protestant thought, even Catholic Ireland. God has promised immortality to His Church, so He sees to it that His representative on earth is inspired when He speaks of things pertaining to the Faith. In that he is infallible and can make no mistakes, but God has never promised immortality to nations and leaves to the people the responsibility of holding the land He has given them, and, if they don't do so, they deserve the misery that comes to them."

"But Irish bishops always denounce the men who are prepared to fight to deliver their land."

"A French bishop burnt Joan of Arc," said the Abbé, "but what does that prove? Only that the bishops are very fallible and should not be followed when they give wrong advice. Look at the carvings on our cathedrals and you will see the devil prodding many mitred heads and sending them all to hell. These things should not make you hold aloof from the Church and cut yourself off from the great spiritual strength of the Mass. But I have no doubt you will come in; I can wait.

I have asked a whole convent of nuns to pray for you; some of them are very holy women and their prayers will prevail."

I felt a little frightened, for I knew that in Ireland, in many tiny cottages in the mountains of Mayo and Donegal, the Rosary was being recited for me with the same intention. I didn't feel myself worthy of so many prayers and I was also afraid of the inevitability of their success.

Canon Dissard and I formed a lasting friendship which ended only with his death. He received me later into the Church in the chapel of the Carmelite convent of Laval and he stood firmly by me when I sought the civil dissolution of my marriage. He knew all the circumstances, which others did not.

To Ella Young, a great friend of mine, I told of Father Cavanagh's and Canon Dissard's predictions. She was more troubled than I was about them. She came from a presbyterian family from Antrim and though she often accompanied me to Mass, shared her family's fears of priestly interference in national affairs. She thought that, if I became a Catholic, my power to work for Irish independence would be curtailed. I was bound to agree with her that, historically and actually, that power had not helped to free Ireland from the English, though the persecutions following England's acceptance of Protestantism may have helped to keep the Irish a distinctive race.

Ella had made a great study of Irish mythology and loved the ancient gods. To-day she is professor of Celtic mythology in a Californian university. She had left George Russell's group of mystics, feeling that Eastern mysticism was not suitable for Ireland's needs, and had in 1900 formed a group of her own called the *Fine* (the fingers) after long meditations on the Swastika and long before anyone had heard of Fascism; strangely enough, also, the salutation between members of the

Fine was the raising of the hand, almost like the Fascists. Ella said it was the old form of Gaelic salutation. The object of the *Fine* was to draw together for the freeing of Ireland the wills of the living and of the dead in association with the earth and the elements which to her seemed living entities. In the *Fine* Ella had chosen Ireland's Eye as the representative of Irish Earth and often we went to that lonely island, for Ella loved boats and was clever in their management.

She was an extraordinary woman, very frail in appearance but with an iron will. On Ireland's Eye amid the seagulls we often lit the Bealtaine fire of the old Gaelic festival, now represented by the fires of St. John's Eve. It served to boil our tea kettle and to destroy all vestiges of the picnic, for Ella was very careful that the land should not be disfigured. At the last she would kindle from it a tiny fire in which she burnt herbs she had gathered from different parts of Ireland, as she said, to unite all,—which sent up a sweet scent like incense. Ella would then talk of the ancient gods and invoke them to help bring back the Lia Fail. Helena Molony and I were often on these excursions and Maureen Fox and Susan Varian. We would sit round the fire, telling of strange, inexplicable incidents, which I think occur to most people if they only noted them. Ella had a great gift for making plants live. Her garden was always full of bloom even in seasons when one did not expect flowers; she presented me with a small stone in which she had induced to grow six different little mountain plants and mosses which actually flowered. She said plants responded to human love and often carried about with her some stone which she was cultivating in this way; she would hold it and cover it with her delicate white hands when she wanted the tiny plants to flower. She was always extraordinarily happy and I loved being with her and missed her greatly when she went to America. She had the gift of making life colourful.

I never doubted the existence of spiritual forces surrounding us, some friendly, some hostile, more completely blind to human needs, pursuing their own existence with the same disregard of us as the birds or the insects. I knew it was possible to break the dividing barrier which separates us from this world and once had been eager to do so in the hope of gaining power to further the cause to which I had devoted my life. Then I had realised the danger of playing with forces without sufficient knowledge,—danger to one's own sanity and still more danger to those one loves and may be unable to protect. I looked on the Catholic Church as the repository of spiritual knowledge and sometimes I longed for its protection and guidance.

I believe every political movement on earth has its counterpart in the spirit world and the battles we fight here have perhaps been already fought out on another plane and great leaders draw their often unexplained power from this. I cannot conceive a material movement which has not a spiritual basis.

It was this that drew me so powerfully towards the Catholic Church and tempted me to accept a long-standing invitation of Canon Dissard to visit the convent to which he was chaplain. I made the acquaintance of its Reverend Mother in a strangely tragic-comic way. The Masonic persecution of the Church was at its height in France; the religious orders were being expelled and scandalously robbed. Canon Dissard had been in Paris often, seeing numbers of deputies trying to save the convent of Laval.

One day, when I was returning from a walk, Marguerite the maid told me two ladies were waiting for me in the drawing-room.

"Take care, Mademoiselle," she said, "I think one of them is a mad woman."

The strangest figure I ever saw rose to greet me. A tall woman of my own age with a beautiful clear complexion, dressed exactly like a statue of Our Lady of Lourdes in a white robe and sky-blue cloak, but on her head, covered with much fuzzy fair hair, instead of a veil, was perched a rakish brown hat with blue and white ostrich feather plumes.

"I have a letter of introduction from Canon Dissard which I was going to send and ask if I might call on you to-morrow, but something awful has happened in this dreadful Paris and I want your help."

To gain time I glanced at the letter. Could this be the Reverend Mother of the Carmelites? I begged her to sit down and ordered Marguerite to bring tea. Then I heard the tale. She and Sister Catherine had come to Paris to interview a manufacturer of 'passementerie' who had agreed to give work to the convent.

"My dear daughters are wonderful embroidresses; we have the most beautiful vestments of all convents in France and all embroidered by ourselves," she said proudly, "but we don't understand the sort of embroideries he wants and he was not satisfied. It is so important to keep the order that I had to come to Paris to see exactly what he needs. You see, we must establish what they call a *"raison sociale"* to prove we are earning our living and employing workers or the Government will close our convent and we shall be all cast out on the world. When we got off the train at the Gare St. Lazare and came out of the station, people followed us. I was asking the way to the street where the manufacturer lives; there was a strong wind and Sister Catherine's hat was blown off and with it her wig to which it was pinned; I had to clutch mine tightly or it would have been blown off too. Our heads are shaved and the wigs don't hold well. Sister Catherine was running after her hat; a crowd of horrid, jeering people surrounded me and I got so frightened I began to cry. Then a kind gentleman got a *fiacre* and put us into it and I gave your address to the driver. I hope you don't mind."

"Of course I don't. I am very pleased to meet you, for Canon Dissard has spoken so much to me of you; but where is he? Why didn't he come with you?"

"He was away when the letter from the manufacturer came, saying the embroidery sent was all wrong and threatening to withdraw the order. The Canon had said I might have to go to Paris to learn the kind of work that was required. To keep the order is so important, for Government inspectors may come any day, so I decided I must go to Paris at once."

"Did Canon Dissard help to choose your dress?" I ventured.

"Oh no. That was the choice and the work of my dear daughters, but we ordered the wigs from the best hairdresser in Laval and my hat from the best milliner because we knew it was important to be "*à la mode*" and to have things that people are wearing so as not to be remarkable."

I tried not to laugh and while we drank our tea I learnt that she had never left the cloister since she had entered it as a girl of sixteen.

"Perhaps my dress is not quite right," she said, doubtfully. "The people in the streets were saying such terrible, horrid things."

"Well, light colours are not much worn in the street," I answered, "but you and I are much of a height. Would you mind wearing one of my dresses?"

"Oh, thank you! Sister Catherine, how right we were to come here,—the Good God sent us."

We went into my bedroom and soon the Reverend Mother was transformed from an image of our Lady with a rakish hat to a tolerably dressed lady in a dark blue costume, rather too tight for her, for she was plumper than I was, and the fair curly wig held in a close-fitting black hat with a little veil. As to Sister Catherine, her costume, cut out of the brown material of the Carmelite habits, made her look quite an old-fashioned lady's maid. I accompanied them to the Catholic hotel where they had written to reserve rooms; we despatched a telegram to Canon Dissard to come and retrieve them and until his arrival I promised to accompany them in their walks abroad in that terrible Paris which I found they were both most interested to visit.

I received a friendly invitation to come and stay at the convent whenever I liked,—an offer of which I often availed myself. Canon Dissard and the bishop succeeded in saving it from liquidation and robbery by a compromise. While holding fast to their ancient rule within the walls, the Reverend Mother and several of the lay sisters had to assume ordinary dress, to receive Government inspectors and to appear occasionally in the streets of Laval. They called themselves the Association of St. Thérèse, working at an industry in which a few outside workers were employed as well. The Carmelite order had been expelled from France, so all its members had to choose either to become ordinary citizens or go into exile. Canon Dissard considered the compromise justified because it saved many of the old nuns who had lived forty or fifty years in the convent from being sent suddenly adrift into the world. The bishop's chief preoccupation was to save church property, and he and the Canon quarrelled ten years later when the bishop decided the huge convent was too big for so small a number of women and turned it into a Seminary. Many of the old nuns had died, some had gone into exile and no new postulants could be recruited. The Association of St. Thérèse was accommodated in a small country manor-house belonging to the rich family of the Reverend Mother. I am afraid even the Church is inclined to treat the rights of women lightly.

When I stayed in the convent it was a very peaceful place. I occupied a room near the Reverend Mother's in that part of the Convent prepared for Government inspection, but was free to wander anywhere in the big gardens or farm and came in contact with many of the nuns who were all praying for my conversion.

It was in their beautiful chapel that I was received into the Catholic Church.

CHAPTER XXVII

DUSK

PEOPLE SAID THE Boer War was nearing its end. De Wet and President Steyn of the Orange Free State were still gallantly holding their own. President Kruger was in Europe, making a vain appeal for belated assistance. The German Emperor, probably from family feelings for his grandmother Victoria, refused to allow him to go to Berlin. I loved the French people for the magnificent reception they accorded him. However pro-English the French government might be, it could not stand against the tremendous surge of popular enthusiasm, but the great welcome was from the people and hardly official. Cheering crowds thronged the boulevards and stood all day round the Grand Hotel where he was staying. It was with difficulty that I and a few members of the Paris Young Ireland Society pushed our way through to present the address from Ireland. Some French students recognised me and cheers for Ireland mingled with the cheers for the Boer Republics and way was made for us.

President Kruger was a tragic, broken-hearted old man, with rugged dignity. He looked very weary. He put his hand on my shoulder, as he took the scroll on which the address was written, and kept me near him awhile though the rooms were crowded with delegations waiting to present addresses. He said:

"The Irish have proved their sympathy by fighting for us. The Irish Commando has done fine work."

I answered: "There are thousands of Irishmen waiting to get out and join."

He shook his head: "It is a different kind of war now. No more big battles; only guerilla war; to be of use men must know the country and speak our language, but we will wear the English down, we will not give in."

A year later the peace of Vereeniging was signed and two years later President Steyn, slowly recovering in Paris from a paralytic stroke due to the terrible hardships of the campaign, told me:

"Thank God this hand of mine was paralysed so I could not sign that treaty; when I signed the order for the Orange Free State to go into the war I was very sad, knowing the suffering it would entail on our people, but I was far sadder when that peace treaty was signed, for I knew then that if we had held out a little longer,—and we could have done it,—we would have won. De Wet was a great general; he would have worn the British out."

Some months later, in Dublin, I got a letter from MacBride. He was returning to France and asked me to meet him in Paris. He had asked me to marry him in America and I had replied that marriage was not in my thoughts while there was a war on and there was always an Irish war on. I feared it might be that personal reason that was bringing him to France, but I hoped there might be a more interesting reason. When I met him he was very disheartened. The Boer War was almost over and, except for the Irish Brigade and Luke Dillon's gallant attempt on the Welland Canal, Ireland had done nothing.

"What are you going to do in Paris?" I asked him.

"Earn my living, I suppose," he answered, "and wait for the chance of a fight."

I told him I was speaking at a great French pro-Boer meeting in the *Salle Wagram* and suggested that I should tell the organisers he would also speak. He had met Colonel de Villebois Mareuil shortly before he was killed and de Villebois Mareuil was a hero to the French people.

MacBride accepted and got a great ovation, though his French was so bad that everyone thought he was speaking Dutch.

Without the language, MacBride, I am afraid, had a hard time in Paris; waiting for a chance is always hard. I felt he would have done better to have stayed in America, where he had many openings.

Cumann na nGael was making rapid progress in Ireland. The Parliamentary Party was becoming more and more discredited; large meetings were calling on them to withdraw from Westminster; Griffith's Sinn Fein policy was improving the morale of the people but it was plodding work, not revolution. MacBride could not go back to Ireland and was terribly home-sick. The money he had saved in the Transvaal, before the war, was nearly exhausted and he could get no job, but he always kept a cheerful face and said luck would turn and he would get another chance of fighting England.

One day he arrived in great spirits. "I have got a job!" The correspondent of the *American Sun* and Laffan's Bureau had engaged him as secretary at £2 a week.

"But, John," I said, "that man is pro-British and was nearly expelled from France."

"Oh, the French see spies everywhere," he replied, "he isn't a bad sort. I admit he used to be an English Liberal and a follower of Gladstone but he is Irish and I have been converting him and his family to Irish Republicanism."

"Well, take care; it was the French anti-English Intelligence service who warned me against him; I think it is strange he should take you as secretary. How can you help him in his work with your bad French?"

"He lives outside Paris and wants me to send off his late cables. I don't need much French for that."

Perhaps it was all right; and as I knew John could hold his tongue and keep his own counsel better than most, I hoped for the best and was delighted that he had got work to occupy his mind and enable him to live. I was often worried about how some of the young Irishmen in the Paris Young Ireland Society existed. They were usually cheerful, but I suspected they often dined on a crust of bread; they were morbidly sensitive, too, about their lack of money, and it required real strategy, when they insisted on taking me out, to avoid going to places where they would have to pay, and many is the time when, though very tired, I had to say I wanted a walk to avoid taking a *fiacre*,—the gay little Paris cab,—for which they would never have let me pay. The French students would laugh gaily when, at the end of term, they were "sans le sou", but the Irish boys hated admitting the fact. I only met a Japanese student who was even more sensitive. He came to interview me for a Japanese paper; he looked like a sick monkey and, because I like monkeys, we became good friends. I noticed that, when tea was served, he generally refused to eat. A French student told me later, after he was dead, that it was because he was so hungry and was afraid anyone might think he was. He died of starvation and would let none of his French comrades help him.

MacBride lived in a tiny attic in the Rue Gay de Lussac. One day, after a lecture by d'Arbois de Joubainville in the Quartier Latin we had both attended, to avoid going to a café, as he suggested, I insisted instead that he should give me tea in his room, where we would be quieter for a talk,—really because I knew the money he would have spent at the café would have probably meant no dinner for him the next day. I think he was shocked at the suggestion, till I told him he must get rid of the English idea that a bedroom was a less proper place than a sitting-room, for he was full of queer conventions.

The room was very tidy and very bare, but MacBride was quite an adept at making tea and many were the fantastic plans we discussed in that little attic and in the more comfortable drawing-room of my flat in the Avenue d'Eylau. Most of these plans did not bear fruit, though indeed he got his chance of another fight against the English for Irish freedom, when he took his place among the sixteen men of imperishable glory who were executed in 1916.

We were both rather desperate about the chances of bringing off a fight with neither arms nor money, but John was always hopeful that European complications would give us a chance. Since the shipwreck of all I had worked for in France I saw little hope of getting arms there now. The Entente Cordiale was in full swing. Clemenceau had triumphed. After having been kept out of public life for many years, he was again in the ascendant. Edward the Seventh had succeeded, as Grand Master of English Freemasonry, in accomplishing what his mother's Ministers had failed to do. French Freemasonry belongs to the rite of the "Grand Orient" which directs its war against religion in general, while English Freemasonry belongs to the "Scotch Rite", professes a belief in the "Great Architect", and is a bulwark of the British Empire and a subterranean enemy of the Catholic Church. French Masons considered it almost a Protestant institution and in league with Protestant Germany. Edward the Seventh succeeded in smoothing out Masonic differences and now the English and French Lodges, working together, had carried through the English Alliance, and a war between France and Germany was coming nearer,—for politically Masonry was a strong force.

Sitting at the window in the little attic I said:

"The Boer War is over but our war is always on so long as England holds Ireland. I think it should be waged on English soil."

"Or on the sea," put in John.

"Yes, that would be equally good. Either way there could be less reprisals taken on our unfortunate people at home. The English people are more easily panicked than most others."

And I recalled the difference between Irish crowds and the huge English crowd I had seen run before fifty policemen in Trafalgar Square.

Even that small notice in an American newspaper, that the *Clan-na-Gael* had bought a destroyer and was going to sink English shipping, sent Insurance rates up and closed two Lancashire cotton mills. "If only that had been a fact and not a rumour," I said.

"Perhaps it was more than a rumour," said John darkly, but he would say no more. He was sometimes very mysterious.

I knew that if some British ships had been sunk, England would never have admitted anything but accidents, and there had recently been a great many accidents. English statesmen are very much alive to the danger of disturbing the happy sense of security of their people. It ought to be possible to destroy that sense of security. It was the heroic attempt of Captain Mackey and his comrades to blow up Westminster and London Bridge that had converted Sir William Harcourt and many other Liberals to Home Rule and had really secured the few "concessions" the Parliamentary Party boasted of. It is the English way to grant concessions to enhance the prestige of those whom they can count on to repudiate the acts which obtained them. That is the only explanation of Parnell having allowed Tom Clark and John Daly and their comrades to be forgotten all those years in Portland prison.

"Such acts as those of Captain Mackey should be successive and continuous," I said. "It was the plagues of Egypt, successive and continuous and well advertised by Moses, that brought Pharoah to his senses, to let the Israelites escape, and broke the morale of the Egyptian people so much that they all lent money to the Israelites to clear out,—and when Pharoah heard of it, he hurried after them but failed to retrieve. There is a lot to be learnt from that old story, but in our war we have no Moses, we have only Bishops denouncing instead of blessing, and Parliamentarians repudiating instead of glorifying, and our people get so confused that it takes them a generation to realise the truth, and do honour and justice to the men who sacrifice their lives and liberty for them. If the Phoenix Park Invincibles had had men to succeed them and every Chief Secretary or Lord Lieutenant (or better still, every English king) were shot one after the other, Ireland would soon be free with small sacrifice of life. It is the want of continuity that makes such acts almost futile."

John shook his head: "I don't believe one could get that continuity. Men who would face certain death in battle couldn't be counted on in that way; moods change, nerves give way under strain. The Russian Nihilists must have tried it and they have not succeeded."

"The Russians are a different proposition from the English," I answered. "In Russia I heard it said that neither Czar or Nihilists could be terrorised and the mass of the people is too inert to be stirred. Russians have not the smug security of the English and those I have met wouldn't like it if they had."

One day John told me he thought our work in America was bearing fruit. Friends of his were coming over from America; he was to meet them in Spain. Something might be done at last.

I was giving up my apartment in the Avenue d'Eylau and had spent all day packing and making my will, leaving my cousin May guardian of Iseult, to whom the day before I had said good-bye in the quiet garden of the convent at Laval.

She was such a beautiful and such a strangely wise child. She had cried when I told her I was getting married to MacBride and said she hated MacBride. I had felt like crying too. I told her I would send her lovely things from Spain, where we were going for our honeymoon, but she was not consoled. Canon Dissard, of whom she was very fond, was delighted about my marriage and told her we would have a great time when I returned and he would give a banquet in our honour in his little house outside the big convent gate and she would be dressed as a queen on our return. She had only cried the louder and clung to me, and Sister Catherine had had to drag her away.

The hearth was full of burnt papers and the rooms looked very desolate, all ready for the *déménageurs* who were coming next morning to take my furniture to store. MacBride was calling for me to dine at a restaurant, for everything was packed in the flat. It was growing dusk and, very weary, I lay down on my bed to rest. I closed my eyes and tried to think of nothing, but did not sleep. Then I heard Tommy's voice, heard it as I had heard it twice before.

"Lambkin, don't do it. You must not get married."

The bell rang; MacBride was waiting for me in the dismantled drawing-room.

"How tired you look," he said when he came in. "Are you ill?"

"No, but I have just had a warning. Tommy says we must not get married."

MacBride said nothing for a while; then:

"My mother says the same thing," and he pulled out a letter, with the Westport postmark, from old Mrs. MacBride and handed it to me and sat on the arm of my chair while I read it.

It was a very loving letter, telling the son, whom she longed so to see but could not, that she thought the marriage unwise.

"I have seen Maud Gonne. She is very beautiful; she is a great woman and has done much for Ireland but she will not make you happy. You will neither be happy, she is not the wife for you. I am very anxious. Think well what you are doing."

"Joseph has written too," he said, and handed me a letter from his brother. This was less complimentary to me.

"You know of course what you are doing, but I think it most unwise. Maud Gonne is older than you. She is accustomed to money and you have none; she is used to going her own way and listens to no one. These are not good qualities for a wife. A man should not marry unless he can keep his wife . . ." and so on.

I smiled at Joseph's letter. "Give me those letters on the mantelpiece," I said. There was a huge pile, many of them unopened, letters of congratulation,—and on the floor lay scattered newspapers with both our portraits announcing our engagement. From the bundle of letters I picked out one from Arthur Griffith, and John read it over my shoulder. It read like this:

"Queen, forgive me. John MacBride, after Willie Rooney, is the best friend I ever had; you are the only woman friend I have. I only think of both your happiness. For your own sakes and for the sake of Ireland to whom you both belong, don't get married. I know you both, you so unconventional,— a law to yourself; John so full of conventions. You will not be happy for long. Forgive me, but think while there is still time."

We both sat silent; then I got up and laughed.

"John, those whom the gods love die young,—a short life and a merry one. Let us go to dinner. We must hurry or we will be too late for the love of the gods or for dinner. I am thirty-six, you are thirty-five and it is ten o'clock."

Next morning we were married in the church of St. Honoré d'Eylau and started on our honeymoon from which we both thought there was great chance we would never return.

The little stones on which the feet of Cathleen have rested disappear in the dark loneliness of night.

What does it matter? She finds other stones on which to spring as she crosses the shaking bog. The sunrise which will crown her glory will warm all of them, for fire is the heart of the stone.

It is blessed to have been for a moment one of those little stones.

NOTES

Toward the close of the eighteenth century a group of young men inbued with the ideals of the French Revolution formed the United Irishmen, a secret, pluralist oath-bound society dedicated to the formation of an Irish Republic with complete political separation from Britain. One of their leaders, Wolfe Tone, sought military help from France. His first expedition with General Hoche was prevented from landing in Bantry Bay in south-west Ireland because of bad weather in December 1796. The leaders were arrested and the rising was abortive, but the people rose in various parts of the country. They were eventually crushed with dreadful atrocities occurring on both sides by July of 1798. It was at this stage that another French expedition landed in Killala in Co. Mayo, led by General Humbert. Joined by the local people, the French marched inland defeating the government forces at the Races of Castlebar, and the Republic of Connaught was declared on 31 August, but on 8 September the French force was defeated at Ballinamuck, Co. Longford and their Irish followers massacred. Tone, captured at Lough Swilly, where another small French fleet landed, was sentenced to be hanged but committed suicide in prison. The British Government pushed through the Act of Union, joining the Irish Parliament to that of Westminster, which took effect from 1801.

From then on the fight for securing Irish independence was fought on different fronts, a parliamentary one seeking repeal of the Act of Union and the re-establishment of the Irish Parliament and home rule, the other seeking complete separation and the United Irishmen's ideal of an independent Irish Republic. Daniel O'Connell dominated the political scene for the early part of the nineteenth century; a barrister and very successful mass orator, he was the first Catholic of modern times to be allowed to sit in Westminster. He disagreed with an offshoot of his Repeal of the Union movement, the Young Irelanders, over the question of physical force. They believed (and their views were put strongly in their paper, *The Nation*) in the spiritual rebirth of the nation through cultural identity, and in the necessity of the use of physical

351

force. They attempted an abortive rising in 1848 during the potato famine. The Government introduced the Treason Felony Bill, which gave them special powers to impose heavy penalties on instigators of rebellion and the leaders were transported.

Two exiled leaders, James Stephens and John O'Mahony, founded the next political revolutionary movement in 1858. In Ireland it was an oathbound and secret organisation called the Irish Republican Brotherhood and in America an open organisation, pledged to support and finance it, known as the Fenians. Fenian became an umbrella name for both organisations. James Stephens founded a paper in Dublin in 1863, the *Irish People*, whose co-editor was John O'Leary, a young man inspired with the ideals of the Young Irelanders. The paper was seized in 1865 and O'Leary sentenced to 20 years' imprisonment. There was an abortive rising early in 1867 with continued disturbances in Ireland and England, including the Clerkenwell explosion which occurred as part of an attempt to rescue a Fenian prisoner. It was during this period of tension that the army in Ireland was increased, forces coming from England to avoid infiltration. At this time Captain Thomas Gonne was appointed Cavalry Brigade Major at the Curragh Military Camp in Co. Kildare.

In 1867 Clan na Gael was founded in New York and became the official wing of the IRB in America. In 1873 Fenians adopted a new constitution which stated that the promised war against England would wait until the majority of the Irish nation were in favour of it. In the meantime the movement remained active as the extreme wing of Irish nationalism, keeping alive the ideals of Irish Republicanism while partaking prominently in open political activities such as the Amnesty movement for the release of the Fenian prisoners, founded in 1869, and in election campaigns. In 1868 Gladstone, at the head of the Liberal party, formed his first Government, turning his attention to Ireland with a new approach. In 1875 Charles Stewart Parnell was elected to parliament and in a few years led the Irish Home Rule party into greater prominence. In 1879 John Devoy, the main power in Clan na Gael, proposed a new policy of cooperation between the republicans, the constitutionalists and the agrarian movement; this was approved by Clan na Gael, which became known as the

New Departure, but a formal alliance with either the parliamentarian or land reform politicians was not accepted by the IRB.

Because the economic situation was increasing the hardships of tenants James Daly and Michael Davitt founded the Tenant Right Movement, also in 1879. This became known as the Land League, with Parnell as its President, and with a strong Fenian membership, so that it was indirectly working towards the objectives of the New Departure. The Land War for tenant protection commenced in earnest with tenants withholding rent, keeping evicted farms empty, with mass meetings and civil disobedience. The Land League was outlawed in 1881 and the Irish National League was formed in its place. Basically it was a political machine to support the Irish Home Rule party, with 1,262 branches throughout the country by 1886, with younger men coming to the fore.

The party now consisted of eighty-five MPs committed to a liberal alliance with Gladstone. Tim Harrington, William O'Brien and John Dillon launched the Plan of Campaign, renewing the land war by collective bargaining on selected estates, its effective period of operation being between 1886-90. The number of evicted tenants involved was probably not more than one and a half thousand, but the expense of looking after them amounted to more than a quarter of a million pounds by 1893. The problem of the displaced tenants still persisted in 1899 when Francis Tully asked Maud Gonne for help. The Conservative Chief Secretary, Arthur Balfour, used consistently ruthless coercion which had a weakening effect upon the movement.

In 1887 the London *Times* published an article, which included a letter supposedly written by Parnell condoning the Phoenix Park murders of 1882. A commission set up to investigate the matter exonerated him, finding the letter to have been forged by Pigott. But the great days of Parnell's Irish Party were coming to an end. In 1889 Captain O'Shea, a member of the party, sued for divorce, naming Parnell co-respondent. As a result there was a split in the party in 1890, with a small Parnellite section led by John Redmond and an anti-Parnellite section lead by John Dillon.

In the early 1880s Alexander Sullivan had become head of Clan na Gael in America; with two others he formed what was

known as the 'Triangle'. It became a political machine attached
to the Republican Party and bitterly opposed by John Devoy,
who disapproved of their dynamite campaign in England of the
early 1880s and their neglect of those men caught and imprisoned in England at that time—the Treason Felony prisoners for
whom Maud Gonne worked. He also opposed Sullivan's
successor, Lyman, under whose auspices Maud Gonne made her
first visit to the United States. This split in the American
movement was also reflected in Ireland, but in spite of these
differences every shade of nationalist opinion was struggling to
make headway. This was a time of phenomal cultural growth
when the Gaelic Athletic Association and the Gaelic League,
fostering Gaelic games and the Gaelic language respectively,
grew rapidly, and the literary movement, with the encouragement of literary clubs in London and Ireland, fostered the
reawakening of a cultural heritage, something attempted by the
Young Ireland Movement, from which grew the Irish Literary
Theatre and the Abbey Theatre. O'Grady, O'Leary (who had
returned from exile in 1885) and Yeats played a large part in
this. Maud Gonne was also involved, but her strength was in her
campaign of publicity throughout Ireland, up and down
England and in France, with meetings, lectures, and demonstrations mostly connected with the Treason Felony prisoners,
evictions and famine; these activities frequently crossed the
divide between parliamentarianism, land agitation, the literary
movement and advanced nationalism, as the more extreme
wings of the movement were called. Towards the end of the
century it was decided that a well orchestrated Centenary
celebration of the 1798 rising might help to unify the various
factions and raise the nationalist consciousness.

Arthur Griffith, newly returned from South Africa, and his
friend Willie Rooney, founder of the Celtic Literary Society,
started a paper, the United Irishman, in 1899, a separatist organ
of advanced nationalist views. In 1898 William O'Brien had
founded the United Irish League, a new land reform organisation which spread rapidly and forced the unification of the
Parliamentary party in 1900. The IRB and Clan na Gael also
united. In 1903 Parliament passed the Wyndham Land Act,

practically completing the work commenced by Davitt enabling tenants to purchase their holdings, so that by 1920 nearly nine million acres had passed from the landlords to the tenants.

From 1902 Griffith commenced promulgating his policy of self-reliance and independence in the *United Irishman*, a policy which eventually became that of Sinn Fein. It was finally put into action when a majority of Sinn Féin candidates won the 1918 general election. The Parliamentary party had been working towards Home Rule, with an act on the statute book, postponed by northern unionist opposition and the commencement of the First World War. The IRB, however, whose members had grown to maturity in the previous two decades and had become strongly influenced by Tom Clarke, one of the Treason Felony prisoners, distrusting the likelihood of Home Rule being enacted, decided that England's difficulty was Ireland's opportunity, and organ-ised a rising on Easter Monday, 1916. The ruthlessness of its suppression lead to strong nationalist reaction and to the success of Sinn Féin in the 1918 election. The War of Independence, known as the Black and Tan war, followed, ending in a truce and the Treaty of 1921 which excluded the six northern counties, whose mainly Unionist population had objected to the previous Home Rule Bill. There was a bitter division between those in favour and those against the Treaty. With the death of Griffith and Collins in 1922 the situation was even more polarised. Maud Gonne and her son Seán MacBride took the anti-Treaty or Republican side and remained in opposition to the new Free State government.

In the bitter aftermath of the Civil War Maud busied herself with protests and concern for the well being of the many political prisoners still in gaols. De Valera, elected to power in 1932, gave her hope of more kindness to the republicans, but she was soon disappointed, and went back to her concerns for prisoners. She stood unsuccessfully for election in her son's new party, Cumann Poblachta na hEireann. De Valera brought in a new constitution in 1938, advancing the state nearer to separation than the Treaty had left it. In 1947 Sean MacBride was a member of a new coalition government which withdrew Ireland completely from the British Commonwealth and declared Ireland a Republic.

NOTES ON PERSONS AND ORGANISATIONS MENTIONED IN
A SERVANT OF THE QUEEN

Amnesty Associations. An amnesty association was first started in 1869 to help the Fenian prisoners, including O'Donovan Rossa and John O'Leary.

It held mass meetings of up to 250,000 people. The Limerick Amnesty Association was founded in 1889. Maud Gonne belonged to The National Amnesty Association of Ireland and the English based Amnesty Association of Great Britain, formed in 1892. The associations worked for the release of all prisoners 'incarcerated in English and Irish prisons on charges arising out of political struggle in Ireland, to protect their interests, and to give such aid for the support of their families as may be necessary; and also to secure that the prisoners shall be visited when permission can be obtained' (Rules of the Irish National Amnesty Association, 1896). Both Associations wound up their business in 1899 when all the prisoners had been released. In their final balance sheets both attributed the largest sums collected to Maud Gonne with her American and European lectures.

Blavatsky, Mme Helen Petrovna (1831-91), born in Russia, was the founder of the Theosophic Movement. She spent many years wandering in Europe and India. With an interest in spiritualism she founded the Theosophical Society in New York with Colonel Olcott in 1875 and came to London with him in 1884, establishing the Blavatsky Lodge there in 1887. She wrote *Isis Unveiled* (1877) and many other books on theosophy.

Boulanger, General Georges, was appointed Minister of War in France in 1886, and became a national figure around whom opposition from left and right gathered, his following being a strange mixture of republicans, royalists and socialists, with many supporters in the Army and the Church. He and his party won overwhelming victories in by-elections and the Paris election of January 1889, when his supporters and the Ligue de Patriotes were ready to follow him in a *coup d'état*, but he failed to seize the opportunity. Believing himself in danger he fled the country and his movement collapsed. He committed suicide in Brussels in 1891.

Clarke, Thomas (1857-1916), emigrated to the USA at twenty-one, joined Clan na Gael and went to England on the dynamiting campaign of 1883. Sentenced to life imprisonment, he was released in 1898 and went back to the USA. He returned to Ireland in 1907, his newsagency in Dublin becoming the centre of IRB organisation. Elected to the IRB Supreme Council in 1915, he was executed after the 1916 rising.

Connolly, James (1868-1916), born in Scotland of Irish parents, founded the Irish Socialist Republican Party in 1896 and worked with Maud Gonne at various times in the next few years. He lived in America from 1902-10, being active in socialist affairs. He became Ulster organizer of the Irish Transport and General Workers' Union in 1910, and led the workers after Larkin's arrest in the 1913 Dublin strike and lock out. He organized the Irish Citizen Army which participated in the 1916 rising and was military commander of the Republican forces in Dublin. He was executed for his part in the Rising.

Daly, John (1845-1916), of Limerick, an IRB man, was imprisoned for life in 1884, having been falsely charged under the Treason Felony Act and released in 1896. It was to effect his release that the Amnesty movement grew out of the Limerick Amnesty Association in the early 1890s. He became Lord Mayor of Limerick and bestowed the Freedom of the City on Maud Gonne and on his fellow Treason Felony prisoner, Tom Clarke, who married his niece.

Dissard, Canon was born in 1860, ordained in 1886 and became secretary to the Bishop of Laval in 1896. He sought Maud Gonne's assistance when the Carmelite nuns in the town were being secularised in 1901. At that time some of the nuns left, but those that remained founded the Association des Dames de Sainte Thérèse and had to have a *raison sociale* to continue in their convent. They eventually had to leave after a dispute with the bishop.

Davitt, Michael (1846-1906) emigrated from Mayo as a child, and lost his right arm in a Lancashire mill accident at eleven. He joined the Fenians in 1865 and was sentenced to fifteen years' penal servitude in 1870 but released seven years later. He went to America where he worked with John Devoy on the New

Departure for the nationalist movement, endeavouring to combine home rule and land reform as he always worked to reconcile constitutional and revolutionary politics. He formed the National Land League in 1879, and was elected MP while in prison in 1882. He encouraged Parnell to form the National League when the Land League was supressed. He was elected as an anti-Parnellite MP in 1892, and later co-founded the United Irish League with William O'Brien in 1898.

Déroulède, Paul, poet-politician, founded the Ligue des Patriotes in 1882 to help to revive the French national spirit by mass appeal; it was ready to support Boulanger's expected *coup d'état* in January 1889 which failed to materialize. In 1892 he attacked Clemenceau in the chamber of deputies over the Panama affair which resulted in a duel and the hounding of Clemenceau out of public life for a time, with charges of corruption and being an English agent. In 1899 he led a *coup d'état* (which was a total failure), at the funeral of the President, Félix Foure.

Devoy, John (1842-1928), born in Co. Kildare, joined the Fenians and was in charge of Fenian infiltration of the British Army. Arrested in 1866, he was released into exile in 1871. On going to America he became prominent in Clann na Gael, opposing Sullivan and Lyman when Clan na Gael split. He kept a close interest in everything that occurred in Ireland, financing many projects up to independence. He founded the *Irish Nation* in 1882 and the *Gaelic American* in 1903 which he edited until his death.

Dillon, John (1851-1927), MP from 1879-1918, he supported the Plan of Campaign. In 1891 he opposed Parnell and became the anti-Parnellite leader. In 1900 he supported United Irish League and Redmond as leader of reunited Parliamentary Party. He became its leader in 1918 on Redmond's death but lost his seat to de Valera in the elections of that year.

Egan, James, imprisoned with John Daly, on his release became the paid organiser for Mark Ryan, dealing with money sent from the USA by Lyman; he was therefore of great value to Maud Gonne on her first tour in the United States under Lyman's auspices. Later he secured a post with the Dublin Corporation as Sword Bearer but remained active in political circles, being a vice-president of Griffith's Cumann na nGaedheal.

Gonne, Kathleen (1868-1919), at 21 married an army officer, Captain (later Major-General) Thomas David Pilcher (1858-1928). She had three sons and one daughter. While her husband was stationed in Ireland she lived in Dublin for a while in the late eighteen nineties. She divorced her husband in the first decade of the century. It was Kathleen — and not Maud, as their father had feared — who developed tuberculosis. She suffered recurring bouts of illness and eventually died in Switzerland early in 1919.

Gill, Thomas Patrick (1858-1931), MP from 1885 to 1892. He was on the staff of Sir Horace Plunkett's Irish Agricultural Organisation Society, and editor of his *Dublin Daily Express* from 1898 to 1899.

Gregory, Lady (1852-1932), born Isabella Augusta Persse in Co. Galway, she married Sir William Gregory of Coole Park, Gort, Co. Galway who died in 1892 leaving her with one son Robert. She met Yeats when she was 42 and again two years later when she invited him to visit Coole. He told her of his plans for an Irish Theatre in which she became deeply involved, founding the Abbey Theatre in Dublin with him. From 1897 he spent every summer at Coole for twenty years, collecting folk lore and writing.

Griffith, Arthur (1871-1922), from a Dublin working class background, he became an apprentice printer and compositor. A member of the IRB for a time, he went to South Africa in 1896, returning to Ireland in 1898 when he started the *United Irishman* with William Rooney. His advocacy of independence and self-sufficiency led to the formation of Sinn Féin (Ourselves Alone), a non-violent separatist organisation. Griffith remained aloof during the 1916 Rising but was arrested several times; he was elected Sinn Féin MP for East Cavan in 1918. Civilian leader of the Irish Provisional Government, he headed the Irish delegation in the negotiations of 1921 which led to the establishment of the Irish Free State, of which he was the first President. He died suddenly on 12 August 1922.

Harrington, Timothy (1851-1910), a journalist, barrister, MP and leading Land League organiser for Co. Kerry. He devised the Plan of Campaign with William O'Brien in 1886. While editing the *United Ireland* in 1898 he persued a campaign for national unity and joined William O'Brien and Michael Davitt in founding the United Irish League. He was Lord Mayor of Dublin (1901-4).

Holmes, Augusta (1850-1903), born in Paris of Irish descent, was a composer of symphonies, operas, choral works and songs. She studied under César Franck. Her symphonic poem *Irlande* was first performed in 1882 in Paris, and later in many European cities as well as Dublin.

Hyde, Douglas (1860-1949), poet, scholar and translator, he founded the Gaelic League in 1893 and became the first President of Ireland in 1937.

Johnston, Anna (1866-1902), wrote and published poetry under the name Ethna Carbery. She was the daughter of Robert Johnston, an influential IRB man from Belfast. She was co-editor with Alice Milligan of the *Shan Van Vocht*. She married the writer Seamus MacManus.

L'Irlande Libre, issued in connection with the Paris '98 Centenary Committee and the Paris Young Ireland Society, was designed to further the nationalist cause in France with information and articles. The first issue appeared on 1 May 1897, and the journal was published every month until October 1898. In 1900, on the occasion of the Queen's visit to Ireland a *numéro exceptionnel* was produced.

Lynch, Arthur (1861-1934), an Irish-Australian working as a journalist in Paris, and a member of the Paris Young Ireland Society, he went to South Africa during the Boer War with a 2nd Irish Brigade, which never took part in any major action. Elected MP (1901-18), on arriving in England to take his seat in Parliament he was arrested on charges of high treason and condemned to death, but was later reprieved. He was a colonel in the British army (1918).

MacBride, Dr Anthony (c. 1866-1942), born in Westport,

received his medical degree from the Royal University of Ireland, practised in London and returned to Ireland about 1905. He was Mayo County surgeon, attached to Castlebar Hospital, from 1907-40. While living in London he was a friend of Dr Mark Ryan, was an active member of the IRB and took part in all nationalist activities.

MacBride, Major John (1868-1916), a brother of Anthony Mac-Bride, was born in Westport, educated there and in Belfast. He became a Fenian at fifteen. While working in Dublin he was a friend of John O'Leary and Arthur Griffith. He emigrated to South Africa in 1896, where Griffith joined him for a while. He formed an Irish Brigade at the outset of the Boer War in 1899. While in South Africa he was defeated as a candidate for Davitt's vacated seat in Mayo. When the brigade was disbanded he went to Paris, then lectured in the United States of America where Maud Gonne joined him. They were married in France on 21 February 1903. The marriage was not happy, and Maud Gonne fought for divorce. Because of a Liberal landslide MacBride did not incur the same risks as Arthur Lynch on returning to Ireland, where he lived in Dublin, playing an active part in IRB politics. He took part in the rising of Easter Week and was executed on 5 May 1916.

MacKenna, Stephen (1872-1934), worked as bank clerk and journalist before moving to Paris. He joined an international brigade to fight for Greece against Turkey. He then worked as European correspondent of the *New York World*, but, wanting to return to Ireland, became leader writer on the *Freeman's Journal*. He translated the work of the Greek philosopher Plotinus (1917-1930).

Milligan, Alice (1866-1953), a poet, was a member of the Gaelic League. With Anna Johnson (the poet 'Ethna Carbery') she founded and edited *Shan Van Vocht*, a nationalist monthly published in Belfast from 1896-1899. Her play *The Deliverance of Red Hugh* was produced by Inghinidhe na hEireann in 1901.

Martyn, Edward (1859-1923), a wealthy Catholic landlord who lived in Co. Galway, was co-founder, with W.B. Yeats, Lady Gregory and his cousin George Moore, of the Irish Literary Theatre in 1898. He wrote some plays, was president of Sinn Féin (1904-8), and founded the Palestrina Choir in the Pro-Cathedral, Dublin.

Millevoye, Lucien (1850-1918), came from a wealthy family, was the grandson of the poet, Charles-Hubert Millevoye, a magistrate, and respectably married. He became a member of the House of Deputies in 1889 as a representative of the National Party at the time of Boulanger's success and collapse. He was political editor of *La Patrie* from 1895 until his death. By the time he met Maud Gonne, when Boulanger was in the ascendant, he was a politician, publicist, orator, a specialist in foreign affairs interested in a Franco-Russian alliance, and had been to Russia for General Boulanger. Later he was chairman of the French army's committee on aviation. He died on 25 March, 1918.

Moore, George Augustus (1852-1933), a Catholic landowner in Mayo, he spent some time in Paris studying art before turning to writing. He was a very successful novelist, living in either Ireland or London. He helped Lady Gregory and Yeats found the Irish Theatre. In his fictional memoirs, the trilogy *Hail and Farewell* (1911, 1912 and 1914), he satirised life in Dublin in the early part of the century.

O'Brien, William (1852-1928), edited Parnell's *United Ireland* from 1881, was Secretary of the National League (1882), and MP from 1883 to 1919. He devised the Plan of Campaign with Harrington in 1886, edited the *Irish People* (1899), and founded the United Irish League with Harrington and Dillon, which aimed at redistribution of land using methods similar to those of the Land League (such as agitation, boycott and intimidation) to put pressure on the government. The organisation grew rapidly and worked with the united Parliamentary Party.

O'Delaney, Mary Barry, left Ireland for France in 1883 and earned a living at journalism. She helped Maud Gonne as assistant and researcher and was the secretary of the Paris Young Ireland Society when it was formed in 1897, reporting its activities in all the Irish nationalist papers also writing many articles under various pseudonyms such as MB, MO'D, and MD.

O'Donovan [Rossa], Jeremiah (1831-1915), joined the IRB in 1856, was Business Manager of *The Irish People* in 1863, arrested in 1863 with John O'Leary and sentenced to penal servitude for twenty years under the Treason Felony Act. In prison he conducted a strenuous campaign against the cruel conditions which resulted in some improvement in them. He was freed into exile in 1871, going to the United States where he edited *The United Irishman* and published an account of his prison experiences. A member of Clan na Gael, he organised the funds for the dynamiting campaign of the early 1880s.

O'Donnell, Frank Hugh (1848-1916) was MP for Galway and Dungarvan. His renomination was refused by Parnell in 1885. He was castigated by Michael Davitt as a 'distinguished self seeker and egoist'. He was introduced into the IRB by Dr Mark Ryan and was referred to by Yeats as 'a certain mad rogue'. At the time Maud Gonne refers to him (1900) he was publishing numerous anonymous pamphlets and articles which caused considerable concern, particularly to Yeats, Maud Gonne and Davitt.

O'Leary, John (1830-1907), from a well-to-do background in Tipperary, he became editor of the *Irish People*, organ of the IRB, in 1863. After twenty months the paper was suppressed and its editors and many IRB leaders were arrested and tried under the Treason Felony Act. He was sentenced to twenty years' penal servitude in Portland Gaol. In 1871 he was released on condition that he went into exile. After living in Paris, he was allowed back into Ireland in 1885. He became influential in the Young Ireland Society, with Yeats and Maud Gonne as his disciples. Yeats said he had 'the moral genius that moves all young people'.

Oldham, Charles Hubert (1860-1926), a barrister and distinguished economist, founded the Contemporary Club in 1885 and the following year established the Protestant Home Rule Association.

Redmond, John Edward (1856-1918), MP from 1881 to 1918, led the Parnellite minority of the Parliamentary Party in 1891 and the reunited party in 1900 which finally secured the introduction of the third Home Rule Bill in 1912. He supported the British government during the 1914-18 war, encouraging Irishmen to join the British forces. He opposed Sinn Féin and deplored the 1916 Rising.

Redmond, William (1856-1917), John Redmond's younger brother, MP from 1883 to his death, was a follower of Parnell. When his brother John called for Irish volunteers at the outbreak of war in 1914, William joined the British army; he was killed in action in June 1917.

Rolleston, Thomas William Hazen (1857-1920), educated at Trinity College, Dublin, and in Germany, was a poet, translator and critic. He founded the *Dublin University Review* in 1885 and was the first Secretary of the Irish Literary Society in London.

Rooney, William (1873-1901), was of Dublin working-class background, worked as a clerk from the age of twelve, continuing his education at night. He founded the Celtic Literary Society in February 1893. One of the first to make speeches in Irish, he spoke on many platforms with Maud Gonne. With Griffith he founded the *United Irishman*, writing large sections of the paper under many different pseudonyms. With Griffith he launched Cumann na nGaedheal in 1900. He died, aged twenty-seven, in May 1901. He had had a great influence on his generation including Maud Gonne. His *Poems and Ballads*, were published in 1902, his *Prose Writings* in 1909. Yeats dedicated the first edition of *Cathleen ní Houlihan* (1902) to his memory.

Russell, George William (1867-1935), whom Yeats met at the School of Art in Dublin, was a mystic. He wrote poetry and plays under the pen name AE, and his mystical paintings represented some of his visions. He became an official of the Irish Agricultural Organisation Society in 1897, Yeats having recommended him to Sir Horace Plunkett. He edited *The Irish Homestead*, its journal (1905-23), and was editor of *The Irish Statesman* (1923-30).

Ryan, Dr Mark (1844-1940), the guiding spirit of Irish nationalists in London for forty years, was a member of the Supreme Council of the IRB and helped to form the Parnell Leadership Committees through which the IRB supported Parnell in his last fight. In 1892 he founded the Amnesty Associations. With many of the London IRB he followed Sullivan and Lyman when Clan na Gael split, which was the cause of much of the confusion when Maud Gonne went to the United States for the first time in 1897.

Sainte-Croix, Mlle Ghénia de (1856-1938), later Madame Avril, was a journalist writing under the name of Savioz, and a reformist feminist. She was secretary of the National Council of French Women (founded in 1900) an affiliation of sixty-seven societies concerned with questions affecting women and children. In 1901 she founded *L'Oeuvre Liberatrice* to help prostitutes.

Sigerson, Dr George (1838-1925), a medical doctor, a member of La Société de Psychologie Physiologique de Paris, became Professor of Botany and Zoology at the new University College established in Dublin in 1908. His main literary interest was in Gaelic poetry and he published *Bards of the Gael and Gall* in 1897.

Synge, John Millington (1871-1909), well known Irish writer, born in Dublin, travelled in Italy and France, where he met Yeats and Maud Gonne in Paris in 1897, joining the Paris Young Ireland Society for a brief period and working with D'Arbois de Jubainville. Yeats advised him to go to the Aran Islands and seek Irish themes. He was a Director of the Abbey Theatre, which produced all his plays. He died of Hodgkinson's Disease.

McGregor Mathers, Samuel Liddell (1854-1918), was one of the founders of the Hermetic Order of the Golden Dawn in 1887. Becoming powerful within the organisation, he turned it towards the study of magic. He married the painter Moina Bergson (sister of the French philosopher Henri Bergson) in 1890. When he lost his post as curator of the Horniman Museum in London in 1892, he and his wife went to Paris where he lived until he died. He became a supporter of Scottish nationalism, adopting the title of Comte de Glenstrae and dropping the name Mathers. When he became too autocratic he was expelled from the Golden Dawn in April 1900 and the rift between him and Yeats was never healed.

Teeling, Charles MacCarthy, a vice-president of the Young Ireland Society in 1885, he was expelled by the committee of the Society. He appeared at nationalist demonstrations on a white horse. He expected to play a part in the '98 celebrations as he was the great nephew of Bartholomew Teeling of the United Irishmen who was hanged in Dublin in September 1798.

Yeats, William Butler (1865-1939), son of the artist John Butler Yeats, he spent his childhood in London, Sligo and Dublin, studied at the School of Art in Dublin and decided to become a poet. He met Maud Gonne in 1889 and fell in love with her, writing her many poems over the years. Interested in magic and mysticism, he wrote decorative, defeatist and beautiful poetry in the 1890s, often called the Celtic Twilight style (after his prose book of that title). He co-founded the Abbey Theaue and was its manager until 1910. He married in 1917, lived part of each year in a tower in Co. Galway, returning to Dublin in 1922, when he became a Senator. Winner of the Nobel Prize for Literature in 1923, he demonstrated an impressive, new kind of energy and poetic vitality in *The Tower* (1928) and *The Winding Stair* (1933). He continued to write vigorously up to his death.

Young, Ella (1867&8-1956), a mystic poet, was a member of George Russell's Theosophist group. She joined Inghinidhe na hEireann and later Constance Markiewicz's Cumann na mBan. She became Professor of Celtic Mythology in the University of California at Berkeley in 1925. She wrote poetry and stories which were published in Ireland and the United States of America. Maud Gonne illustrated her *The Coming of Lugh* (1909), *Celtic Wonder Tales* (1910) and *The Rose of Heaven* (1920).

INDEX